Starving the South

Also by Andrew F. Smith

The Oxford Companion to American Food and Drink

Eating History: Thirty Turning Points in the Making of American Cuisine

The Tomato in America: Early History, Culture and Cookery

Pure Ketchup: The History of America's National Condiment

The Saintly Scoundrel: The Life and Times of Dr. John C. Bennett

Popped Culture: A Social History of Popcorn in America

Souper Tomatoes: The Story of America's Favorite Food

Rescuing the World: The Life and Times of Leo Cherne

Peanuts: The Illustrious History of the Goober Pea

*Real American Food: Restaurants, Markets,
and Shops Plus Favorite Hometown Recipes*

The Encyclopedia of Junk Food and Fast Food

The Turkey: A Social History

The Oxford Encyclopedia on Food and Drink in America

Hamburger: A Global History

Starving the South

HOW THE NORTH WON THE CIVIL WAR

ANDREW F. SMITH

ST. MARTIN'S PRESS ❈ NEW YORK

www.stmartins.com

Library of Congress Cataloging-in-Publication Data

Smith, Andrew F., 1946–
    Starving the South : how the North won the Civil War / Andrew F. Smith.—
1st ed.
        p. cm.
    Includes bibliographical references.
    ISBN 978-0-312-60181-2
    1. United States—History—Civil War, 1861–1865—Food supply.   2. United
States—History—Civil War, 1861–1865—Economic aspects.   3. United
States—History—Civil War, 1861–1865—Blockades.   4. Confederate States of
America. Army—Supplies and stores.   5. United States—Army—Supplies and
stores—History—19th century.   6. Confederate States of America—Economic
conditions.   7. Food industry and trade—United States—History—19th
century.   I. Title.
    E468.9.S65 2011
    973.7'1—dc22

                                                                2010043557

First Edition: April 2011

10   9   8   7   6   5   4   3   2   1

Contents

Starving the South

Prologue

American farms of the late eighteenth century had much in common with European farms of the Middle Ages. By nature, farmers were conservative, and little had changed on American farms and plantations since early colonial times. Farming was labor-intensive: Fields were cultivated, plowed, and harrowed with horse-drawn equipment, while the crops were seeded, weeded, harvested, threshed, and winnowed largely by hand. Farmers ate much of what they grew; excess produce was sold to or bartered with people they knew at local markets.

A major challenge for America was how to acquire the labor needed to operate farms and plantations. Slavery existed in both the North and South, but only in the South did it flourish. In colonial and early America, slaves were particularly efficient on large plantations that raised cash crops, such as tobacco, indigo, and rice, and to a much lesser extent on those that grew cotton. The cotton gin, invented in 1793, radically changed Southern agriculture. The gin efficiently removed seeds from the cotton balls, a task previously done by hand. Cotton grew easily in the South, where slaves could cultivate and harvest it. Low-cost cotton became the fabric of choice in the United States, as well as in England and France. No other place in the world at the time could produce such high-quality cotton in such vast quantities and at such a low cost as did the American South, and slave-produced cotton became king in Southern agriculture.

Local economies shaped regional lifestyles, affecting, among other things, what people ate. As a result of the cotton-slavery connection, Southern per capita income rose steadily during the first decades of the nineteenth century; by 1860 it was almost twice that of the North. Southern wealth, however, was distributed disproportionately. The rich were *very* rich, and this wealth was manifested in their culinary lives as they enjoyed generous servings of meat and expensive imported foods accompanied by the best European wines and spirits. The second social rung consisted primarily of rural whites who relied on what they could grow and raise on small farms. It was extremely difficult for small farmers to compete with large plantations powered by slaves. The third rung consisted of poor whites, whose subsistence diet was supplemented with game and fish they killed or caught themselves. The lowest group in Southern society consisted of the enslaved blacks, who in many places outnumbered the whites. They ate what their owners gave them and whatever garden crops and livestock they could grow or raise on small plots of land.

The Line of Civilization Moves Westward

The North also needed agricultural labor, but slavery was not the answer, and Northern states gradually abolished slavery before the Civil War. The North was, however, the beneficiary of massive immigrations, especially from Ireland and Germany, beginning in the late 1840s. Immigrants supplied the North with low-cost labor that fueled its industrialization, and factories were established throughout the region. When the Civil War began, many immigrants joined the Union army. Others worked on construction crews building the railroads that were rapidly expanding throughout the North and Midwest. Immigrants who settled in the Midwestern cities, such as Chicago, Cincinnati, and

St. Louis, established stockyards, slaughterhouses, and meat-processing facilities, which would become essential to the Union war effort.

Before the Civil War, the prairies of the Midwest were opened for settlement and vast new areas began to be converted into agricultural land. A self-polishing steel plow, patented by John Deere in 1837, made it easier to break up the sod, and prairie farming expanded. Widespread adoption of this and other equipment signaled a change in American agriculture from hand power to horse power.[1]

Harvesting grain was one of the farmer's most vexing challenges. Farmers had some flexibility in deciding when to plow, sow, weed, winnow, and thresh their grain, but harvesting was a high-stakes task that had to be completed within ten to fourteen days—sometimes less, depending on the weather. In 1830, farm workers harvested wheat by hand, an arduous and exhausting task.[2] Since the late eighteenth century, British and American inventors had tried unsuccessfully to create a workable mechanical reaper.[3] That soon changed, however. Beginning in 1831, Cyrus McCormick, a farmer in Virginia's Shenandoah Valley, invented, refined, and patented various designs. Since slavery dominated Southern plantation agriculture, there was less interest in the South in a labor-saving device such as a mechanical harvester.

There was great interest in reapers and other mechanical devices in the Midwest, where labor was scarce and land was cheap. Recognizing this geographical advantage, McCormick moved his operation from Virginia to Chicago in 1847. Due largely to its strategic location as a transportation hub, the city was growing rapidly. In this more advantageous environment, sales of McCormick's reapers skyrocketed. By 1860, thanks to the mechanization, wheat production in Midwestern states—Ohio, Indiana, Illinois, Wisconsin, and Iowa—soared to half the national total. In 1860, William H. Seward, a U.S. Senator at the time and the future Secretary of State under President Abraham Lincoln, concluded, "Owing to Mr. McCormick's invention, the line of civilization moves westward thirty miles each year."[4]

Transportation Revolution

It was relatively easy for Midwesterners to send their agricultural goods to the South via the Mississippi River system, but in the mid-nineteenth century the river was filled with rapids, and shifting sandbars, while low water obstructed travel for much of the year. Midwesterners faced an additional problem when it came to sending grain to market on the East Coast or overseas. The shallow mouth of the Mississippi prevented large ships from steaming upriver to pick up or discharge goods. Midwestern grain had to be transferred at New Orleans from river boats to small coastal freighters that would then sail to Eastern cities with deepwater ports, such as New York, Baltimore, Philadelphia, and Boston, where their cargo would be transferred again to larger oceangoing vessels for shipment to Europe. If Midwestern farmers could send their agricultural commodities directly to the East Coast, transportation costs—and thus the cost of food—would drop dramatically.

The North invested vast sums of money in constructing canals and railroads to tap the agricultural wealth of the Midwest. In New York, for example, construction of the Erie Canal from the Hudson River to Lake Erie was the largest single public works project in America up to that time. The canal was a financial success well before its completion in 1825. After the canal opened, trade between New York and the Great Lakes and the Midwest escalated exponentially. The financial success of the Erie Canal set off a frenzy of canal building, but there were relatively few places where canals were cost-effective. In the decade beginning in 1830, canal mileage swelled from 1,270 miles to 3,320 miles—and most of this new construction was in the Midwest.[5] These canals and waterways created aquatic "superhighways" that permitted goods to be transported quickly and inexpensively from the Midwest to the South and the East Coast.

The success of canals spurred the construction of railroads, which could connect places that were unreachable by canals or navigable rivers. When the steam railroad engine *Tom Thumb* went into operation in August 1830, there were only 23 miles of track in the United States. Within a decade, this had surged to 2,800 miles. By 1860, the United States had more than 31,000 miles of railroads, 90 percent of which were in the North and Midwest.[6] With railroads located closer to farms, farmers could now grow specialty crops to which their land was best suited instead of only those crops needed for subsistence. As a result, farmers began specializing in particular crops, livestock, or related industries. More food was produced and farmers used increased profits to purchase new equipment, which increased their crop yield even more.

East-west railroads were completed just in time to meet increased demand for Midwestern goods. The grain harvests in England and France were dismal in 1860, and large quantities of Midwestern grain were dispatched eastward via canals and railroads and then transshipped from Eastern ports to Europe. As one observer wrote, railroads and canals had "rolled back the mighty tide of the Mississippi and its ten thousand tributary streams until their mouth, practically and commercially, is more at New York and Boston than at New Orleans."[7]

Regional Specialization and Internal Trade

Improved internal transportation throughout the U.S. gave rise to regional specialization—banking, merchandizing, manufacturing, and shipbuilding in New England and the mid-Atlantic states, domestic food production in the Midwest, and export crops, such as cotton, sugar, molasses, and tobacco, in the plantation South. Beginning in 1815, internal commerce rapidly expanded, continuing to grow through 1860. It became less costly and more efficient for Southern plantations to purchase food from the Midwest than to grow it themselves.[8] Other than a few commodities, such as sugar, the South had little that the Midwest needed; what that region wanted was manufactured goods that were available from the East Coast. The North needed food from the Midwest and cotton from the South, and the North's manufactured goods were needed in both those regions.

Thanks to slavery, the South was the most productive agricultural region of the United States. Many plantation owners chose to grow cotton and tobacco, simply because they were much more profitable than food crops. Had they devoted their land to growing wheat or corn or sweet potatoes, or to raising cattle or pigs, Southern farmers and plantation owners could easily have produced enough food to feed the entire continent. But even with so much acreage devoted to cash crops, in 1860 the fifteen slave-holding states produced a considerable quantity of provisions, including all the nation's rice and sugar, more corn than the North, and almost as much wheat; the South was also nearly self-sufficient in meat production.[9] The prewar South exported mainly cotton, tobacco, hemp, indigo, rice, and sugar, and imported, as one Southerner proclaimed, "hay from Maine, Irish Potatoes from Nova Scotia, Apples from Massachusetts, Butter and Cheese from New York; Flour and Pork from Ohio or Beef from Illinois." To that list could be added wheat and pork from the Midwest, salt from Wales, and industrial equipment and finished goods from the North. With the exception of salt, direct imports from Europe were minor, as most of the South's European trade went through Northern ports, such as New York. These goods were then transported by coastal steamer to Southern ports.

At the beginning of the Civil War, Northerners were well aware of the South's dependency on food from the Midwest. The idea that the Confederacy could be starved into submission was discussed in the North—at least in newspapers. The *New York Times*, for instance, noted that the Confederacy had plenty of cotton, which the South "can neither eat or drink—and nor can they wear it, unless they first send it North to manufacture it." But Southerners ridiculed the notion that they could be starved out. As one Southerner bragged, it was impossible "to starve the South. They have food enough, and as they are diminishing the production of cotton, they will next year have a superabundance of corn, beef, pork, rice, sugar, whisky, and tobacco. Did a people ever yield to a blockade that possessed these necessaries, because they were deprived of tea, wine, and coffee? Would it not be unmanly to think of it?"[10]

I

Lincoln's Humbug of a Blockade

braham Lincoln was elected the sixteenth president of the United States on November 6, 1860. He opposed the extension of slavery into new territories, and his election convinced many Southerners that it was time to leave the Union. By the time of Lincoln's inauguration on March 4, 1861, seven slaveholding states had seceded, immediately expropriating as much Federal property as they could, including arsenals, forts, military camps, and the United States Mint in New Orleans. Eight other slave-holding states remained in the United States, but any precipitate action by the new administration might tip them into seceding as well.

The Lincoln Administration confronted many crises, but the most volatile was what to do with a few remaining Union-held forts in states that had seceded. Fort Sumter was the flashpoint: It controlled the entrance to Charleston, South Carolina's largest port. The fort was garrisoned by a small army detachment commanded by Major Robert Anderson, a pro-slavery, former slave owner from Kentucky. Anderson attended West Point, where he met Kentucky-born Jefferson Davis and tutored a Creole from Louisiana named Pierre T. G. Beauregard. In 1861, the commander of the Confederate troops stationed in Charleston was Beauregard, who under orders from Jefferson Davis, then the provisional president of the Confederacy, refused permission for Anderson's garrison to buy food and supplies in Charleston. Instead, Davis and

Beauregard demanded that Anderson surrender the fort. Anderson refused. By early March 1861, the fort began to run out of provisions. Anderson told the War Department that "unless we receive supplies I shall be compelled to stay here without food, or to abandon this post."[1]

All Loyal Citizens

Lincoln's cabinet was divided about whether to send provisions to the garrison. William Seward, the U.S. Secretary of State, favored withdrawal, as did Simon P. Cameron, the Secretary of War, and Gideon Welles, Secretary of the Navy. Relieving the fort, they argued, would require an army and a navy that the United States just did not have. Others disagreed. Salmon P. Chase, Secretary of the Treasury, and Montgomery Blair, the Postmaster General, thought that surrendering the fort would be treason, and any such action would dampen the morale of the many Unionists who lived in the slave-holding states. Others feared that withdrawal would be tantamount to official recognition of the Confederacy.

Lincoln concluded that if the Union troops evacuated Fort Sumter, the nation would be irrevocably split in two. At a cabinet meeting on March 28, 1861, he made the decision to send provisions to the Union garrison at the fort. A small flotilla of vessels loaded with supplies left Northern ports on April 5. When the ships arrived off the coast of South Carolina six days later, Beauregard gave Anderson a choice of immediately surrendering or facing bombardment. Anderson declined to surrender, and at 4:30 a.m. on April 12, 1861, batteries fired on the fort.[2] The cannonade continued through the following day, until Anderson agreed to a cease-fire. On April 14, Anderson and his men lowered the American flag, boarded the ships that had come to supply the fort, and headed north. Thus ended the first military engagement of the Civil War.

Even before the Confederate artillery fired the first shots of the Civil War, various proposals were circulating in Washington on how best to encourage the South to return to the Union. Winfield Scott, the General-in-Chief of the U.S. Army and a Virginian by birth, is credited with the proposal to blockade the Confederacy's Atlantic and Gulf ports and then to take control of the Mississippi River. Such actions would prevent war materiel from coming into the Confederacy from abroad and would split the Confederacy in two. After the South stagnated commercially, it would then peacefully rejoin the Union, or so proponents believed. The plan was leaked to the press, where it was disparagingly referred to as the "boa-constrictor," the "anaconda," or "Scott's Great Snake."[3] The press and the public wanted no part of it. Northern newspapers demanded the immediate conquest of Richmond and a speedy end to secession.

On April 15—one day after Fort Sumter surrendered—Lincoln issued a proclamation calling for the mobilization of 75,000 volunteers to suppress the rebellion. In the North, the proclamation generated widespread support and unity. In the South, four states responded to Lincoln's call by seceding from the Union, and strong secession movements pressed the remaining four slave-holding states to follow their example.

Within the Lincoln Administration, debate ensued about whether to declare a blockade of the Confederacy. It was Jefferson Davis's action that tipped the debate in favor of doing so. Two days after Lincoln's call for volunteers to suppress the rebellion, Davis invited applications for "Letters of Marque" authorizing Confederate agents to seize and destroy American merchant ships. On April 19, Lincoln responded by declaring a blockade of Southern ports with the intent of preventing cotton, tobacco, and sugar from being exported and military equipment and supplies from coming into the South from abroad.[4]

Declaring a blockade was easy; enforcing it was another matter. The

South had nine major ports and more than 3,500 miles of coastline, and it would be impossible for the North to prevent small ships from landing goods along thousands of bays, inlets, rivers, and islands. The Federal navy had only ninety ships at the beginning of the war, and more than half of these were outmoded sailing ships, many of them unseaworthy. As soon as Lincoln declared the blockade, the Navy Department recalled naval ships from foreign waters, purchased merchant ships, which were quickly converted into gunboats, and launched a major shipbuilding program. Within weeks, the United States had 150 ships ready for duty, and construction had begun on another 50 ships.

As ships returned from abroad and new ships came on line, the blockade became more effective. By December 1861, the navy had 264 ships on line, and the effects of the blockade were "severely felt" in the Confederacy.[5]

The Provision Blockade Is Nothing

Most Southerners did not see the blockade as a serious threat. Some, in fact, welcomed it. Jefferson Davis called it "a blessing in disguise," believing that the blockade would force England and France "to a speedy recognition of the Confederacy, and to an interference with the blockade." Even if the blockade became effective and England and France were not drawn into the conflict, Southerners concluded that "Lincoln's humbug of a blockade" would still not succeed because of the South's abundant food supply. As one Confederate officer in Nashville proclaimed, "The provision blockade is nothing; we shall have wheat, corn, and beef beyond measure, besides tobacco, sugar, and rice." No one imagined that the blockade of the Atlantic and Gulf ports would have much of an impact on the availability, distribution, or cost of food in the Confederacy.[6]

Although the Anaconda plan was never officially approved, a modified version of it shaped Union strategy after the Northern defeat at Bull Run in July 1861. Southerners were well aware of the supposed "anaconda" strategy of the North, and many called it a "starvation policy." This Anaconda strategy was well understood in both the North and South, and regular mention of the serpent—"contracting coils of the anaconda," the "embraces of the Northern anaconda," "the great anaconda has begun to enfold," or "strangulation by the great anaconda,"—appeared in both Northern and Southern newspapers and magazines as the war progressed.[7]

An assistant to Jefferson Davis accurately foretold Union strategy, which was "to take our chief sea-coast cities, so as to cut off all supplies from foreign countries, get possession of the border States of Kentucky, Missouri, and Tennessee, which are the great grain-growing States, properly belonging to the Confederacy; cut the railway connections between Virginia and the cotton States, and cut the cotton region in two divisions by getting full possession of the Mississippi River by getting possession of the sea-coast cities on the one side and the principal grain-growing region on the other; by separating the cotton region of the Confederacy from Virginia and cutting it into two separate divisions; by commanding completely the Mississippi River, they expected to starve the people into subjection."[8]

Severely Felt

The U.S. Navy needed coaling and supply depots in the South to resupply blockading ships. On August 28, 1861, Federal forces captured Fort Hatteras and Fort Clark on Cape Hatteras Inlet on North Carolina's Outer Banks, and later captured Roanoke, New Bern, Elizabeth City, and Plymouth. In South Carolina, U.S. Army and Navy units seized

Fort Walker and Fort Beauregard, guarding the entrance to Port Royal Sound. On November 24, 1861, the North seized Tybee Island in Georgia near the Savannah River estuary and immediately began constructing long-range batteries to fire on Confederate-occupied Fort Pulaski, which surrendered months later. From forts and fortified positions on offshore islands, Federal gunboats prevented coastwise trading. These conquests also gave the United States access to the South's food production areas, among them the fertile strip of land along the coast of the Carolinas and Georgia; raiding parties ventured far into the hinterland confiscating commodities, dismantling the dikes, and flooding the rice fields. As a result, rice and other food production in these areas nosedived.[9]

From the beginning, the blockade reduced food imports into the South. Coffee, tea, spices, and wine quickly became difficult to acquire. More important losses from a nutritional standpoint were apples and dairy products, such as butter and cheese, which had been imported from New England; citrus fruits, dates, pineapples, and vegetables, which had been imported from Bermuda and the Caribbean islands became scarce, as did salt (used as a preservative), which had been mainly imported from abroad before the war. The nutritional effects of these losses increased as the war progressed.

The Confederacy did permit ships, mainly operated by private enterprises looking to make sizable profits, to run the blockade. Blockade-runners brought in much needed military equipment and supplies, but the most profitable part of their cargoes consisted of luxury goods, such as silks, laces, spices, molasses, liquor, sugar, coffee, and tea. What the South needed was machinery, salt, zinc, iron, steel, and copper, but these were heavy and bulky, and these items produced much smaller returns. The Confederate government tried to regulate blockade-runners, but this usually lessened the willingness of private entrepreneurs to risk having their ships and cargoes captured. Although the Confederacy finally outlawed the importation of alcoholic beverages and some other luxury goods, bans proved ineffective and these items were available in the Confederacy up to its final days—for those able to pay for them.

Starving the People of New Orleans

The most important port on the Gulf Coast was New Orleans—the largest city in the Confederacy. Southern officials believed that the city's formidable forts and some hastily converted and constructed naval vessels were powerful enough to repulse any possible Union invasion coming from the Gulf, so the regular military units stationed in New Orleans were sent northward to block the expected Federal campaign down the Mississippi River from Illinois. This left only an inexperienced home guard in the city proper, with limited supplies. When the Mississippi was closed to traffic in August 1861, the flow of grain and other foodstuffs from the Midwest to New Orleans was halted. During the following eight months, the city's storehouses were depleted. The food situation became desperate enough for city officials to make the outlandish request that Virginia send a trainload of grain every day to prevent famine in New Orleans.[10]

On April 24, 1862, the Union Flag Officer David G. Farragut, a Tennessean by birth, achieved strategic surprise when he led a flotilla past the forts protecting New Orleans and sank the ships sent to stop him. After an intense bombardment, the two forts surrendered, and the flotilla turned upriver toward New Orleans. The Confederate home guard evacuated the city, fearing that the meager supplies of flour and meat would not hold out during a siege.[11] Northern troops occupied New Orleans, and the South lost its largest city, with its strategic location on the Mississippi River, its ship-building facilities, and its large industrial base.

When the Union military arrived in New Orleans, they had to offer provisions to "the starving people of New Orleans," as *Harper's Weekly* reported it. The city's former Confederate authorities were blamed for the famine situation in New Orleans. The article continued, condemning Confederate officials: "If the leaders of this accursed rebellion could have looked upon the sight and reflected upon their responsibility for all this misery, it would have been strange if they had not experienced some dark forebodings of the terrible punishment that surely awaits them in another world, however easily they may escape a just retribution in this."[12]

Farragut wasn't satisfied with just taking New Orleans. In a lightning move, he sent a small flotilla under the command of Commander S. Phillips Lee up the Mississippi River. The flotilla occupied Baton Rouge on May 5, and Natchez five days later. On May 18, the ships arrived before Vicksburg and fired a few shots into Confederate positions. But the Confederates in Vicksburg refused to surrender, and Commander Lee's few troops were unable to take the city, so the flotilla turned back to New Orleans. Thus ended the first feeble Union attempt to take Vicksburg, a key port on the middle section of the Mississippi River.

With the occupation of New Orleans, Baton Rouge, and Natchez, the Union solidified its control of the lower Mississippi; this gave Federal troops access to rich agricultural areas in Louisiana and Mississippi. Beginning in the fall of 1862, Union troops under the command of Major General Benjamin Butler began to confiscate or destroy agricultural commodities and production facilities in lower Louisiana. Some plantations were deliberately reduced to ashes by Union troops in order to prevent food from falling into Confederate hands. Other plantations succumbed to the foraging activities of both armies. Still other plantations were simply abandoned by their owners, who took their slaves to more protected places further inland. Levees in Louisiana wore down or were torn down and agricultural machinery fell into disrepair or was destroyed. Louisiana produced 270,000 tons of sugar in 1861, but three years later production had dropped to a total of only 5,400 tons.[13] Similar declines in the production of other agricultural commodities turned much of eastern Louisiana into an agricultural wasteland.

The Federal presence in New Orleans and along the Gulf Coast was enough to encourage slaves to flee plantations. Eight months after the occupation of New Orleans, more than 150,000 slaves were behind Union lines. In the State of Mississippi alone, an estimated one third of the slaves left their plantations in 1862 and more would leave later. Since slaves grew much of the surplus food in the South, their absence meant a decrease in agricultural production.[14]

The Cotton Famine

For decades, American newspapers, magazines, and political leaders had extolled the power of Southern cotton, and for good reason: it accounted for 85 percent of all the cotton fabric manufactured in the United States, Great Britain, and France. Many Southerners had come to believe that without its cotton, the North's textile industry—America's largest and most lucrative business—would collapse, leading to economic ruin. Long before this happened, proclaimed Southerners, the North would call a halt to the war and recognize the South's independence. For the same reason, many Southerners predicted that Great Britain and France would recognize the Confederacy as an independent nation just as soon as their existing supplies of cotton were exhausted. Southern newspapers hailed the coming of the "cotton famine" believing it would force England and France to break the blockade. Jefferson Davis, a major cotton grower and a strong believer in cotton power, boasted that Southern "cotton would pay all debts of war and force New England into penury and starvation."[15] As it turned out, Davis was wrong on both counts: cotton did not pay for the Confederacy's war, and cotton did not force New England into penury or starvation.

Many secession leaders believed that the best way to hasten the cotton famine would be to embargo the export of cotton.[16] They petitioned the Confederate Congress to stop its export, but the legislation never passed, in part because many Southern legislators were major cotton growers. So embargo supporters launched a vigorous campaign pressuring plantation owners to stop exporting cotton. Pro-embargo sentiments filled Southern newspapers and magazines, and the campaign did influence the passage of state laws restricting the planting of cash-crops, mainly cotton and tobacco.

The embargo's success had some ironic results. According to international law, for blockades to be considered legal, they had to be effective. By restricting the export of cotton early in the war, the embargo made it appear as if the blockade was more effective than it was. Southern plantation owners, who had strongly supported secession and observed the embargo, were financially ruined because their finances depended on exporting their cotton crop. Conversely, plantation owners who did not observe the embargo generated substantial profits from the export of their cotton, as the embargo greatly reduced the amount of cotton available on the world market and escalated the price of cotton to astronomical heights.[17]

Despite the informal embargo, the peer pressure, and the legal restrictions, plantation owners continued to grow cotton and store it on docks and in warehouses. The South produced large cotton crops in 1861 and 1862. Growers had projected that the war would be of short duration and they expected to make a killing when they sold their bales after the war. Some cotton was run through the blockade or traded to the North, but most of it rotted or was burned by Southerners trying to prevent its capture by Union soldiers. Although cotton production appreciably declined during the following years, the South continued to raise twice as much cotton as was necessary for its needs. Stanley Lebergott, a professor of economics at Wesleyan University, pointed out that despite a rapid reduction in cotton growing, the number of people "growing cotton far exceeded the average size of the Confederate armies."[18] Had the manpower devoted to excess cotton production been diverted into producing foodstuffs, it might well have made a difference to the outcome of the war.

The alternative to the embargo was to trade as much cotton as possible at the beginning of the war before the blockade became effective. This was argued by Judah Benjamin, then the Confederate Attorney General. Early in 1861, he proposed that the government buy 100,000 bales, ship them to Europe, and pocket $50 million in specie, or use the money to buy 150,000 guns, munitions, and pieces of military equipment, which the Confederacy desperately needed at the beginning of the war. This might well have stabilized the Confederate financial system, but the Confederate government rejected the proposal.[19]

After two years of serious disruption in textile manufacturing in Britain, France, and New England, imports of cotton from Egypt and India surged and the demand for cotton textiles shrank as other fabrics were substituted. This brought an end to talk of the cotton famine, yet Confederate leaders continued to oppose selling or trading cotton long after this served any useful purpose.

The Salt Famine

Prior to the Civil War, Southerners used an estimated 450 million pounds of salt annually. Very little salt was produced in the antebellum South; most of it came from Wales on ships, which carried salt as ballast when they sailed to Southern ports to pick up cotton. In the nineteenth century, salt was used for commercial purposes, such as tanning leather for use in making harnesses and shoes. Salt's most important use, however, was as a preservative. In an age without refrigeration, virtually all pork and beef that was not cooked and served immediately after slaughter was preserved in brine. Salt was used to preserve fish, and other foods, such as butter, had to be salted. Salt was also used in cooking and was added as a condiment at the table. At the time, Americans consumed more salt than any other nation in the world, and more salt was used in the South than in any other region of the United States.

Once the blockade was declared, ships no longer brought salt into Southern ports. New Orleans had large stockpiles of salt, but this accumulation had shrunk to nothing by the fall of 1861. The price for salt surged so high that many farmers who raised hogs were unable to preserve them because they had no salt. One farmer wrote to the governor of Mississippi: "With a great many now, the deepest anxiety prevails to keep our families from suffering for want of salted provisions. Meat is now ready to be slaughtered."[20]

The shortage of imported salt was only one reason for its rising price; another cause was speculation. An editor of a Mississippi newspaper reported in November 1861 that "all the salt in New Orleans and elsewhere is now in the hands of speculators. . . . Something must be done in the matter, and be done quickly. We are willing that speculators should reap a rich profit, but we are not willing for them to suck the very life blood out of the people, if we can avoid it."[21]

The salt famine became severe in 1862. In March of that year an Alabama official reported that speculators were using "every artifice and fraud" to acquire salt. In May 1862 the editor of Atlanta's *Southern Confederacy* announced that "we will be in a dreadful condition unless we get salt." In December twenty women from Greenville, Alabama, became fed up with the salt famine. They marched on the local railroad station shouting "Salt or Blood," and forced an agent to give up the contents of a large sack of salt.[22]

Facing severe shortages, Southern leaders encouraged domestic salt production. States offered rewards for locating salt deposits and bonuses for its production. Southerners began to manufacture salt from salt lakes, saline artesian wells, and seawater. While such domestic production helped families and small farmers, these sources did not produce enough salt to meet the military and civilian needs of the Confederacy. Only five areas in the South had sufficient concentrations of salt to produce the large quantities needed to replace imported salt. These were the Great Kanawha River, near Charleston, then in Virginia; Goose Creek near Manchester, Kentucky; the salt wells in Clarke, Washington, and Mobile counties in Alabama; the saline wells near New Iberia in northern Louisiana; and the great saline artesian wells in the extreme southwest corner of Virginia, near Saltville. In addition, large-scale operations to convert ocean water to salt emerged in Florida. These operations produced enough salt for military, industrial, and civilian needs, but it was difficult to transport due to the lack of railroads in Florida.[23]

When the price of salt skyrocketed in early 1862, Daniel D. Avery and his son-in-law, Edmund McIlhenny, began working the salt springs on Avery Island, not far from New Iberia, about 140 miles west of New Orleans. By accident, Avery discovered a source of dry, pure rock salt a mere fifteen to twenty feet below the surface. Avery and McIlhenny began to quarry this salt in May 1862. A Confederate agent sent out to evaluate the site claimed that the mine could supply "the Confederacy if properly managed." As the Union forces controlled New Orleans, salt from Avery's Island had to be shipped by a circuitous route overland to the Red River, and to the Mississippi, where it could then be distributed throughout the eastern Confederacy.[24]

Union forces were well aware of the importance of salt to the

Confederacy, and they targeted salt production facilities. The salt manufacturing areas around Kanawha Valley in Virginia and Goose Creek in Kentucky were taken or destroyed by the North early in the war. In Louisiana, Union forces seized New Iberia and took control of Avery Island in 1863. Saltville, Virginia, was regularly targeted, but it wasn't finally captured until December 1864. Meanwhile, the Union navy conducted continuous amphibious efforts to disrupt salt manufacturing in North Carolina and repeatedly assaulted saltworks and plantations along Florida's Gulf Coast. Many plantation owners took their slaves inland, where, often, both master and slave became subsistence farmers.[25]

Another solution to the salt famine was for Southerners to curtail their use of salt. Those living near the coast cooked rice, grits, and hominy in seawater. Civilians were encouraged to eat tinned corned beef, which didn't need salt added at the table. Southern newspapers, journals, and books published dozens of recipes made with little salt. Salt conservation and even salt recycling became common practices. Southerners collected and reused loose salt grains from cured meat. Troughs and barrels used for brining meat were dried and the salt recaptured for future use. The floorboards in salt houses were ripped out and soaked in water, which was then boiled down to produce a little salt. People even dug up the soil under old smokehouses and recovered salt, which was fed to cattle and horses. In addition to conservation and recycling efforts, Southerners experimented with numerous methods for curing meat with little or no salt, but the meat often spoiled. Experimenters also produced a substance that tasted somewhat like salt, according to Varina Davis, the wife of Jefferson Davis; however, this had no preservative property.[26]

Without salt, Southerners frequently went without meat, and as time went on, things only got worse. After the occupation of Avery Island and New Iberia by Union forces in 1863, a resident of the area told the

Confederate Congress that those living in "Louisiana lying east of the Mississippi River are starving for the want of salt and salt meat." Southern governors spoke of "salt famines" and established programs for citizens to buy salt cheaply, yet the price continued to rise.[27] Despite these efforts, the salt famine meant shortages of pork that would previously have been preserved. The beef supply also dwindled because salt was essential to the diet of cattle, and without it, the animals did not fatten up. Likewise, cavalry and artillery horses sickened from the absence of salt (a necessary electrolyte for animals kept hard at work) in their diet. By the end of the war, Confederate leaders were offering exorbitant fees for blockaders to bring in salt and salted meat. Had the South just figured out a better way to tap the natural salt deposits that they had, imports would have been unnecessary. Then there was the transportation problem.

Unable to Meet Requirements

As the blockade prevented coastwise shipping and Union gunboats raided rivers, railroads took on a crucial role for transporting goods, troops, and military equipment. Prior to war, the South had imported virtually all of its railroad equipment. The Confederacy had few factories that could build train engines, rolling stock, rail track, or the machinery and equipment needed to sustain the region's transportation needs, and there was no great encouragement by the Confederate government to launch such efforts. Early in the conflict the South failed to centralize its railroads so that they might run more efficiently, and it did not encourage blockade-runners to bring in heavy equipment for railroads, when doing so might have made a difference.

The Confederacy did appoint a railroad czar without much authority or power. In December 1861 he requested that the government exempt from conscription skilled railroad men, and supply much-needed equipment to repair the railroads. If this were not done, he warned, "the railroads will very soon be quite unable to meet requirements of Government." In April 1863, the *Richmond Sentinel* pointed to transportation as the bottleneck in the supply system, and recommended that the Southern railways be coordinated by a "master mind" in order to transport provisions from where they were grown to where they were needed.[28] These suggestions, which had been made by others, fell flat, thanks to the laissez-faire economic policies of the Confederate government.

The railroads slowly deteriorated, making food distribution increasingly difficult. When the main railroad lines began to give out, Southerners cannibalized smaller trunk lines, decreasing the number of miles served by railroads, thus weakening the overall system. The railroads, even when not interdicted by Union soldiers, could not transport enough food to feed civilians, the military, cavalry horses, and draft animals. Even when food was available, inefficiencies resulted. Civil War railroad historian George Edgar Turner concluded: "Tons of bacon, rice, sugar and other perishable foods spoiled in accumulated masses while soldiers in near-by Virginia famished for want of them." Historian Charles W. Ramsdell pointed out that Lee's army starved, "not because there was no food in the Confederacy, for it was plentiful in many portions of Georgia, Alabama, and Florida, but because the railroads simply could not carry enough of it." When Petersburg and Richmond were cut off, and "the remnant of the feeble roads wrecked by Sherman's destructive march through Georgia and the Carolinas," Ramsdell continued, "the stoppage of all supplies followed, and the long struggle was over."[29]

The South also had problems with its roads and wagon transportation. The roads were mainly unimproved, which meant that when it rained, they were filled with mud and were impassable. Even in good weather, the South's wagon transportation was inadequate, largely because of the scarcity of draft animals, thousands of which had annually come from the Midwest before the war.[30] Southern armies purchased or expropriated large number of mules, oxen, and horses, and these had to be replaced regularly. The animals had to be fed as they traveled. Transporting bulky and heavy forage required even more draft animals. The military often commandeered or impressed animals from farmers as needed, which caused yet more problems: Without draft animals, farmers could not plant, harvest, or transport their crops, further contributing to food shortages.[31]

Blockade Effects

Historians have lavished attention on the success of blockade-runners. Indeed, an estimated 300 steamers made an estimated 1,300 attempts to test the blockade, and about a thousand of these runs were successful. Citing the success of these blockade-runners, some historians have pronounced the Union operation a failure. However, the 1,000 successful blockade attempts should be compared to the 20,000 ships—many of them much larger than the sleek blockade-runners—that arrived or departed harbors in what became the Confederacy during the four years prior to the war. The amount of supplies imported and cotton exported during the war was a small fraction of what had been transacted in the prewar period. What was brought in through the blockade did not even come close to fulfilling Southern wartime needs.

The revenue from cotton exported through the blockade generated substantial profits—mainly for shipbuilders, blockade-runners, and insurance companies. Blockade-running did little for Confederate finances. The profits on exports were not adequate to establish credit, acquire large loans, or bring in specie to support the Confederate currency. Blockade-running did, however, contribute to inflation and escalating food prices.

The willingness of wealthy Southerners to pay exorbitant prices for scarce items made it more lucrative for blockade-runners to carry luxury goods rather than much-needed staple foods.[32] Many Southerners greatly resented the blockade-runners, the traders who sold the luxury goods, and those who purchased them—all while most Southerners suffered severe privations.

The blockade may not have stopped all goods from entering the Confederacy, but it greatly reduced the amount of large bulky items, such as foodstuffs, railroad equipment, and raw materials, and jacked up the cost of all imported goods. Over time, the blockade contributed to the South's demoralization and its ultimate defeat. No one can seriously believe that the North could have won the war without the blockade.

2

Scarcity and Hunger

On January 23, 1863, General Robert E. Lee informed President Jefferson Davis that "unless regular supplies can be obtained, I fear the efficiency of the army will be reduced by many thousand men, when already the army is far inferior in numbers to that of the enemy." Three days later, Lee reported that his army was down to an eight-day supply of fresh and salted beef. He wrote, "I am more than usually anxious about the supplies of the army, as it will be impossible to keep it together with-out food."[1]

Lee defused the immediate crisis by sending two divisions—one fourth of his army—to Suffolk, in southeastern Virginia, where there was ample food. This left two fewer divisions to feed in northern Virginia, and the men he transferred could help acquire food for the rest of the army. There was a drawback, however. When Lee wanted to take the offensive in early April 1863, he was unable to do so because the Army of Northern Virginia was scattered. It would not be reunited again until later in the month, when the Union army was once again on the march. This Union offensive ended in defeat at Chancellorsville; the battle, however, took the lives of many Southern soldiers, including that of Thomas "Stonewall" Jackson, one of the South's best military commanders. Lee's biographer Douglas Freeman has speculated that, if the Army of Northern Virginia had been well fed and at full strength in early April 1863, Lee might have assumed the offensive with the added leadership of Stonewall Jackson "and with the strength of the men who fell at Chancellorsville"; then the outcome might have been very different from the Gettysburg defeat in July.[2]

Starved Out at Manassas

The lack of provisions influenced Confederate military movements from the beginning of the war. When Union forces gathered in Washington and Alexandria, Virginia, the Confederate army assembled at Manassas Junction under the command of Brigadier General P. G. T. Beauregard, now identified as the "Hero of Sumter." His superior, Brigadier General Joseph E. Johnston, was stationed in the Shenandoah Valley, but he planned to join Beauregard as soon as the Union army was on the march. Johnston, a Virginian by birth, had graduated from West Point and had served with distinction during the Mexican-American War. When the Civil War broke out, he was the Quartermaster General of the U.S. Army. When Virginia seceded, Johnston resigned his commission and joined the Confederate army.

The Confederate army in Manassas rapidly expanded as new units arrived. An obvious problem was that there were no warehouses or storage facilities in the area and none were built by the soldiers stationed there. Food either remained in freight cars on sidings or was unloaded next to the tracks. As there were no tarpaulins to cover the food, it rotted in the hot, humid days of summer. Simultaneously, the Confederate Commissary-General Lucius Northrop decided that subsistence purchasing should be centralized through his office in Richmond, so commissaries in Manassas were limited in the amount of provisions they could buy locally. When the Confederate army was small, this worked. As soldiers poured in, Richmond was hard-pressed to provide enough food.[3]

At the battle of Bull Run, on July 16, 1861, the Confederates won despite serious supply deficiencies. Their army might have been able to follow up this victory with an assault on Washington—which at the time was largely defenseless. Beauregard evidently wanted to do just that, but Johnston vetoed the move because the army was low on supplies. There was not one day's rations of food for the entire army. One Confederate soldier described the situation this way: "two days after the battle we were literally starved out at Manassas, and were forced to advance to Fairfax Court House in order to get the supplies which the Union army had left in abundance." One week after the battle, Johnston begged for supplies: "We are almost destitute and in danger of absolute suffering." On July 29, Beauregard told Davis that "some regiments are nearly starving." In another letter he claimed that "The want of food and transportation had made us lose all the fruits of our victory. We ought at this moment to be in or about Washington." He then asked, "Cannot something be done towards furnishing us more expeditiously and regularly with food and transportation?"[4]

Historian Richard Goff, who extensively studied the Confederate supply system, concluded: "The abandonment of the 'on to Washington' scheme is the first, and quite possibly the most important, instance of the manner in which supply deficiencies shaped strategy."[5] Had the Southern army destroyed the remnants of the defeated Union army and captured Washington in July 1861, the war might well have ended there with the Confederacy's independence.

It Will Feed Our Armies

The South was agrarian, but much of its best farmland was devoted to nonfood crops, such as cotton and tobacco. Southern leaders were well aware of the need to increase food production for the war effort, which

meant growing less cotton; they encouraged cotton and tobacco planters to convert to agricultural crops to avoid famine. Specifically, farmers and plantation owners were encouraged to grow wheat, which was a
winter crop. Once the wheat was harvested in the spring, the same
land could be used for growing other crops, particularly corn, which
required less labor and could easily be grown throughout much of the
South. Because of the cornerstone Confederate belief in the principle
of states' rights, however, the Confederate Congress never passed legislation making the changeover mandatory. The Confederate Congress
did place a tax on cotton exports, which was intended to generate revenue and encourage plantation owners to grow food crops. However,
the tax was largely ignored, and only about $6,000 in taxes was col-
lected.[6]

All Confederate states eventually restricted the amount of cotton
that could be grown, but none banned it. When the Georgia legislature
passed a resolution discouraging the production of cotton and encouraging food crops, Jefferson Davis wrote to the governor of Georgia,
complimenting him and sharing his concerns about shortages: "The
possibility of a short supply of provisions presents the greatest danger to
a successful prosecution of the war. If we shall be able to furnish adequate subsistence to the Army during the coming season we may set at
defiance the worst efforts of our enemy."[7]

In 1860, the United States had slaughtered and packed three million
hogs, of which only about 20,000 were produced by the states that later
seceded. Instead, Southern states imported 1.2 million hogs from the
North. Beginning in February 1861, the Confederate subsistence department began buying as much meat as possible from border states, and
20,000 hogs that came from within Federal lines.[8] To alleviate future
problems, Nashville was established as the Confederacy's meat-packing
center and supply depot for the Confederate armies in the west.

When the Federal government finally broke off trade with the Confederacy in August 1861, it became impossible for the South to acquire salt pork from the Midwest. Hog production in the South could be increased, but not enough to meet everyone's needs: The Southern armies alone would require an estimated 500,000 hogs annually, projected the Confederate Commissary-General, Lucius B. Northrop. He calculated that it would be possible to produce only about one third of that quantity within the Confederacy.[9]

The Confederacy turned to beef. In October 1861, an estimated 40,000 cattle were available in the Southern states east of the Mississippi River. The Army of Northern Virginia alone consumed 1,000 cattle per month. Even with expanded production, the South's total beef stock east of the Mississippi dropped to 30,000 head by 1862, and this decline continued, falling to 20,000 by 1863 and less than 6,000 by 1864. Exacerbating the problem was the fact that the South had few slaughterhouses and salt was at a premium. Also, the Southern transportation system was so erratic that fresh beef often spoiled before it could be distributed to the troops. Many Southerners, who were more familiar with pork, did not even know how to cook beef.[10]

Despite all the problems, food production swelled in the South during the first year of the war. The so-called "bread statesmen," who advocated growing grain over cotton, won a stunning victory in 1861, when the states of the Confederacy produced the largest amount of food in their history. Corn was particularly prominent in this expansion, increasing from 30 million bushels in 1860 to 55 million bushels in 1861. As the editor of the *Southern Cultivator* noted in January 1862, this was an encouraging development, for "Corn makes bread and bacon and poultry and beef, and fat horses and mules. It is good for 'man and beast'—it is the 'all in all'—the 'staff of life' for the South—it will feed our armies and help vanquish our foes!" The *Columbus* (Georgia) *Sun* put it more succinctly: "Plant corn and be free, or plant cotton and be whipped."[11] Samuel Phillips Day, a pro-Southern British journalist who traveled throughout the South in 1862, proclaimed enthusiastically that the Confederacy had major reserves of food and concluded that "Southern production and resources will serve to exhibit the utter impossibility of the blockade necessitating a scarcity of provisions— much less 'a famine in the land,' as some Northern croakers prophesied at the commencement of the civil war."[12] As it turned out, Day was wrong and the croakers were right.

Swineflesh, of the Most Miserable Description

The Confederate-controlled Fort Henry and Fort Donelson protected major agricultural areas in western Tennessee as well as crucial railroads and rivers on which provisions were transported within the Confederacy. These forts were also the gateway to Nashville, the major supply center for Confederate armies in the west. Fort Henry fell to Union naval forces, and the Union army proceeded overland to take Fort Donelson. Despite its strategic location, the garrison in Fort Donelson ran out of provisions, which was one reason for its commander's surrender. The Union victories at these forts in February 1862 gave them access to central Tennessee and forced Confederates to withdraw from Kentucky. Most significant, the Confederates also evacuated Nashville, but they had no plan for the removal of all supplies collected in the city. The retreating army left behind "an immense amount of flour, beef, pork, bacon, &c., which they had been accumulating for the supply of a great army for a long campaign," crowed the *New York Herald*. These lost provisions had to be replaced by supplies coming from the northern counties of Alabama and Mississippi, and food prices in the area shot up. The effects of these losses were felt as far east as Macon, Georgia, where beef prices went from ten to twenty cents a pound in a few days, and "swineflesh, of the most miserable description," surged "from thirty-three to forty cents per pound." Due to the loss of these supplies, and the loss of large food-producing areas in Kentucky and Tennessee, the Confederate War Department ordered a severe reduction in the meat ration for all Confederate armies.[13]

The scarcity of provisions for the army and price increases for food in the marketplace caused concern throughout the South. In May 1862 the *Richmond Dispatch* reported that the Southern "panic on the subject of a scarcity of food is one of the most causeless imaginable." It further noted that the railroad from Danville to Greensborough was under construction, and once completed, would "open North Carolina, Tennessee, and even Georgia and South Carolina, for supplies to feed the whole state of Virginia." The *New York Times* republished the *Richmond Dispatch*'s article; an editor there dryly observed that the same *Richmond Dispatch* issue also reported the cost of butter in Richmond at $1.40 a pound, an unheard of price at the time.[14] As high as this may have seemed in 1862, it was just a fraction of what butter would cost in the South a few years later.

Simultaneously with the North's advance into Kentucky and Tennessee was a planned campaign to take Richmond. As the Union army—more than 110,000 strong—began to assemble around Washington, Joseph E. Johnston decided that his army's position in northern Virginia was indefensible, and he made the decision to retreat southward. However, the army did not have a plan for removing the vast reserve of food—estimated at one million pounds—they had accumulated at Manassas Junction and Thoroughfare in northern Virginia. When the army left on March 8, some of the provisions from these depots were distributed to local residents, and the rest were torched, including 370,000 pounds of meat at Thoroughfare and virtually all the supplies at Manassas. Confederate General Jubal Early wrote after the war that the loss of these stores "was a very serious one for us, and embarrassed us for the rest of the war, as it put us at once on a running stock."[15]

Rather than heading directly south as Johnston anticipated, the Union army embarked on ships and shifted its operations to Fort Monroe in southeastern Virginia. As Union forces pushed up the peninsula, Confederate forces retreated from Norfolk and Williamsburg, resulting in yet another large loss of supplies and foodstuffs. While marching from Yorktown to Richmond, one Confederate soldier wrote, "I came nearer starving than I ever did before."[16]

General Johnston was wounded at the Battle of Seven Pines, and on June 1, 1862, Robert E. Lee took command of the Confederate army. Lee had graduated from West Point and served in the prestigious army Corps of Engineers constructing forts on the East Coast. He served with distinction during the Mexican-American War and remained in the army after the war. Four days after the surrender of Fort Sumter, Lee was informally offered the command of what would become the Army of the Potomac, but he declined when Virginia seceded a few days later. Lee was appointed Lieutenant General in the Confederate army and served in various capacities during the early war years. Lee's subsequent victories in the Peninsula Campaign saved Richmond and forced the Union army to retreat. Lee then took the offensive and thrust into Maryland, but the campaign ended in defeat at Antietam in September 1862.

In the retreat from Maryland, the Confederates were unable to supply their army. The diet consisted of apples, green corn, and short rations of beef and flour. "Our army," a soldier reported is, "almost starved out." When the Confederate army returned to Virginia, however, this was rectified. As the Army of Northern Virginia had largely subsisted on food taken from farmers and Union supplies captured in Maryland, the Confederate commissary had been busy stockpiling foodstuffs in Virginia. Richmond had ten days' worth of food for 100,000 men, while the supply depot at Lynchburg held five million bacon rations and 10,000 cattle; additional supplies were available at other nearby depots.[17] With these stockpiles, there should not have been any sustenance problems for the Army of Northern Virginia during the winter, assuming that provisions were in as good supply in the autumn of 1862 as they had been in the autumn of 1861.

Who Can Fight Starvation

But what a difference that year made. By late 1862, major food-producing areas of the South were under Federal control. Union-occupied Kentucky and Tennessee contained important wheat-growing and hog-producing areas that had previously supplied one third of the hogs packed for the Confederate armies. What's more, the Federal occupation of central Tennessee allowed Union cavalry and gunboats to raid northern Mississippi, Alabama, and Georgia, confiscating provisions, burning crops, and disrupting supply lines.[18] All along the coasts of the Confederacy, Union amphibious forces conducted raids that demolished war-related installations, mills, salt-making facilities, warehouses, and crops, and killed or confiscated livestock and beasts of burden. This further undercut the total availability of food in the South.

Just as Confederate food supplies were shrinking, a burgeoning number of Southern civilians needed to be fed as a torrent of refugees, often with their slaves, flooded into the Confederacy from Kentucky, Tennessee, and northern Virginia. By the war's end, an estimated 400,000 Southerners had left their homes—in many cases, farms or plantations—and many had taken refuge in Southern cities.[19] As a result, less food was being produced in what remained of the Confederacy while the need for food was growing, especially in urban areas.

In addition to the loss of crops due to military actions, nature also contributed to the growing food problems in the South. Throughout the summer of 1862, much of the Confederacy east of the Mississippi River suffered from drought. As a result, only one fourth of the usual wheat crop was harvested in Virginia. That same year, the corn crop failed entirely in sections of Georgia and the Carolinas. This meant not only less grain for human consumption but also less feed for animals, requiring their early slaughter before they had been properly fattened. Pork production thus took a dive. Texas beef cattle could not easily be driven to other areas of the Confederacy because there was little fodder or forage to sustain them. By the fall of 1862, the Confederate commissary department projected a 25-percent deficit in hog production and a 90-percent deficit in beef for military needs during the upcoming year. Commissary-General Northrop warned that unless "something is done to afford transportation for all the wheat that can be procured, I do not see anything but failure and ruin to our Army."[20]

Weather, refugees, and loss of agricultural land were not the only reasons for the Confederacy's growing food crisis. Northrop and Jefferson Davis also contributed to it. The two had met at West Point, and they became kindred spirits when the two second lieutenants served together at Jefferson Barracks near St. Louis. When Davis became president of the Confederacy, he appointed Northrop to the position of Commissary of Subsistence, responsible for making sure that Confederate armies were well fed. Northrop had good qualities—he was honest and he was loyal to Davis. He believed in economy in government, which during normal times would have been greatly admired. However, it was wartime and his attempts to keep costs down would contribute to the food problems in the Confederate army. Northrop's main problem was that he had no experience running large organizations or bureaucracies, no experience with agriculture or food management, and little experience as a quartermaster while in the army. Despite numerous and frequent charges of gross incompetence, Davis retained Northrop in this position until early 1865. According to Richmond diarist Mary Chesnut, Northrop was "the most 'cussed' and vilified man in the Confederacy. He is held accountable for everything that goes wrong in the army."[21] Northrop wasn't responsible for everything that went wrong in the army, but he was responsible for the state of subsistence in the Confederate army.

Solutions to the Confederacy's food problems were offered—and they might just have worked. One potential solution was to exchange cotton for provisions with the United States. This idea had been raised previously, but Davis opposed it, believing that it would demoralize civilians as well as the army, among other reasons. On October 30, 1862, the Confederate Secretary of War, George W. Randolph, sent a letter to Jefferson Davis stating that "the Army cannot be subsisted without permitting trade to some extent with Confederate ports in the possession of the enemy. The alternative is thus presented of violating our established policy of withholding cotton from the enemy or of risking the starvation of our armies."[22] Northrop agreed with Randolph. Davis refused to sanction the trade. Randolph resigned.

On January 3, 1863, the new Secretary of War, James A. Seddon, diplomatically told Davis, "The harvests of the past season have not generally proved propitious, and notwithstanding the much larger breadth of land devoted to the culture of cereals and forage, the product in many extensive districts of the Confederacy is below the average, and in some threatens scarcity." Davis paid no attention. In February 1863, the editor of the *Daily Southern Crisis*, a newspaper published in Jackson, Mississippi, put it less diplomatically: "There is more to fear from a dearth of food than from all the Federal armies in existence." He then asked, "Who can fight starvation with hope of success?"[23]

We Have Tried to Get Help but Can Not

Food production in the South was also adversely affected by labor shortages. The large percentage of men under arms in the South meant that there were far fewer farm laborers, and thus less food production, especially on small farms. As the agricultural historian Charles Ramsdell wrote of Southern agriculture, "There were large sections of the country—the small farm sections, primarily—almost bare of agricultural labor. The result was a marked decline in production." In 1862 a woman wrote to her brother serving in the Confederate army about their corn crop: "I expect we will have to let some of it go. We have tried to get help but can not."[24] While this loss of labor greatly affected the families living on the farm, most of these were subsistence operations and did not produce agricultural surpluses.

Food surpluses were mainly grown on large farms and plantations, which were powered by slaves. Many owners avoided serving in the army and were able to secure exemptions for their sons and overseers. But there was a loss of labor on these as well. Owners moved their households and slaves away from Union lines. This often removed productive agricultural land from cultivation and also brought more hungry mouths deeper into the South. Slaves who remained on plantations became less willing to work, especially when experienced overseers and plantation owners were away fighting the war. Other slaves headed for Union lines, taking whatever opportunities they could. By the war's end, the total number of former slaves behind Union lines numbered one million, many of whom joined the Union army or worked on Union-controlled plantations.[25] As a result, labor on Southern farms and plantations declined steeply.

This loss of manpower should not necessarily have affected overall food output. Cotton was a labor-intensive crop, while corn required far fewer workers. As cotton production declined, corn output soared, but food production could have risen to even greater heights had the slaves been mobilized for growing food. However, 20 percent of slaves served as domestics and did not contribute to food production, and a large number of other slaves were kept at work in the production of cotton. Even with the weather problems, the loss of significant agricultural land, and the decrease in the total number of slaves, the South could still have produced food surpluses.

Grovelling Speculators

The Confederacy faced serious economic problems from the beginning of the war. The Confederate government was unwilling to tax citizens, which would have been a violation of states' rights, and it was opposed to selling cotton, which would have generated considerable revenue and loans from abroad. With a dwindling gold reserve, the Confederate government began floating loans and printing money to pay its bills. This caused inflation, which averaged 10 percent per month during much of the war. The value of the Confederate currency dropped precipitously and the price of staples shot up: The most rational economic behavior was to buy and store commodities, whose values at least kept pace with inflation. It was in the financial best interest of those with Confederate currency to exchange it as quickly as possible for commodities that could be stored and sold at a later time for more money. Hoarding became common throughout the Confederacy.

The inclination to hoard provisions was understandable for other reasons. Since many kinds of foods were more available at harvest time, in the late summer and autumn, buying quantities when plentiful meant lower prices, and would also ensure a supply during the lean months of winter and spring. Food availability also depended on the weather; crops could be reduced by storms, hail, or drought. The war brought additional uncertainty: Where the armies fought or marched, troops devastated crops, tore down fences, demolished mills, and looted or burned warehouses—all of which could affect food production for months. It made sense to stockpile food as a hedge against all contingencies.

Also contributing to the problem were speculators, who bought up as much food as possible in hopes of reaping financial rewards by selling it at much higher prices in times of scarcity. Politicians and newspapers frequently targeted speculators, who were identified as the cause of skyrocketing food prices. Governor Z. B. Vance of North Carolina told his state legislature: "The demon of speculation and extortion seems to have seized upon nearly all sorts and conditions of men, and all the necessaries of life are fast getting beyond the reach of the poor. Flour, which if properly left to the laws of supply and demand could not have risen to more than double peace rates, can now be used only by the rich."[26]

The *Richmond Dispatch* claimed that the real instigators of the food crisis were speculators: "The Yankees are monsters enough to starve us to death if they could, but they can't; whilst the speculators can and are doing it, and then lay the blame upon the Yankees!" Jefferson Davis also blamed food scarcity on "grovelling speculators" who attempted to "forestall the market and make money out of the lifeblood of our defenders." Southern newspapers agreed with Davis's sentiments. The *Richmond Dispatch* later proclaimed that speculators were "rendering more aid and influence than all the combined armies of Yankeedom to accomplish the avowed purpose of this war." A woman wondered why Davis just didn't take food from those who were hoarding it and send it to those who needed it: "Monopolists and misers hold enough meat and grain in their clutches to feed our army and Lincoln's."[27]

Shall We Starve?

Substantial responsibility for food scarcity can be attributed to actions and policies of the Confederate government and military. When the food crisis hit in the early months of 1863, military leaders began to restrict the movement of commodities out of their areas of responsibility and began to accumulate as many provisions as possible. This was understandable: Inflation affected not only individuals, but also the government. It was in the best interest of quartermasters to invest government funds in commodities that could be sold at a later time as a hedge against inflation (or to generate personal profit). This practice became so common by 1862 that orders were issued targeting military officers who bought "supplies for the purpose of selling them again at a profit," and the following year the Congress passed a law against officers and government officials speculating in food and other goods. The legislation proved ineffective, however, and some quartermasters and commissaries got rich.[28] The consequences of private and governmental speculation led to further increases in food prices and a drop in the value of the Confederate currency.

When food became unaffordable for many Southerners, the Confederate government stepped in and tried to place price controls on various commodities in the hope of keeping prices down. However, farmers hoarded staples rather than sell them at the artificially low prices, resulting in less food on the open market.[29] Price controls were discontinued, but inflation then ran rampant.

The scarcity of provisions was a particularly serious problem in northern Virginia. John B. Jones, a clerk in the Confederate War Department, asked, in January 1863, "Shall we starve?" He wrote that "none but the opulent, often those who have defrauded the government, can obtain a sufficiency of food and raiment." The Army of Northern Virginia was also in trouble. Jones observed that units looked "pale and haggard" and remarked that "we are approaching the condition of famine." He concluded that "the army must be fed or disbanded, or else the city must be abandoned."[30]

As the situation worsened, the Southern military had no choice but to expropriate provisions when needed just to keep soldiers alive. The confiscation of goods, called impressment, was a time-honored practice that armies and navies had engaged in for centuries. From the beginning of the Civil War, Confederate armies engaged in impressment when necessary, taking civilian property in exchange for currency or notes indicating that the farmer would be paid at some future date. As the food supply for the military dwindled in the early months of 1863, impressment sharply increased, and this caused a political backlash. Governor Joseph E. Brown of Georgia wrote to Jefferson Davis that "the little supplies of provisions in the hands of a few is being seized by Confederate officers, leaving none to distribute to relieve those likely to starve. If this continues the rebellion in that section will grow, and soldiers in service will desert to go to the relief of their suffering families."[31]

Had agents paid market rates for impressed goods, the system might have worked. But as contemporary observers and subsequent historians have pointed out, the prices paid for impressed goods were far below market value. For instance, farmers were paid only about 10 percent of the value of the flour and meat that were impressed. Rather than have their provisions, horses, and mules impressed, many farmers hid them. Others raised just enough food for their own family needs. The result was a general disappearance of provisions that were impressed, such as wheat and corn, while foods that were not impressed, such as fruits and perishable vegetables, were generally available. Impressment constricted the supply of staple provisions for both the military and civilians.[32]

When there was no other choice, Lee impressed goods for the Army of Northern Virginia, but he was not sanguine about the practice. "Wholesale impressments will give us present relief," he wrote, "but I fear it will injure our future supplies. It will cause concealment and waste, and deter many farmers from exerting all their efforts in producing full and proper crops. Already I hear of land in Virginia lying idle from this cause."[33] This is precisely what happened: Farmers stopped growing crops that they knew would be impressed, hid what they did grow, and hoarded surpluses for their own use or to make money.

Farmland around Richmond went fallow or was not used to its fullest agricultural potential simply because Confederate governmental policies discouraged the planting of crops that could be impressed.

The Confederate Congress passed a law on March 26, 1863, making impressment legal. The passage of this law recognized what, in fact, had been going on for two years. The law, however, caused an uproar even among those firmly committed to the Southern cause. It created such a political firestorm that Congress rescinded it a few months later. Despite the change in the Confederate law, the practice of impressment continued, for without it the Confederate armies could not survive.

Impressment generated resistance to the government in the forms of speculation, hoarding, and evasion. Southern newspapers condemned hoarding and speculation, but they railed most loudly against impressment. As constituents complained to their representatives, Congress passed bills intended to ameliorate the worst aspects of impressment.[34] The economist Stanley Lebergott concluded that impressment "proved the most decisive possible way to acquire material," but that "it slowed the flow of goods to markets and speeded up feelings of outrage among a wide population." He observed further that "because impressment bore disproportionately on the farms of common soldiers," it "induced disproportionate despair among them and fostered desertion."[35]

As an alternative to impressment, in April 1863 the Confederate Congress created a 10-percent in-kind tax on agricultural products. The tax applied to foods grown during that season, which meant that it did not take effect until the fall, so it did nothing toward solving the army's immediate food problems. But the tax had the desired effect: Rather than accept worthless Confederate currency for their crops, farmers just gave a portion of their harvest. After the currency reform of February 17, 1864, the printing of Confederate currency was greatly restricted, making the cumbersome system of bartering virtually the only way to exchange goods. As currency disappeared, soldiers were often paid late, or not at all, for months at a time.[36] For those soldiers with families, no pay meant that their families might well suffer from malnutrition and hunger. When faced with the choice between obligation to their state and obligation to their families, thousands of soldiers deserted.

Loyalty by Starvation

In early 1863, the Army of Northern Virginia was in desperate need of food. Lee's lieutenants recommended a strike at the Baltimore & Ohio railroad, an important supply line for the Union army in northern Virginia and for Washington, D.C. If it could be cut, it might upset Union plans for an expected spring offensive. Lee told those leading the raid that the "collection of horses, cattle, provisions, &c, is of primary importance to us—as much so as the destruction of the railroad. I request, therefore, that nothing be neglected on your part to obtain as large a supply as possible." It was also hoped that this raid on the B & O might recapture western Virginia for the Confederacy. The raid disrupted Union railroad traffic for a few weeks, but the railroad was quickly repaired. The Confederates captured only a thousand cattle, which did not solve the sustenance crisis faced by the army. Moreover, the raid did not prompt western Virginia to reconnect with the Confederacy; a few weeks after the raiders left, West Virginia was admitted to the Union as a state.[37]

Still desperate for food, Lee sent three expeditions into different parts of Virginia, hoping to obtain supplies for his army. These expeditions produced a total of 700 cattle, 200 sheep, and 7,000 pounds of bacon—not much of a haul. Commissary-General Northrop also sent agents out to procure all provisions in the Richmond area. They paid for wheat, corn, and meat, but as usual offered far less than the going rates on the open market. These agents operated under few rules and were not subject to supervision. Some were lazy, confiscating food by whatever means proved easiest. This usually meant impressing food from those who were least able to resist, such as farms being run by the wives of absent soldiers. Small farms suffered more from impressments than did large plantations, which were generally owned by rich and powerful individuals. Worse still, Southerners believed that impressment agents were paying the bare minimum and then selling provisions to the government at a higher price, thus making handsome personal profits.[38]

Officials tried other solutions to the subsistence problems. North Carolina helped ameliorate the shortages by "lending" the Confederate government a portion of 50,000 bushels of corn, which the state had accumulated to feed the families of soldiers. Corn and other provisions from Atlanta were sent to the Army of Northern Virginia. In addition, Confederate forces quietly began trading cotton across the lines for meat, coffee, and other provisions.[39]

Despite such efforts, many Confederate troops remained on short rations, and for those on active duty in the field, a plummeting food supply impaired performance and certainly affected troop morale. When scurvy appeared in the Army of Northern Virginia, in March 1863, Lee directed each regiment "to send a daily detail to gather sassafras buds, wild onions, garlic, lamb's quarter, and poke sprouts,"[40] some of which do, in fact, supply the needed vitamin C.

By April 1863, Lee reported that rations were down to "one-fourth pound of bacon, 18 ounces of flour, 10 pounds of rice to each 100 men about every third day, with some few peas and a small amount of dried fruit occasionally, as they can be obtained. This may give existence to the troops while idle, but will certainly cause them to break down when called upon for exertion."[41] Not until late April, however, were supplies for the Army of Northern Virginia available in sufficient quantities to permit the army to take the field again.

Confederate food supply problems were not limited to Virginia. As the planter, politician, journalist, and historian J. F. H. Claiborne told Mississippi's governor in August 1862, "We are now proving our loyalty by starvation—by the tears of our women and the cries of our children for bread." John C. Pemberton, the Confederate commander of Vicksburg, placed a restriction on shipping food out of Mississippi, and then sent agents into neighboring Alabama to acquire more supplies, thus stripping Mobile of its normal food sources, and civilians suffered more as a consequence. There were also serious problems in the Carolinas. General Beauregard declared that in South Carolina the food supply was "getting rapidly exhausted." In North Carolina, Governor Vance told Jefferson Davis: "In the interior of the State there is much suffering for bread already, and will be more on account of the failure of the crops from drought, and the Legislature made a large appropriation of money to enable me to purchase corn and transport it west to feed wives and children of soldiers." A private letter from a North Carolinian reported that they were on the "verge of starvation." Another observer in Raleigh wondered how the poor would survive and asked, "What are we coming to?"[42]

Effects of Scarcity

Before the railroads began to deteriorate, before hyperinflation set in, and before the destruction or union occupation of a significant amount of agricultural land, the Confederate food system was already strained. When these difficulties became acute in late 1862, Confederate leaders failed to resolve them, and these early failures had serious consequences. Southern military campaigns, especially in northern Virginia, were adversely affected. Farmers and plantation owners were discouraged. Strong supporters of the Confederacy were alienated. Civilians, especially in

Richmond and other cities, became demoralized. Soldiers' families were hard-pressed to grow their own food, and begged husbands, sons, and brothers to return home to plant or harvest crops. Confederate armies were frequently undermanned, partly because soldiers were furloughed to help their families plant or harvest crops—and, increasingly, because men were deserting due to the lack of food.

As Federal armies gained control of more Confederate territory, food-producing areas were cut off from the Southern states, and total food production declined. Other agricultural areas still in the Confederacy, such as northern Virginia, much of Louisiana, and the region north of Vicksburg, Mississippi, were devastated by the war. And droughts, speculation, and hoarding exacerbated the food crisis.

Confederate military and political leaders were constantly distracted by food-supply issues throughout the war, while their counterparts in the North had few such concerns. One wonders what might have happened if the Southern leaders had not been preoccupied with feeding their armies and cities, and instead had concentrated on winning the war.

3

Bread Riots

On the evening of April 1, 1863, a few hundred women met at Belvidere Hill Baptist Church in Richmond. The attendees were mainly from the surrounding working-class area. One person who was outspoken at the meeting was Mary Jackson, a 34-year-old woman who bought and sold veal at one of the Richmond markets. Another speaker was Minerva Meredith, a 40-year-old, butcher's apprentice. Others worked at the Tredegar Iron Works, which produced most of the South's artillery during the conflict. Still others were the wives of civil servants. The reason for the meeting was simple—the attendees could not feed their families. Even though the attendees were employed, as were their husbands, food prices had skyrocketed during the past several months in Richmond. This is not to say that there was no food in the city. There were government warehouses in the city that served as supply depots for the Army of Northern Virginia. Many stores did have food that was purchased by the city's well-to-do. For working-class families, however, the available food was beyond their means.

The attendees at the meeting were also convinced that the stores with food were deliberately hiking up prices and that speculators were holding back supplies of food so that they could make more profits as the price of food escalated. They agreed to meet the next morning and take their grievances to the Virginia governor. Should their requests to the governor not produce food, the women were determined to acquire it by any means in order to feed their families.

On the following morning a few hundred women and children rendezvoused at the Belvidere Hill Baptist Church. They meant business, for they were armed with stones, clubs, knives, hatchets and guns. At 9 a.m. the women headed for the governor's residence on Richmond's Capitol Square. Thus began the largest riot in the Confederacy during the Civil War.

Novel Impressment

The Richmond Bread Riot was not the first—or the last—food disturbance in the Confederacy. The increasingly effective Union land and sea blockades and the policies of the Confederate government contributed to food shortages throughout urban areas in the Confederacy. Such shortages of food and other supplies, in turn, contributed to civil unrest. In December 1862, women in Greenville, Alabama, forced a railroad agent to open the door to a supply depot and hand over sacks of salt destined for the Confederate army. In early February 1863, women in Bladen County, North Carolina, calling themselves "regulators," raided the Bladensboro grain depot and took six sacks of corn and one sack of rice. Five of the women were later convicted of breaking into the warehouse.[1]

On March 16, 1863, about twenty women, one of whom carried a revolver, went around to grocery stores in Atlanta, "seizing bacon, meal, and vegetables, paying such prices as they thought proper." This "riot" was broken up by the police, but the event was duly reported in Southern newspapers, occasionally with admiration. The *Charleston Mercury* reported in an article titled "Novel Impressment," that "the women were only imitating the example set them by Government officials."[2]

Two days later, in Salisbury, North Carolina, a "company of females," forty to fifty of whom were wives of soldiers, armed themselves with hatchets and raided a government depot where a speculator from Charlotte had stored flour. When the agent tried to stop them, three women forced their way in, leaving the agent "sitting on a log blowing like a March wind." They removed ten barrels of flour from the depot. They then targeted merchants whom they believed were speculators. Store owner Michael Brown saw the crowd coming and locked his door. When the women began hacking the door down, he agreed to give them ten barrels of flour, provided that the women would thereafter leave him alone. The women agreed and Brown rolled out the barrels. The women next visited the store of a Dr. John H. Enniss, coproprietor of Henderson & Enniss, who gave them another three barrels of flour. From other merchants, the women seized more flour, salt, other provisions, and twenty dollars in cash. From a store owned by a William Welch, the women took several barrels of molasses. As Welch was a strong supporter of impressment, the *Raleigh Standard* asked rhetorically how Welch liked "the principles of impressment as applied to this case?"[3]

In the wake of this event, Salisbury's local newspaper, the *Carolina Watchman*, criticized not the women, but the county Board of Commissioners who were charged with responsibility for distributing $50,000 earmarked for the relief of soldiers' families. The editor opined that the commissioners, who had failed to provide food for the soldiers' families, should all be "blushing with shame for the scene enacted in our streets." The women also had considerable support within the community. Throughout the riot, the mayor of Salisbury and the city justices just watched "dispassionately." The women were never prosecuted.[4]

About the same time as the Salisbury women were liberating goods, women plundered a government supply center at Sander's Mill, North Carolina. This time the press was not as supportive of the rioters. The editor of the Greensborough *Patriot* identified the rioters as unchaste females who "wage eternal war against society," and the editor believed that "society must wage eternal war" on such females. On April 1, 1863, soldiers' wives and other women "rose en masse" in Petersburg, Virginia, where they broke into "stores of the mercenary speculators who have been enriching themselves by holding all necessities of life at an enormous prices, helped themselves forcibly to what they wanted, pitching out goods to the poor and needy as they went." In Georgia, riots hit Columbus, Macon, and Augusta. Commenting on the riots, the editor of the *Raleigh Standard* wondered: "Bread riots have commenced, and where they will end, God only knows."[5]

Fasting in the Midst of Famine

When Richmond became the capital of the Confederacy, politicians, civil servants, and military officials flocked to the city. On top of this, military operations in northern Virginia during the first two years of the war sent a deluge of refugees into Richmond—many of them penniless, jobless, and occasionally homeless. Due to the war, Richmond also attracted some of the dregs of the South so that the city's crime rate soared. The poor grew more numerous in the city, and their ranks were inflated by an influx of soldiers' families. Many widows also came to Richmond looking for employment because they were unable to keep their farms going, but few jobs were available. By 1863 Richmond's population had grown to an estimated 120,000 people—three times its prewar size.[6]

Coinciding with Richmond's swelling population was the shrinking regional food supply base. This was caused by the wartime destruction of farmland in northern Virginia, declining agricultural production resulting from the loss of farm labor, an increasingly inefficient transportation system, and the military's impressment of the food that was available. In the early months of 1863 supplies dwindled further as heavy rains made many roads impassable. By February 1863 the price of flour had more than doubled. Bacon, which cost $1.25 per pound in 1860, sold for $10, while the price of sugar increased more than fifteen-fold and coffee cost forty times what it had previously. The *Richmond Whig* proclaimed that the citizens were being "gouged by heartless extortioners and robbed by official rogues."[7]

Rapidly escalating prices encouraged hoarding and speculation, which drove prices up even more. Since the salaries of soldiers, government workers, and factory laborers were fixed—or at least did not rise quickly enough to cover inflation—food became unaffordable for many of the city's most important workers, as well as for poor people. According to one contemporary source, "Females had begged in the streets and at the stores until begging did no good, and many had been driven to robbery to sustain life."[8] Other women became prostitutes in a desperate effort to earn enough money to put food on their table.

The emerging food calamity in Richmond continued to worsen. Eight inches of snow fell on the city on March 19, and snow continued to fall on and off until March 29. According to the Richmond war clerk John B. Jones, the snow placed an "embargo on the usual slight supplies brought to market, and all who had made no provision for such a contingency are subsisting on very short commons." He noted that there were "some pale faces seen in the streets from deficiency of food." When the storm finally abated, the muddy roads further delayed supplies from reaching the city. Food prices ballooned to such an extent that, on March 22, a soldier wrote that "the price of looking at foods in Richmond is five dollars."[9]

Contributing to the dearth of food was the way impressment was conducted around Richmond. Rather than head out to farms to gather provisions, agents waited on the roads leading into the city. As farmers brought food to city markets, officials stopped them and impressed their goods. The folly of this policy was obvious: Farmers stopped bringing food into Richmond, and they only grew "so much corn as will suffice for their own use," claimed Robert Garlick Kean, a Confederate official. Farmers particularly resented the schedule of impressment prices, "which are often 50% below the market or neighborhood price," observed Kean. He believed accurately that impressment caused universal withholding, "surplus-secreting and non-production. The army will be starved, and famine will ensue in cities unless the Secretary changes his policy and buys in the market for the best prices. The Government will have to outbid the traders; else *neither* will get anything of the present scanty stock, and no future stock will be produced." When impressments didn't generate enough food, Commissary-General Lucius Northrop sent agents to seize flour stocks, beef, bacon, and other provisions. Farmers believed they had been cheated and many began hiding foodstuffs to avoid confiscation: this generated fears among city dwellers of a "famine in the land."[10]

By the end of March, the food that was available in Richmond was so expensive that it was beyond the ability of many Richmonders to buy it. Confederate Senator Clement Clay wrote to his wife of the dire situation in Richmond:

A general gloom prevails here because of the scarcity and high price of food. Our soldiers are on half rations of meat, one-quarter pound of salt, and one-half pound of fresh meat, without vegetables, or fruit, or coffee or sugar! Don't mention this, as it will do harm to let it get abroad. Really there is serious apprehension of having to disband part of the army for want of food. In this city the poor clerks and subaltern military officers are threatened with starvation, as they cannot get board on their pay. God only knows what is to become of us, if we do not soon drive the enemy from Tennessee and Kentucky and get food from their granaries.

Richmond diarist Edmund Ruffin, an ardent supporter of the Confederacy who has been credited with firing one of the first shots that hit at Fort Sumter in 1861, wrote: "It seems to me that our country & cause are now, for the first time during the war, in great peril of defeat—& not from the enemy's arms, but from the scarcity & high prices of provisions." Others were deeply "fearful of starvation." On March 30, Jones wrote in his diary that "The gaunt form of wretched famine still approaches with rapid strides." Two days later, Kean ominously observed the same: "Indications of famine thicken."[11]

Apparently oblivious to the emerging food crisis, Jefferson Davis, the president of the Confederacy, declared March 27 as a day of fasting, humility, and prayer. Davis's proclamation did not go over well with many of Richmond's city dwellers, who were already struggling to find food. This may have been the spark that ignited the fireworks that followed. When Jones heard about Davis's proclamation, he exclaimed in his diary: "Fasting in the midst of famine! May God save this people."[12]

The Riot Act

The few hundred women who had gathered at Richmond's Belvidere Hill Baptist Church on the morning of April 2, 1863, were determined to see Virginia Governor John Letcher, whose residence was on Richmond's Capitol Square. By the time they arrived in the Square, the marchers had grown to several hundred women and children. One marcher stopped for a few minutes and spoke with Sara Agnes Rice Pryor, a bystander in the crowd that had gathered to watch the march. According to Pryor, the marcher was "a pale, emaciated girl, not more than eighteen, with a sun-bonnet on her head, and dressed in a clean calico gown." The girl told Pryor: "We are starving. As soon as enough of us get together we are going to the bakeries and each of us will take a loaf of bread. That is little enough for the government to give us after it has taken all our men." The conversation ended abruptly when the girl said, "I'm going to get something to eat!" Pryor called after her, "And I devoutly hope you'll get it—and plenty of it."[13]

Governor Letcher was already at work, or so the crowd was told. A delegation of women met with his aide, S. B. French, and requested that food be sold to the public at government rates. French declined to do anything about the women's grievances and asked them to leave. Their abrupt dismissal incited the crowd, which had grown to a few thousand people, including some unsavory sorts who had gathered to see what was happening. Rather than take no for an answer, the angry mob proceeded out of the square and into the city's ten-block business district, breaking into stores and government warehouses, according to an observer, helping themselves "to hams, middlings, butter, and in fact every thing eatable they could find. Almost every one of them were armed. Some had a belt on with a pistol stuck in each side, others had a large knife, while some were only armed with a hatchet, axe or hammer. As fast as they got what they wanted they walked off with it." Observers did not put a stop to this "shameful proceeding," but "cheered them on & assisted them all in their power."[14]

Colonel William Munford, the head of Richmond's Young Men's Christian Association, quieted a portion of the crowd and invited anyone needing food to follow him to the association's office, where he would give them food. Some women and children followed him, but the majority continued looting. Shops bolted their doors and shuttered their windows, but the mobs just broke them down. Looters turned their attention from acquiring food to expropriating nonedibles, including clothing, dry goods, fancy goods, jewelry, and many other items. One merchant alone claimed that he'd been robbed of more than $13,000 worth of goods.[15]

Governor Letcher, Richmond's Mayor Joseph Mayo, and Jefferson

Davis all hurried to the town square. Davis addressed a portion of the mob, saying that their actions would bring famine upon Richmond because "it would deter people from bringing food into the city." Taking out his wallet, he said he'd give them all the money he had, and promptly flung his Confederate dollars into the crowd. According to one foreign eyewitness, the mob declared the money worthless and they drowned out Davis's voice "amid cries for 'bread!' 'the Union!' 'No more starvation!'" Letcher ordered out the Public Guard and Richmond's mayor read the unruly mob the "Riot Act."[16]

What happened next has been debated since 1863. Davis claimed, and others agreed, that he gave the mob five minutes to disperse or the Public Guard would be ordered to shoot. Governor Letcher and other eyewitnesses proclaimed that it was he—Letcher—who gave the order to disperse. Still others claim that it was Richmond's mayor, Joseph Mayo, who gave the order. Whoever gave the order, it was enough to persuade the mob to disperse. Two hours after the women had entered Capitol Square, the riot ended. The police then arrested more than sixty women and men caught with stolen property. During the next few days these individuals were tried, and most were convicted: Some paid fines, others served sentences in jail.[17]

The number of people who participated in the Richmond riot has been variously estimated at between 2,000 and 10,000. As the riot occurred in several sections of the city, eyewitnesses did not have bird's-eye views of everything that happened. After reviewing contemporary estimates, historian Michael Chesson concluded that the several hundred women who launched the protest were joined by thousands of others, some bystanders simply interested in seeing what was happening, and others opportunists who joined in to plunder. Chesson speculated that the number of people who participated in or witnessed the riot was probably closer to 10,000—about one tenth of the city's entire swollen population.[18]

Rumors spread that another riot was planned for the following day. When women began standing on street corners demanding food, public officials decided to defuse the situation by giving it to them. Officials also decided on a show of force: the City Battalion marched down the streets of Richmond at midday, and cannons were placed on city streets. Rumors of yet more demonstrations circulated during the following week, and the Public Guard was reinforced by military units, but no further demonstration materialized.[19]

Yankee Conspirators in Cheap Jewelry and Hoop Skirts

No mention of the April 2, 1863, riot appeared in Richmond newspapers the following day. Government officials had tried to hush it up by requesting newspapers to "refrain from any present notice of it on account of the misrepresentations and exaggerations to which a publication would give rise." Officials feared that accounts of the event might be "misconstrued" in the Confederacy as well as abroad. Richmond's telegraph company was asked not to send any information about the bread riot over its wires, and a "special appeal" was made directly "to the editors and reporters of the press at Richmond, and earnestly to request them to avoid all reference directly or indirectly to the affair. The reasons for this are so obvious that it is unnecessary to state them, and the Secretary of War indulges the hope that his own views in this connection will be approved of by the press generally. Any other course must tend to embarrass our cause, and to encourage our enemies in their inhuman policy."[20]

Word of the riot leaked out anyway, and Southern newspapers began describing the event in detail. They were uncomplimentary to the rioters. Mary Jackson, the supposed leader of the riot, was vilified as an "amazonian huckster" who had "the eye of the Devil." Another newspaper referred to her as "an extortioner" and claimed that the riot was "simply a plundering raid under female impunity." Yet another newspaper called the leaders of the riot "professional thieves, prostitutes and gallows birds of every hue and nationality." Most Southern newspapers claimed that there was no reason for the riot. The Mayor of Richmond asserted that the poor were well taken care of and the riot "was not for bread. Boots are not bread; brooms are not bread; men's hats are not bread, and I have never heard of any body eating them." Yet another Southern observer claimed that the "so called" bread riot "was nothing more than an impudent attempt at wholesale robbery on the part of a vile gang of thieves and brigands." The perpetrators were "cowardly men, operating on the worst passions of abandoned women."[21]

The *Richmond Examiner* called the mob "a handful of prostitutes, professional thieves, Irish and Yankee hags, gallows-birds from all lands but our own." These "gangs, foreigners and Yankees the organizers of them" were determined to commit "plunder, theft, burglary, and robbery." The *Southern Confederacy* identified the "rioting women" as "very wicked and ignorant women, generally instigated thereto and led on by some rascally individual who aims at plunder and robbery." Other newspapers identified the "leaders and instigators" as "in the pay of the Yankee Government." Still others went further, claiming the riot was a "premeditated affair, stimulated from the North, and executed through the instrumentality of emissaries."[22]

These sentiments struck a responsive cord with Southerners. Another letter writer alleged that the riot leaders weren't Southern women after all—they were "Germans and Irish, chiefly, with Yankee conspirators in cheap jewelry and hoop skirts."[23] No evidence was offered then or since indicating that the riots had been influenced by the United States government or its agents with or without hoop skirts.

Other newspapers concluded that the real cause of the bread riots was the Union policy to starve out the Confederacy. The *Memphis*

Daily Appeal proclaimed that the bread riots had reawakened "the hopes of the Lincolnites in the efficacy of the starving out policy." It maintained that the Northern policy was to wait until famine had so "weakened the Confederates as to make further resistance useless." The *Charleston Mercury* proclaimed that the United States had boldly avowed the purpose of creating "famine and starvation—and in accordance with this avowal, they carry off our laborers, burn fences, mills, factories and bridges, steal horses and mules, destroy implements of husbandry, slay milch cattle and brood stock, trample down growing crops, pillage or fire granaries, and by every appliance and agency of destruction attempt to carry out their fiendish design."[24]

After the "it was the Yankees' fault" excuse ran its course, attention turned to blaming speculators and hoarders. As the *Richmond Sentinel* claimed on April 7, "It was no cry for bread. It was no hunger riot." The rioters were really just opposed to the high prices that merchants, speculators, and "extortioners" were charging. Of the speculators, one contemporary hoped "that these hard-hearted creatures could be made to suffer! Strange that men with human hearts can, in these dreadful times, thus grind the poor."[25]

It wasn't just the poor who suffered. It was also those who had been used to luxuries, but who were now enduring hardship. As Richmond resident and diarist Sallie A. Brock noted, "The real sufferers were not of the class who would engage in acts of violence to obtain bread, but included the most worthy and highly cultivated of our citizens, who, by the suspension of the ordinary branches of business, and the extreme inflation in the prices of provisions, were often reduced to abject suffering; and helpless refugees, who, driven from comfortable homes, were compelled to seek relief in the crowded city, at the time insufficiently furnished with the means of living for the resident population, and altogether inadequate to the increased numbers thrown daily into it by the progress of events."[26]

Bread or Blood

After the Richmond riot, other Southern cities followed suit. On April 10, 1863, about three hundred "well clothed" women in Milledgeville, then the capital of Georgia, raided a dry-goods store owned by a Mr. Gaus, and seized only the "fine things," according to a local newspaper account. Although this raid was not connected with bread, accounts of the event were published in various newspapers, and these may well have encouraged women in other cities to take similar action. About the same time, women in Columbus, Georgia, "turned out en masse and broke open the stores for food and clothing. Provisions were very scarce and at very high prices. The troops wrote to their wives and families that they will soon lay down their arms and give up fighting if the rebel Government does not provide for their families."[27]

Another riot took place in Mobile, Alabama, in the fall of 1863. At the beginning of the war, well-to-do residents of Mobile feasted at sumptuous dinners. An English visitor in 1861 found people eating oysters "as if there was no blockade, as though oysters were a specific for political indigestion and civil wars." Then the prices for food in Mobile began to rise as shortages became common. These price increases were particularly hard on the families of soldiers, who could not afford to buy food on their low fixed income. The situation became so desperate that in late November 1862, E. S. Dargan, a member of the Confederate Congress representing Mobile, wrote to Jefferson Davis stating that the inhabitants in Mobile were "in an awful condition" mainly because farmers refused to bring food into the city, fearing that impressment agents would seize their goods. Davis responded by ordering a halt to impressment, but this didn't solve the problem. The city's food supply was also restricted for other reasons. Mobile traditionally acquired many of its provisions from Mississippi, via the railroad. When Confederate

General John C. Pemberton began preparing for a possible siege at Vicksburg, Mississippi, he issued orders preventing meat and grain from being shipped out of his department. This meant that provisions could no longer be shipped to Mobile via its most important supply line, the Mobile & Ohio Railroad. By February 1863, the food supply in Mobile had deteriorated sharply. The Mobile *Register,* worried about the lack of affordable provisions, headlined an editorial, "Do You Mean to Starve Us?"[28]

A month later, handbills circulating in Mobile threatened "Bread or Blood," the slogan that women used in revolutionary France in 1789.[29] Posters mysteriously appeared in public places around the city:

BREAD OR PEACE

It has not yet come to be a question of bread or peace with us, but we are fast coming to it. If our Government can compel a man with a family of children to fight for it for eleven dollars per month, it can compel, and must, those who stay at home and enjoy their ease now, and will enjoy our freedom when achieved, to feed the poor children of poor fathers—the widows, whose only sons are fighting the battles and enduring the terrible hardships of the march and camp, foodless, clothless and shoeless. Forbearance will soon cease to be a virtue.

Our wives, sisters and little ones are crying for bread! Beware!! Lest they cry for *blood also!!* We have had enough of extortion and speculation: it is time the strong arm of the law was extended.

The people will rise sooner or later! There are lamp-posts and rope enough to cure this worse than treason—and the remedy will be supplied by an outraged people.

BRUTUS II[30]

Enough food was diverted from military supplies to alleviate immediate civilian needs, but in the summer women in the city began to worry about food supplies for the autumn and winter. Vicksburg had fallen to Union forces in July 1863, and with its fall, supplies coming into Mobile from Mississippi were drastically cut. On the morning of September 4, 1863, about six hundred women, many the wives of soldiers, met on Spring Hill Road in Mobile. Armed with clubs, knives, and hatchets they marched down Dauphine Street holding banners emblazoned with "Bread or Blood." Along the way, they broke into stores and took food and clothes. The Seventeenth Alabama regiment was ordered out to put down the disturbance, but they refused, saying, "if they took any action, rather assist those starving wives, mothers, sisters and daughters of men who had been forced to fight the battles of the rebellion." The Mobile Cadets entered the fray, but they were "driven from the field, or rather streets, by the infuriated women." Mobile leaders promised to solve the food problem and the riot subsided, but participants threatened that "if some means were not rapidly devised to relieve their suffering or to stop the war they would burn the city."[31]

One observer noted that even the well-to-do in Mobile had food problems. They formed a society called the Supply Association, "for the benefit of those who are short of means. They send agents around the country who buy as they can, and the food is retailed by these gentlemen at cost; and I believe besides they see that soldiers' families who can not buy do not suffer for want of food. They also formed a 'free market' which was supported wholly by donations of money and provisions. Many of the planters send all kinds of vegetables to it." Despite the "Bread or Blood" riot and attempts by officials to improve the situation for the families of soldiers and the poor, there was just not enough food to go around. In late January 1864, Mobile diarist Kate Cumming declared that "the whole topic of conversation is, What can be procured to eat?"[32]

Six weeks after the Mobile bread riot, a Mississippi newspaper reported that inflation was "fast reaching a point beyond even starvation prices. We are approaching a state of things that will inevitably culminate in riots and bloodshed among our own people." Food shortages continued, but the riots never turned to bloodshed. Small groups of women, and sometimes men, demonstrated and expropriated foodstuffs from wherever they could find them. In October 1863, women in Wilmington, North Carolina, raided and removed the cargo of a blockade-runner. The local Home Guard refused to fire on them. In March 1864, about twenty "respectable" people, mainly soldiers' wives or relations, engaged in an "insignificant" riot in Raleigh, North Carolina, when they could not purchase corn, wheat, or flour with Confederate money. The women liberated four barrels of flour, wheat, and corn, but evidently paid for their acquisitions with Confederate money.[33]

In April 1864, between fifty and one hundred armed women marched down the streets of Savannah, Georgia, demanding "bread or blood." The women in Savannah "seized food wherever it could be found." Soldiers were called out and, after a brief conflict, three women were arrested and jailed. During the trial that followed, the judge proclaimed, "When women become rioters, they cease to be women." One participant in the Savannah riot responded by printing and distributing a card which stated: "Necessity has no law & poverty is the mother of invention. These shall be the principles on which we will stand. If fair words will not do, we will try to see what virtue there is in stones." The *Savannah News* modestly pointed out that "the present high prices of provisions have provided distress no one can doubt."[34]

Other riots are known to have occurred in Barnwell, South Carolina, and Waco, Texas, and at least one Confederate brigade raided a commissary depot, relieving it of large quantities of provisions. There were likely many more small-scale riots around the South. A self-identified Northern "spy" who had spent five months wandering about the Confederacy alleged in January 1864 that "bread riots are frequent, yet newspapers do not mention them lest the intelligence reach their soldiery. They are not confined to one or two places, but are universal in every town and city throughout the south where the poor, starving families can be brought together."[35]

Food riots continued to occur right up until the end of the war. In February 1865, the *Southern Confederacy*, then published in Macon, Georgia, reported: "A disgraceful affair is now going on up town. A mob of women, with a black flag, are marching from store to store on a pillaging expedition."[36]

Problems and Solutions

The bread riots highlighted serious food problems confronting the Confederacy. Within two days of the Richmond bread riot, the Confederate Congress proclaimed that the Confederacy was engaged in a long war, and that it was "of the utmost importance, not only with a view to the proper subsistence of our armies, but for the interest and welfare of all the people that the agricultural labor of the country should be employed chiefly in the production of a supply of food to meet every contingency." Jefferson Davis followed up this resolution with a self-serving proclamation informing citizens that the cause of the food scarcity was mainly the drought, not the actions or policies of the Confederate government: "The very unfavorable season, the protracted droughts of last year, reduced the harvests on which we depended far below an average yield, and the deficiency was unfortunately still more marked in the northern portion of the Confederacy, where supplies were specially needed for the army." He then urged farmers not to plant cotton and tobacco but "to grow corn, oats, beans, peas, potatoes, and other food for man and beast." Jefferson ended with a rousing question: "If the surplus be less than is believed, is it not a bitter and humiliating reflection that those who remain at home, secure from hardship and protected from danger, should be in the enjoyment of abundance, and that their slaves also should have a full supply of food, while their sons, brothers, husbands, and fathers are stinted in the rations on which their health and efficiency depend?"[37]

In late April 1863, Southern governors met in Milledgeville, Georgia, and discussed the food emergency. The outcome was more proclamations. Some states sent letters to large plantations urging them to voluntarily plant more food. Alabama encouraged every citizen to raise "the largest possible quantity of provisions," in order to supply "the army and support of the people." They noted that Federal forces had occupied portions of the Confederacy that were "well adapted to raising provisions" and claimed that Union soldiers had damaged "farms, houses and fences, plundered and appropriated stock, and destroyed farming implements, under the hope that if they could not conquer us by arms they could subjugate us with the aid of starvation."[38]

Speeches, proclamations, harangues, and letters made good press and they did encourage many farmers and plantation owners to plant more food in 1863, but they did not solve the underlying problems confronting the Confederate food system. The one person who did have a systemic vision was General Braxton Bragg, who proposed a three-part plan for preventing famine:

> The first is that the President, by proclamation, prohibit the raising of any more cotton and tobacco or clearing of new lands until further notice. The second is that, by proclamation, he order all planters to seed a certain number of acres of grain or other articles of necessary consumption, in proportion to the quantity of cleared land and negroes belonging to them. The third is for the Government to take possession of the plantations, or such portion of

them as the owners do not intend to seed with grain, etc., and employ the negroes belonging thereto in raising such agricultural products as may be deemed necessary. Officers and soldiers who have been rendered by wounds and disease unfit for further service in the field could be employed as superintendent and overseers.[39]

Northrop believed that Bragg's plan was "feasible, and entirely the best that can now be adopted." He endorsed the plan with a flourish: "Let the emergency be urged upon the President while there is yet time to save ourselves."[40] Bragg's plan might well have solved the food crisis that was growing in the South: however, like so many other worthwhile proposals, it was ignored. Any plan that called for strong central government action was just too radical for Southerner leaders, who had wrapped themselves in states' rights and laissez faire economic policies.

Another problem that needed fixing was the inequitable distribution of the food that was available. There was plenty of food in Richmond—for those who could afford it. Anyone with money could buy almost anything he or she wanted. This did not sit well with poorer Southerners, many of whom believed that they had ended up fighting the war for the rich, many of them having acquired exemptions from military service and prospered throughout the war. The families of soldiers could not afford to buy food, which was readily available for the well-to-do. Jones pointed out: "These men and their families go in rags and upon half rations," while the rich dine "most sumptuously." He continued: "None but the opulent, often those who have defrauded the government, can obtain a sufficiency of food and raiment."[41] This situation created resentment particularly among Southern women, who had to make do without their husbands who were in the army, and had little money to buy food for their families.

Within a week of the Richmond riot, two men were appointed to each of twenty-four districts to work with the "ladies of the Union

Benevolent Society, to visit each family in the city, ascertain its actual condition, and furnish tickets entitling the holder to such supplies as may be received at the depots." The committee members visited the poor and gave them tickets, which could be redeemed for food. Within two weeks of the Richmond riot, the city council passed an ordinance for "the Relief of Poor Persons not in the Poor House," which set up a free store for the poor to acquire food. At Richmond's Metropolitan Hall, the Ladies' Benevolent Society began distributing 2,400 loaves of bread per month to needy families. Food for the poor was also made available through churches and the YMCA. From July 1863 through April 1864, the Richmond City Council pumped $150,000 more into poor relief.[42] These measures appeared to assuage some of the food difficulties of Richmond's poor, and no further riot occurred in the city until after the evacuation of Confederate forces in April 1865.

Feeling the Effects of Rebellion

Northern newspapers made the most of the riots. On April 8, 1863, the *New York Herald*'s headline read, "Serious Bread Riot in Richmond." The article editorialized that the riots in the South were "very significant of the condition to which rebeldom is reduced. If the people of that city are compelled to break open the public stores to obtain bread, what must be the state of the inhabitants of those districts which produce but little food and raise mainly cotton or tobacco?" Three days later the *Herald* quoted from a witness to the Richmond riot asserting, "The effect of this riot upon the troops about Richmond was very demoralizing."[43] The *New York Times* pointed out that women "do not get up street riots, break open provision shops, and pillage bakeries and flour stores from political sympathies. When their children are in peril of starvation, they become capable of anything." The *Times* concluded that "We have cumulative evidence that a scarcity of food never before paralleled exists in the South, that it is weakening the rebel army, disturbing the rebel rulers, and upturning the most inveterate traditions and usages of Southern Society." Of the Mobile bread riot, the *New York Herald* ran a headline that read: "Terrible Riot of Starving Soldiers' Wives and Children, Bread or Blood, Bread or Peace."[44]

The *Cincinnati Commercial* published an account of a self-identified Union spy who claimed to have "witnessed many of these riots, which he describes as extremely harrowing to the feelings of the humane. To such an extreme are the unfortunate families of soldiers driven that the women in towns and cities, as a last resort, take to a life of prostitution." The editor of the *Village Record* in Waynesboro, Virginia, concluded: "The demand for bread is too imperious to be overlooked, and the rebel authorities must heed it; but how? There is nothing in the confederacy with which to give relief." It concluded: "The plan of starving the south into submission, once so ridiculed, is now deemed feasible." The *Boston Herald* headlined an article "Food Wanted Instead of Cotton." The *Louisville Daily Journal* claimed that the bread riot was the "Rebel Cry for Help."[45]

The drumbeat continued with many more articles and even some cartoons. *Harper's Weekly* published one entitled "The Food Question Down South," which has Jefferson Davis holding up a pair of boots to show the Confederate General P. G. T. Beauregard. The caption has Davis saying: "See! see! the beautiful Boots just come to me from the dear ladies of Baltimore!" Beauregard responds: "Ha! Boots? Boots? When shall we eat them? Now?" The editor of the *New York Herald* doubted that the South could "supply their armies operating at a distance from the food supplying regions." *Frank Leslie's Illustrated Newspaper* published two engravings—one of them showing Southern women encouraging their men to fight for the Confederacy, the second of Southern women, one holding a smoking pistol, storming a bakery with smashed windows, while children cart off loaves of bread. It was titled "Sowing and Reaping," and the caption under the bakery illustration was "Southern women feeling the effects of rebellion, and creating bread riots."[46]

Riotous Effects

With the exception of the Richmond and Mobile events, the Southern bread riots were relatively small affairs and authorities dealt with them easily. There were no deaths, and few injuries were reported. Nevertheless, the bread riots reflected real problems in the South. The riots were yet additional wake-up calls for Confederate leaders to address crucial problems confronting the Southern food system. They responded with proclamations and Band-Aid solutions. Food problems confronting the Confederacy that might have been solved in 1863 became almost insoluble within a year.

The bread riots also created rumors in Europe that the South faced famine, just when the Confederacy needed loans and recognition. On April 15, 1863, the Confederate Secretary of State, Judah P. Benjamin, wrote to John Slidell, the Confederate diplomat in Paris, trying to refute the belief of "our oft-deluded foes" who were "again indulging the hope that we are to lose our independence by starvation." He claimed that the only real problem was meat, because "of bread there is a superabundance and the Southern wheat crops, which are fine, will commence furnishing new flour in Texas in five or six weeks." It is true that Texas had a bumper crop, but before it could be shipped to the Confederate states east of the Mississippi, Grant had shut off the movement of goods from Texas by besieging Vicksburg. Likewise, Florida had a good corn crop, but inadequate rail and sea transportation made it difficult to move it from where it was grown to other Confederate states.[47] It is unknown to what extent the bread riots caused Europeans to be cautious about giving loans or extending credit to the Confederacy. But the fact that the Confederate Secretary of State would feel pressure to reassure Europeans suggests that there was some concern in Europe about the chances of the Confederacy's survival. Few loans were given to the Confederacy by Europeans, and this failure caused more economic distress in the South as the war progressed.

4

Abundance and Organization

*M*ajor Henry C. Symonds, Commissary of Subsistence for the Federal supply depot in Louisville, Kentucky, was partly responsible for feeding the Union armies that operated west of the Alleghenies. His depot began by producing 3,000 rations a day in 1861 and expanded production to 300,000 per day in 1864. To accomplish this, Symonds opened factory-scale bakeries to produce crackers and bread, constructed three slaughterhouses, and established a soldiers' rest facility that daily served 5,000 to 15,000 meals. Symonds also organized the processing and distribution of large quantities of coffee, tea, sugar, vegetables, salt, ale, beer, whiskey, fresh beef, dried beef, fish, butter, cheese, potatoes, sauerkraut, pickles, and canned food.[1]

Symonds' Louisville depot was just one of many supplying Northern armies, and their total output was stupendous. During an eight-month period between January and August 1864, three supply depots west of the Alleghenies acquired, produced, and processed 65 million rations of salted meat, 26 million rations of fresh beef, 63 million rations of sugar, 83 million rations of salt, 54 million rations of breadstuffs, 70 million rations of vegetables, 70 million rations of coffee, 10 million rations of tea, 60 million rations of pepper, 30,095 pounds of dried beef, 133,000 pounds of butter, 349,410 pounds of dried apples, 1.6 million pounds of potatoes, 333,395 gallons of whiskey, 21,939 pounds of eggs, 134,280 units of canned food (two pounds each), and much, much more.[2] These provisions fed Union armies in Kentucky, Missouri, Tennessee, and Georgia, and the excess would make it possible for the well-supplied army commanded by Major General William T. Sherman to cut his supply lines and march across Georgia to capture Savannah in late 1864.

The variety and quantity of food that was available in the United States during the war is somewhat surprising in light of the labor shortage on Northern farms prior to the war. Although the North was far more populous than the South, the difference was due to the rapid growth of cities—partly from rural populations migrating into urban areas and from recent immigrants, such as the Irish, who mainly settled in cities. Northern farms had to produce more with comparatively fewer farmers just to feed the fast-growing cities. During the Civil War about 20 percent of farm workers eventually served in the Union army, and on the farm labor shortage became acute. How was it possible for the non-slaveholding, more urbanized North to provide abundant supplies to its armies and civilians and still have plenty of surplus food to export?

Diversity

Prior to the war, the North had developed a diversified agricultural system with different localities specializing in grains (wheat, corn, oats, and barley), poultry (chickens, turkeys, and ducks), fruits (apples, berries, cherries, grapes, peaches, pears, and plums), vegetables (potatoes, beans, peas, and tomatoes), meat production (pork, beef, and mutton), and dairying (milk, butter, and cheese). The North also raised large numbers of horses, mules, sheep, and oxen, and produced most of the hay in the United States. Many of these foodstuffs and farm animals were sold to the South. When North-South trade was disrupted in August 1861, the excess livestock and agricultural production in the North provided food for soldiers and civilians, wool for uniforms and clothes, horses for the cavalry and artillery, and draft animals for pulling wagons and farm equipment.

The crops that the South exported to the North were mainly nonedibles—cotton, tobacco, and hemp—so the disruption in trade with the Confederacy had little effect on what Northerners ate during the war. The main exceptions were rice and cane sugar, all of which was produced in the South. Rice was not a major ingredient in Northern culinary life, and there were many possible substitutes for Southern rice, but sugar was essential. Substitute sweeteners, such as maple sugar and syrup, were available, but the little that was produced could not meet the demand. Sorghum, which had been raised largely for silage, found some success as a sweetener. Yet another possible substitute was the sugar beet, which could be grown in the cooler Northern climate.[3] Extracting and processing sugar from these sources required extensive labor, and the extra workforce was just not available during the war. Some sugar was acquired in Louisiana after the Federal conquest of New Orleans, but sugar production drastically declined as the war progressed. By late 1862 it was cheaper for the North to import cane sugar from the Caribbean than to try to replace it with homegrown substitutes or revive the sugar plantations in Louisiana.

Mechanized Abundance

Despite the large number of farm workers who joined the army, Northern farms generally maintained something close to prewar levels of production. This was accomplished, in part, by farmers working longer hours and by women, children, and the elderly becoming more involved in agricultural production. In addition, new farms were established by those attracted to cheap land and high commodity prices. A fresh supply of farm labor was provided by immigrants—800,000 newcomers arrived in the United States during the Civil War, and many, particularly Germans and Scandinavians, settled on farms. In just six Midwestern states, 430,000 new farms were established during the war, and more than 2.7 million acres of land went into production for the first time.[4]

This expansion in farming had an especially striking impact on wheat production, which increased by 50 percent during the war. Grain production was greatly enhanced by the accelerated adoption of more animal-powered equipment. The scarcity and high cost of farm labor led to the almost universal adoption of the horse-drawn reaper promulgated by Cyrus McCormick: An astonishing 233,000 reapers helped Northern farmers harvest increased production of small grains with less labor. Each machine freed up an estimated two or three farm workers, many of whom enlisted in the Union cause, while others launched new farms of their own, thus increasing agricultural output.[5]

The reaper was only one of many new types of equipment that enhanced Northern farm production while reducing the need for agricultural labor. The beater press, used in baling, made it possible for farmers to produce and ship much more hay. Jerome Case invented a threshing machine that shelled grain from the seed heads, separated it from the straw, and winnowed it from the chaff. John Deere's improved ox-drawn plows made it easier to break the concrete-hard sod of the Midwestern prairies. Deere's company began selling cultivators in 1863, and production expanded rapidly during the next two years. Threshing machines powered by steam engines, first manufactured in 1862, greatly improved productivity on the enormous Midwestern farms. As the Ohio State Board of Agriculture claimed, "without drills, corn-planters, reapers and mowers, horse-rakes, hay elevators, and threshing machines, it would have been impossible to have seeded and gathered the crops of 1863 with the implements in use forty or fifty years ago."[6]

Increased demand from the military, orders from Europe, and trade with the Confederacy led to rising prices. The initial labor shortage and the high prices paid for farm goods encouraged farmers to mechanize their operations. As their profits rose, farmers became more willing to purchase more farm machinery which, in turn, enhanced productivity. Partly as a result of new labor-saving equipment, many farms shifted from near subsistence to commercial operations producing surpluses.[7]

Transporting Abundance

When the Mississippi River was closed to Northern commercial traffic at the beginning of the Civil War, hard times hit the Midwest. Within months Northern railroads and canals were rerouted and began to ship more commodities from the Midwest to the East Coast. The economic problems of the Midwest eased in 1862, and after the conquest of Vicksburg by Federal forces in July 1863, Midwestern farmers could once again ship their goods down the Mississippi to New Orleans. The Midwest's food surplus, which traditionally would have been sent South, instead fed the Union army, and a large quantity of it was exported to Great Britain and France.

Compared with Southern railways, those in the North were better developed and much more extensive. The North's railroad system permitted relatively easy access to much of the country. Most important, the North had the industrial base needed to repair and manufacture track, locomotives, and rolling stock. Even during the war, railroad construction continued at a fast clip in the Northern states, with 1,800 new lines built in the Midwest alone, whereas new construction was very limited in the Confederacy.

Railroads played a crucial role during the Civil War, permitting the rapid movement of troops and transporting supplies, equipment, and provisions to armies deployed over thousands of square miles of territory. This was made possible by the coordination of railroads for military purposes by Colonel (later General) Herman Haupt, who organized an efficient construction corps and formulated principles of military operation for railroads. Haupt made it possible for the Federal armies in the East to be well supplied with goods, and when armies retreated, he made sure that their supplies were moved or destroyed so they would not fall into Confederate hands. The procedures that Haupt established were used throughout the remainder of the war, and they were particularly important in the Western theater, where railroads played a significant role in supplying the advancing Union armies in Tennessee and Mississippi.[8] By comparison, no such system was devised in the South until late in the war, when its railroads were already in shambles.

The railroads also affected the geography of America's food industry. When the war began, and the Mississippi River was closed to northern shipping, railroad lines through Chicago dominated East-West transportation. Thanks to this transportation nexus, Chicago became an important food-processing center. The Union army contracted directly with meatpackers, particularly in the Midwest, to supply the troops. One contractor was a German immigrant named Nelson Morris, a small Chicago pork packer. Under a single contract, Morris shipped twenty thousand live cattle to the army.[9] Morris had became the largest meat packer in Chicago, and when the war ended, thanks to the railroads, he was ready and able to expand sales of meat to population centers in the East. Prior to the Civil War hog packing was a minor industry in Chicago. Chicago's hog production had expanded from 151,000 in 1861 to 970,000 in 1865—one third of the nation's total production, surpassing St. Louis, Louisville, and Cincinnati. Soon Chicago became the new "Porkopolis of the West," a sobriquet previously bestowed on Cincinnati.[10]

Processing Abundance

This northern transportation system worked well with basics—grains and salt pork, for instance, could easily be shipped great distances without difficulty. But before refrigeration, which was not common until the late nineteenth century, transporting perishables, such as fresh meat, fruits, vegetables, and milk, was another matter. During the summer, these could be bought locally, and many isolated military units lived off the land where local food was abundant. In the winter and spring, or in areas devastated by war, however, perishables were simply unavailable.

One solution was processed food. Before the Civil War, the food-processing business had undergone rapid change, especially in the North. In the arena of meat processing, slaughtering and packing had already become centralized. Stockyards sprang up in major cities, making it easier to purchase and process livestock and meat products. During the 1850s, German immigrants began flooding into the Midwest, bringing new techniques of salting meat, especially pork. German-owned packing facilities in such Midwestern cities as Cincinnati, St. Louis, and Chicago turned out high-quality preserved pork products.

Before mechanical refrigeration, meatpacking was suspended during the summer due to high spoilage rates caused by the heat. In 1854 the Cincinnati inventor John C. Schooley began experimenting with the use of ice to cool packing houses so that pork could be cured in hot weather. The following year, he patented his process. Other inventors improved Schooley's technique, making it possible to pack pork all year round, and many meatpackers installed the equipment, boosting the availability of pork. Midwestern packers began selling large quantities of salt pork to the South to feed slaves on plantations. When the war began, Midwestern packers were cut off from their Southern market, but the army's demand for meat more than made up for the loss. In addition, exports of ham and bacon to Europe rose sixfold, and pork production increased by 50 percent during the war.[11]

On the eve of the Civil War, canned goods were mainly specialty items bought by only the wealthy few who could afford them, or by seamen setting out on long expeditions. The public was leery of both of the high price of canned goods and the potential health risks associated with them. Inventions reduced the cost of the canning process. Isaac Winslow, a corn canner in Maine, decided to experiment with metal canisters to see if he could reduce the health risks. He tried changing the contents of the cans and varied the length of time the canisters were processed in boiling water, finally devising a method that was then used throughout the Civil War. In 1860 Isaac Solomon, a Baltimore canner, made the next important discovery. Rather than boiling the cans in plain water, Solomon added calcium chloride to the processing bath, which made it possible to heat the water above 212°F, to 240°F. This enabled Solomon to reduce the processing time by 4 to 6 hours— down to as little as 25 to 40 minutes.[12] This resulted in faster production, lower energy costs, declining consumer prices, and safer canned food. Solomon did not rest on this success, however. As the Civil War began, he figured out that canning would be even more easier, cheaper, and safer, if the cans were heated in a pressure cooker rather than the traditional open kettle. This further reduced the time for cooking, greatly increased the quality of canned goods, and lowered their cost even more.

Gail Borden was an entrepreneur who had failed miserably at manufacturing dehydrated meat in the form of biscuits. Basically broke, but with financial help from friends, Borden embarked on the creation of condensed milk, a way of preserving milk by adding sugar, heating the milk, and then cooking it to partially evaporate the water content. Just as Borden began shipping condensed milk to New York City, *Frank Leslie's Illustrated Newspaper* broke the shocking story of New York's "swill milk trade," which related to the sale of contaminated fresh milk. In the wake of this nauseating exposé, which went on for months, Borden's canned and pasteurized milk found a ready market.[13] It was not known at the time that canned milk was not as nutritious as fresh milk, but it was so much safer.

Borden's company saw only moderate success until the fall of 1861, when a customer entered the offices of the New York Condensed Milk Company, asked a few questions of its proprietor, and then ordered five hundred pounds of condensed milk. The customer happened to be a commissary agent. The Federal army found it impossible to supply the troops with fresh milk, which spoiled quickly in the Southern heat. The army's commissary department was satisfied with Borden's first shipment of condensed milk, and within months issued orders for much more. Once the military contracts came through, the future of Borden's enterprise was assured. Contracts also came from Sanitary Commissions, which had been set up to nurse sick and wounded soldiers back to health. Soldiers and officers who drank Borden's condensed milk testified that it was "of the most highly commendatory character."[14]

Federal contracts during the war primed the pump for the canning industry. Existing canners expanded their operations and began turning out tens of thousands of cans of food. William Underwood & Co., in Boston, made a fortune selling canned beef to the army, as did the firm Rumery & Burnham in Baltimore. In Indianapolis, Gilbert C. Van Camp packed fruit in large cans for the army. In Camden, New York, Ezra A. Edgett canned corn, chicken, turkey, duck, goose, and beef for the army. Quick profits encouraged others to enter the canning business. In Baltimore alone, the number of canneries rose from thirteen in 1860 to close to twenty-five by the end of the war. Throughout the war, the quality of canning operations improved, as did their efficiency, which reduced costs.[15] Canned goods were soon affordable even for the average wage earner.

Canned goods were used throughout the Union military. Hospitals and ambulance trains were well supplied with condensed milk and canned peaches and tomatoes. Northern troops were fed on canned foods occasionally during the last two years of the war. Sutlers—merchants who sold goods to soldiers—brought canned goods into Federal military camps and sold them. Soldiers often made mention of canned goods in their battlefield diaries and their letters home (and, later, in their memoirs), and wherever Union armies camped, they left piles of empty cans in their wake. The navy provisioned its sailors with canned goods; canned tomatoes were touted as a means of preventing scurvy when fresh vegetables were unavailable. Some enterprising canners manufactured canned goods with fruit or vegetable labels, which were in fact filled with whiskey. Soldiers and sailors purchased these goods and smuggled them into their camps and onto ships. This became so common, especially in the navy, that authorities began inspecting cans as sailors boarded their ships.[16]

Although little commercial canning occurred in the South during the war, Southerners did sometimes eat commercially canned foods. Southern armies often captured Federal supply trains and depots, and Confederate blockade-runners acquired and imported canned goods through Nassau or Bermuda. This trade was so extensive that in February 1864, the Confederate Congress outlawed the importation of "prepared vegetables, fruits, meats, poultry and game, sealed or inclosed in cans or otherwise." The goal was to encourage blockade-runners to import bulkier and less profitable commodities, such as grain and meat. The law was so unpopular, however, that it was repealed four months later. Northern sutlers also sold canned goods to Confederate prisoners in Union camps, and canned goods were sent to Union soldiers in Southern prisoner of war camps.[17] By the end of the war, the majority of soldiers and sailors on both sides of the conflict had had their first taste of canned goods—and they liked them.

Organizing Abundance

It wasn't just the abundance of food in the North that gave the Union a distinct advantage—it was the mobilization of these resources to meet wartime needs. During the first few months of the war, chaos reigned. The War Department's Commissary of Subsistence had but twelve officers. The Federal government was unable to clothe, equip, or feed even the initial 75,000 volunteers that President Abraham Lincoln had requested in April 1861, so each state was instructed to provide uniforms, equipment, arms, munitions, and provisions for its own volunteers; the War Department would then reimburse the states for their expenses. Most food was purchased in metropolitan areas of the North and then shipped via distribution channels consisting of river boats, railroads, and wagons to commissaries of each army. Other foodstuffs, such as beef and flour, were purchased locally, where possible. Cattle were usually herded behind the armies to satisfy the demand for fresh meat. Supply depots were established to facilitate the production and distribution of foodstuffs. During the first year of the war, the Federal government spent nearly $50 million on subsistence, and by the end of the war, the cost of foodstuffs totaled more than $369 million.[18]

The amount of rations each Union soldier received daily was set by Federal law. A large portion of a soldier's ration consisted of salted or fresh beef and flour or bread, including the always available and frequently detested hardtack. Like the Confederate army's, the Union soldiers' diet was high in salt and often lacked fruits and vegetables, and scurvy was common. In addition to the foods supplied by the Union commissary, Soldiers' Aid Societies and Sanitary Commissions supplied quantities of other foods; camp sutlers, commissioned by each state, provided a wide range of items, as long as soldiers had money to buy them. When armies were on the march through Confederate territory, they foraged freely, especially during the last two years of the war.[19]

Each state purchased its provisions by contract on the open market; this created intense competition for limited supplies, so prices and profits shot up, and corruption spread. Newspapers and magazines publicized these abuses, and a Congressional hearing confirmed many of the most serious cases of corruption. *Harper's Weekly* lampooned contractors in a cartoon showing a skinny soldier asking a fat contractor for beefsteak. The contractor responded: "Want Beefsteak? Good Gracious, what is the World coming to? Why, my Good Fellow, if you get Beefsteak, how on earth are Contractors to live? Tell me that."[20]

Edwin M. Stanton, who became Secretary of War in January 1862, instituted reforms that curbed the worst abuses. Georgian-born Montgomery C. Meigs became Quartermaster General and masterminded the procurement, acquisition, and distribution system for the army's supplies. Meigs, a West Point graduate who served for decades in the Corps of Engineers, was energetic, highly competent, and scrupulously honest. He was an organizational genius, and was one of the first Civil War leaders to recognize the importance of logistics in war. He made sure that supplies moved forward with great efficiency, and Union armies were well fed in large part thanks to his efforts. After the war, Secretary of State William H. Seward proclaimed that, without the services of Meigs, "the national cause must have been lost or deeply imperiled."[21]

The Wheat Famine

Beginning in 1860 both England and France had serious problems with grain production because of bad weather. Both countries began importing large quantities of grain from the United States. In 1860 more than 27 percent of the total wheat imported into the United Kingdom came from the United States; two years later that amount had increased to more than 45 percent.[22]

Noting these statistics, U.S. Secretary of State William Seward, and the American ambassador to Great Britain Charles Adams put forth the idea of a "wheat famine" as a counterweight to the "cotton famine" frequently mentioned in the Confederacy. If European countries tried to break the blockade or recognize the Confederacy, Seward threatened to cut off the export of grain to Europe. Northern newspapers proclaimed that a wheat famine would result in England and France if this trade were disrupted. As the *Louisville Daily Journal* editorialized in August 1861, whether the British and French obtained cotton or not, they still needed bread. If, the editorial continued, "the leading European nations can be forced into war with us to reopen the cotton ports, of the seceding States, the first belligerent blow would increase the price of breadstuffs to famine prices." The continued importance of the grain trade was recognized in Britain. In an October 1862 editorial, the London *Economist* opined, "The truth is that without such importations our people could not exist at all."[23]

Historians have debated the significance of the threatened wheat famine for the past century. In 1918 Louis B. Schmidt, an agricultural historian at Iowa State College, picked up on Seward's idea. In an extended analysis of British imports of American wheat during the Civil War, Schmidt came to a startling conclusion: Northern wheat was the decisive factor "in keeping the British government from recognizing the Confederacy." The British public was aware of their nation's dependence of Northern wheat, and at least some British leaders argued publicly for neutrality, using the rationale of the need for American wheat.[24]

The American historian Ephraim Douglass Adams came to the opposite conclusion. It was a mistake, he believed, to equate the two commodities: Cotton "could not be obtained in quantity from any source before 1864," while wheat could be acquired from Prussia and Russia, albeit at a higher price than American grain. Adams found no reference to wheat in the memoranda or notes of British Cabinet officials, while cotton was frequently mentioned. Adams concluded that wheat played a negligible role in the British decision to stay neutral. Likewise, diplomatic historian Frank Lawrence Owsley concluded that Seward's comments about a wheat famine and possible war with Great Britain or France were pure propaganda: There was no evidence that a disruption in the wheat trade with the United States would have produced a wheat famine in either country.[25]

Between 1861 and 1864 the North shipped the equivalent of 203 million bushels of wheat to Europe. Whether the wheat trade made much of a difference in relations with Great Britain is questionable, but the grain trade generated an estimated $265 million for the United States. Furthermore, the North exported large amounts of ham, bacon, pork, lard, corn, and cornmeal to Europe and these exports generated an additional $136 million. Vast quantities of food were also traded or bartered to the Confederacy for cotton, much of which was exported to Britain and France, generating even more export dollars for the United States. The income from these exports allowed the Union to acquire military equipment, supplies, and loans from abroad. This income also helped control inflation in the United States. Retail food prices in the North went up only 1 percent in 1861, 12 percent in 1862, 23 percent in 1863, and 27 percent in 1864.[26] While 63 percent cumulative inflation over four war years seems disastrous, keep in mind that the Confederacy's inflation rate during the same period averaged 10 percent per month.

Abundant Effects

Despite the loss of farm laborers to the military and the disruption of traditional routes of transportation at the beginning of the war, Northern soldiers and sailors were comparatively well fed throughout the conflict, as were most Northern civilians, and no civilian rationing was necessary during the war. Yet, there were some exceptions: Hard-hit were families of Union soldiers, wounded soldiers, and widows. Organizations such as Christian Commissions and Sanitary Commissions were set up to promote clean and healthy conditions in Union camps. Women's groups held "sanitary fairs," which sold donated agricultural machinery, art work, furniture, and many other goods; the monies raised were used to help the neediest cases on the homefront. Members of these organizations also lobbied for improved conditions, ministered to the sick and wounded in hospitals, and distributed food to the troops.[27]

Improved transportation, the industrialization of food processing, the mechanization of agriculture, and superb organization made it possible for the North to feed both its military forces and civilians and still ship a surplus to Europe during the war. While the North's military suffered occasionally from food scarcity, it never faced the constant privations that Southerners confronted during the last three years of the war. While retail prices did increase substantially in the North, there was no rationing. After economic dislocations at the beginning of the conflict, the Northern economy prospered, providing jobs for anyone who could work and creating fortunes for those who had contracts with the government. Southern civilian and fighting men, on the other hand, were increasingly faced with food shortages and threatened with famine as the war dragged on.

Abundant food strengthened the Union army's morale and made it possible for its navy and army to operate hundreds—in some cases, thousands—of miles from their home bases. Well-fed armies do not always win wars, but the superior physical stamina of the well-nourished soldiers and sufficient food on the homefront helped the North win the Civil War.

5

Gibraltar of the Mississippi

On May 18, 1863, the Union army and navy closed in on Vicksburg, Mississippi, one of the most strategically important cities in the Confederacy. Its location, high on a bluff overlooking the eastern bank of the Mississippi, enabled the city's batteries to control river traffic. Because of its strategic importance, the Confederates had been fortifying the city from the beginning of the war. As long as the city remained in Southern hands, supply lines were kept open to Texas. As Texas had a long border with Mexico, virtually anything could be imported into the Confederacy as long as Vicksburg held. Southern control of the river also deprived Midwestern states of a crucial navigation outlet to the Atlantic Ocean.[1] The city's strategic location meant that it had been regularly targeted by Federal forces. Previous Union attempts had failed to conquer Vicksburg, earning it the nickname "Gibraltar on the Mississippi."

After assaulting the city's formidable fortifications and failing to break through, the Union army laid siege in hopes of starving the garrison inside into submission. The Confederates had amassed provisions in the city as a precaution against just such a siege, or so it was believed. Although these provisions would dwindle as the siege wore on, the defenders were confident that Confederate forces outside the city would come to their aid before food ran out. By June 12, 1863, however, there was no sign of a Confederate relief army and the beef ration was almost exhausted. A few days later, when the stock of bacon was used up, soldiers were reduced to eating mule meat. This ration was issued only to those who wanted it, but as the commander of the Confederate army, Lieutenant General John C. Pemberton, optimistically proclaimed, mule meat "was found by both officers and men not only nutritious, but very palatable, and every way preferable to poor beef."[2]

When the supply of mule meat gave out, soldiers and civilians ate rats and some allegedly consumed dogs and cats as well. After forty-seven days of siege it became evident that there would be no last-minute intervention from outside the city, and that famine would soon rage inside the city. On July 4, 1863, the starving city surrendered and the United States had achieved two of its most important strategic goals of the war—control of the Mississippi River and splitting apart the Confederacy.

Distress and Almost Famine

The Union general charged with capturing Vicksburg was Ulysses S. Grant. Born in Ohio in 1822, Grant entered West Point in 1839. After graduating, Grant was assigned to the duties of a regimental quartermaster. During the Mexican-American War, he saw action in three different battles. After the war, he remained in the army and served in several different posts, including the Washington Territory. In 1854, Grant left the army, spending the next seven years at a variety of undistinguished and generally unsuccessful jobs. At the beginning of the Civil War, Grant rejoined the army and recruited and trained volunteers in Illinois. In August 1861, Grant was promoted to Brigadier General and given command of the Southeast Missouri Military District. While serving in this capacity, in February 1862, his troops occupied Fort Henry on the Tennessee River and Fort Donelson on the Cumberland River.

Grant's victories emboldened him to move his army to Shiloh, a small town in southwestern Tennessee. Meanwhile, twenty miles away at Corinth, Mississippi, 40,000 Confederates had assembled without thought as to provisions. Many soldiers had sickened because of inadequate food and bad water. Medical authorities there claimed that "thousands of soldiers" suffered from scurvy caused by the unavailability of fresh fruit. One reason given for attacking Grant at Shiloh was to acquire the Union army's supplies. The Confederates were able to pull off a surprise assault on Grant's lines on April 6, 1862. After initial success, Union reinforcements arrived and Shiloh turned into a Confederate disaster the following day. Poor nutrition may have contributed to Confederate defeat.[3]

In November 1862, Grant began his first advance on Vicksburg, the last major Confederate fortress on the Mississippi River. Vicksburg was under the command of Lieutenant General John C. Pemberton. A Pennsylvanian by birth, Pemberton was a West Point graduate who served with distinction in the United States army during the Mexican-American War. He married a Virginian, and when Virginia seceded, Pemberton resigned his commission in the U.S. army and joined the Confederate army. Jefferson Davis assigned him to command the Mississippi Department in October 1862.

Grant and his army moved down the route of the Mississippi Central Railroad, reconstructing the damaged tracks, bridges, and telegraph lines as they went. Since his supplies came from Columbus, Kentucky, two hundred miles away, Grant established a secondary supply base at Holly Springs, Mississippi, a dozen miles from the Tennessee border. There he stockpiled food and munitions for his campaign against Vicksburg. Such tactics followed proper military procedures. According to Grant, "great armies moving in an enemy's country should start from a base of supplies, which should be fortified and guarded, and to which the army is to fall back in case of disaster." Yet, as Grant casually wrote in his *Memoirs*, "This was a long line (increasing in length as we moved south) to maintain in an enemy's country."[4]

As both Federal and Confederate armies had passed through northern Mississippi, Grant noted that "distress and almost famine" had been visited upon "many of the inhabitants of Mississippi." He mused that humanity dictated "that in a land of plenty no one should suffer the pangs of hunger," and directed military posts to supply provisions to local civilians.[5] Grant would soon be forced to rethink his magnanimous policy of feeding enemy civilians.

Grant left a small force behind to guard the supply depot at Holly Springs while he headed west toward Vicksburg with the bulk of his forces. On the night of December 19, Confederate General Earl Van Dorn passed around Grant's flank and raided Holly Springs. Van Dorn easily captured the town, and liberated $1.5 million worth of supplies. At the same time, Confederate cavalry under the command of Major General Nathan Bedford Forrest swept northward into southeastern Tennessee and Kentucky, disrupting Grant's only supply line, tearing up railroads and destroying bridges.

With most of his provisions gone, and no likelihood of receiving more anytime soon, Grant began to withdraw his forces northward toward Tennessee. Soldiers only had two days' rations when the retreat began, and they received no more supplies from Union depots for many days. With supplies dwindling, Grant told his soldiers to take what they needed from Mississippians as they marched northward. When Grant arrived at Oxford, Mississippi, local citizens rejoiced at hearing that the Federal army had lost all its supplies. The citizens came to Grant "with broad smiles on their faces, indicating intense joy, to ask what I was going to do now without anything for my soldiers to eat." Grant told them that he had "already sent troops and wagons to collect all the food and forage they could find for fifteen miles on each side of the road." He pointed out that the army "had endeavored to feed ourselves from our own Northern resources while visiting them; but their friends in gray had been uncivil enough to destroy what we had brought along, and it could not be expected that men, with arms in their hands, would starve in the midst of plenty." He advised the residents of Oxford "to emigrate east, or west, fifteen miles and assist in eating up what we left."[6]

Grant came to the conclusion that Mississippi was a fruitful state and there was plenty of food and supplies for the taking in the Southern countryside. Grant's troops had no difficulty getting "ample food and fodder from the still luxuriant plantations." Major General William T. Sherman, now under Grant's command, who was engaged in another prong of attack on Vicksburg, had a similar experience. He wrote to his brother: "We found everywhere abundant supplies, even on the Yazoo, and all along the river we found cattle and fat ones feeding quietly. The country everywhere abounds with corn." Not everyone in the Union army benefitted from gastronomical largess on the retreat. A soldier from Illinois complained to his wife that "we have not been on full rations for several days."[7]

According to Sylvanus Cadwallader, a war correspondent for the *Chicago Times*, "Trains of wagons, heavily guarded, were sent out by the scores, for twenty-five miles on both sides of the road from Yocknapatafa to Holly Springs, and stripped the country of all food for men and fodder for animals. Mills were erected, grain ground, fat stock driven in and slaughtered by thousands, and abundant supplies obtained. To people's inquiries as to what the inhabitants should live upon, Gen. Grant advised them to move further south. His army would not be allowed to starve while there was anything to live upon within reach." Grant himself "was amazed at the quantities of supplies the country afforded. It showed that we could have subsisted off the country for two months." According to Grant, "The troops were drawn back gradually, but without haste or confusion, finding supplies abundant and no enemy following." Two days later, Grant told Henry W. Halleck, then commander of the Western Department, that "for 15 miles east and west of the railroad, from Coffeeville to La Grange, nearly everything for the subsistence of man or beast has been appropriated for the use of our army, and on leaving our advanced position I had the principal mills destroyed."[8]

Grant's army was so successful in stripping the land clean of food that by the end of 1862 near-famine conditions prevailed in northern Mississippi, and many civilians repeatedly sought the Confederate governor's assistance for the starving families of absent soldiers. The extreme food shortage mainly affected the civilian population, but its effects were felt in the Confederate army as well. Morale declined as soldiers received letters from home, and desertion rates climbed as fighting men "wanted to go home and take care of their families."[9]

Beef-Cattle and Corn Are Abundant Everywhere

The next campaign against Vicksburg was part of a two-pronged effort to control the Mississippi River. The first prong was launched by Major General Nathaniel Banks in Louisiana. During 1862, Louisianans ferried 30,000 head of cattle across the Mississippi to the lower South "to feed the armies of the Confederacy." Banks intended to stop this trade, and beginning in March of 1863 he sent forces from New Orleans into south-central Louisiana. Banks had a simple view of his mission: he deemed it expedient "to deprive the rebel Government of all possible means of support, to take possession of mules, horses, cattle, and the staple products of the country—cotton, sugar and tobacco." Banks confiscated 20,000 animals, 5,000 bales of cotton, and numerous hogsheads of sugar. After taking New Iberia, Louisiana, all the food, supplies, cotton, cattle, mules, and horses were organized into an eight-mile-long wagon train that was sent on its way to New Orleans.[10] Miraculously, the entire train arrived in the city without any interference from the Confederates, who were in hot pursuit.

Banks next targeted Confederate-held Port Hudson, the only remaining fortified Confederate town along the Mississippi River besides Vicksburg. Its conquest would be necessary to secure the river for the United States and prevent the transfer of cattle and other supplies from the trans-Mississippi. Banks began a campaign against Port Hudson in May 1863. His troops employed the same tactics as they had in Louisiana. As one Union soldier described it, the expedition "collected a large amount of cotton; and we were suffered to kill cattle, pigs, and poultry. All this marauding went on ruthlessly and wastefully. We left the road behind us foul with the odor of decaying carcasses. Cattle were killed, a quarter or so taken out of them, and the remainder left to the buzzards. So with sheep and poultry. Pigs were bayoneted, sugar-houses plundered of sugar and molasses, private dwellings entered; and, if any resistance was offered by the owner, his arms were wrested from him, and he overmastered."[11] Although well supplied, the offensive stalled at Port Hudson, where the Confederate garrison of 7,500 troops held off the Federal army, eventually numbering 40,000. Unable to capture the port, Banks placed the stronghold under siege.

The second prong of the Union strategy was Grant's second effort to take Vicksburg. He had spent the early months of 1863 conducting a series of unsuccessful operations intended to gain access to the Confederate fortress. One such operation involved a massive effort to divert the Mississippi River through bayous to the west of the existing riverbed, so that the river would bypass Vicksburg. When this failed, Grant sent his army to the west around the swamps and marshes, but he had a problem—how to get his army to the eastern bank of the Mississippi from the western side so he could assault Vicksburg.

To camouflage his landing on the eastern side of the Mississippi, Grant devised four diversionary efforts to distract the Confederates. From Nashville, a small Union detachment under the command of Brigadier General Grenville Dodge moved into northern Alabama to raid supplies and dismantle the infrastructure that supported Confederates. Dodge occupied Tuscumbia, where his troops torched 1.5 million bushels of corn and a million pounds of bacon, large quantities of wheat, rye, oats, and fodder, and much of the railroad between Tuscumbia and Decatur. He also demolished "six flouring mills, and we left the country in such a devastated condition that no crop can be raised during the year." A Dr. Cross, who joined the Confederate army and left his wife in charge of their plantation near Tuscumbia, claimed that Federal forces "took every thing" including "upward of seventy negroes, twenty-five thousand pounds of meat, all her live stock, and a large amount of grain, and a large supply of groceries for family use. After they took all of these things, they politely asked Mrs. Cross to leave the house, as they intended burning it."[12]

Simultaneous with Dodge's effort, a cavalry brigade under the command of Colonel Abel Streight moved into northern Georgia, where it assailed supply depots and cut the Western and Atlantic Railroad that supplied Bragg's army in Tennessee. Although Streight and his men did little damage and they finally surrendered, his force attracted the attention of Brigadier General Nathan Bedford Forrest, who went in pursuit. Of all the Confederate leaders, Grant feared Forrest the most, and so Grant was delighted with Forrest's departure.

A more ambitious and effective diversion involved Colonel Benjamin Grierson, a 36-year-old former music teacher, and his 1,700 horse troops. The 600-mile raid commenced on April 17, 1863, from southern Tennessee. Grierson headed south behind Confederate lines, burning commissary stores and government buildings, and severing Vicksburg from all rail connections except the direct line to Jackson, Mississippi. Grierson's cavalry lived off the land for fifteen days before arriving safely in Union-controlled Baton Rouge, Louisiana.

Grant also planned diversions north of Vicksburg. Sherman sent troops to take Greenville on the Mississippi River. These troops then proceeded down Deer Creek, where they confiscated a thousand horses, mules, and cattle along with 500,000 bushels of corn and other provisions that might otherwise have ended up with the Confederates in Vicksburg. When the Federal troops withdrew, the Confederates moved back in, placing their artillery along the river and taking potshots at passing Union ships. Grant again sent more troops into the area, this time with the order to destroy "everything that can be made use of by the enemy in prolonging the war."[13] Sherman's main force then feigned an attack against heavily fortified Snyder's Bluff on the Yazoo River north of Vicksburg. This feint was intended to hold Confederate troops in place north of Vicksburg while Grant's army crossed downriver.

While the Confederates were focused on Grierson to the east and Sherman to the north, Grant sent ironclads and transports down the Mississippi past the Vicksburg batteries at night, suffering only minor losses. He used the ships to shuttle his army to the eastern side at Bruinsberg on April 29 and 30, 1863. Unfortunately, the army had little in the way of supplies and it would be weeks before all the necessary supplies for a major campaign would be assembled. This did not bother Grant. According to biographer Jean Edward Smith, for four days Grant acted "as the Quartermaster he had been in the Mexican-American War, firing off logistical instructions to subordinates, stockpiling ammunition, and dispatching foraging parties into the countryside."[14]

Charles A. Dana, a former managing editor at the *New York Tribune* who, at the time, was a War Department investigative officer assigned to Grant's staff, reported that "Grant made inquiries on every side about the food supplies of the country we were entering. He told me he had been gathering information on this point ever since the army crossed the Mississippi, and had made up his mind that both beef and cattle and corn were abundant in the country." On May 4, Dana told the War Department that Grant intended "to disregard his base and depend on the country for his meat and bread. Beef-cattle and corn are abundant everywhere. The enemy is not suffering for want in the least."[15]

Each day, Grant sent out foragers ten to fifteen miles to gather supplies by making the rounds of the local plantations. Newspaper reporter Sylvanus Cadwallader noted that the wagons returned at nightfall groaning under the weight "of grain, pieces of salted meat, or pails full of butter, eggs, honey or vegetables." As the army was particularly short on transport vehicles, the foragers augmented their wagons with an odd assortment of carriages, phaetons, and surreys filled with an abundance of items—hams, chickens, sweet potatoes, corn, oats, plums, strawberries, figs, pears, bread, biscuits, and animal fodder. These vehicles were drawn by an equally unusual collection of horses, mules, and oxen. In addition, horses, mules, cattle, milk cows, calves, sheep, goats, lambs, turkeys, geese, ducks, and chickens were driven together, frequently in one drove. The only supplies provided by the army commissary were salt, sugar, coffee, and sometimes hardtack. Federal troops were delighted with this state of culinary affairs: As Isaac Jackson of the 83rd Ohio Infantry smugly announced at the time: "We live fat."[16]

When several hundred wagons filled with supplies from the Federal supply depot at Milliken's Bend, Louisiana, arrived at Bruinsberg on May 6, Grant supplied his army with three days' rations and moved out. Rather than move directly northward toward Vicksburg, Grant headed northeast toward Jackson, the capital of Mississippi. Along the way, foragers continued to raid plantations along their line of march. In a series of hard-fought battles, the Union army captured Jackson on May 14, and pushed forces under Johnston's command further east.

While in the city, Sherman destroyed military and commissary supplies, cut the east-west rail lines to Vicksburg, and torched "foundries, machine shops, warehouses, factories, arsenals and public stores." Afterward, Sherman predicted that Jackson would not serve as a Confederate railroad center or supply depot, or house military factories, "for six months."[17]

After their victory at Jackson, the main part of Grant's army reversed course and headed directly west toward Vicksburg, splitting Johnston's army from Pemberton's. The bulk of the Southern troops headed toward Vicksburg, and the others, who wanted to avoid being encircled at the Mississippi port, headed anywhere the Union army wasn't.

Nothing Like Order Prevailed

Even before the siege of Vicksburg commenced, food was a problem in the city. Confederate soldiers engaged in "the customary pilfering—fruits, vegetables, chickens, and livestock disappeared; troops drained the city of supplies, created shortages, and sent prices soaring. Food became scarce. Butter sold for $1.50 a pound, and flour was virtually unavailable. A substance that passed for coffee was brewed from sun-dried pieces of sweet potato" and families "lived on bacon and cornmeal, and salted mackerel was considered a delicacy."[18]

Pemberton prohibited food from being shipped out of Mississippi, he encouraged farmers to grow edible crops rather than cotton, and some farmers and plantation owners did just that. Although food was plentiful outside Vicksburg, as the Union army would later prove, plantation owners were often unwilling to sell food to the military authorities, simply because farmers could get better prices on the open market. Well before the arrival of the Federal army, Vicksburg residents had to drive into the countryside to purchase salt for $45 a bag and turkeys at $50 each, which were unavailable in the city. But even when food was available and owners were willing to sell these goods to the military, there was still the problem of how to get the food into Vicksburg. Pemberton had no control over the railroad lines or steamboats, which often carried considerable private cargo rather than military necessities, and there were not enough army wagons or usable roads to carry the needed provisions into the city, or so he would later complain.[19]

Unlike Grant, Pemberton was unwilling to confiscate private foodstuffs and his supply acquisition was limited. In March 1863, General Edward Tracy reported from Vicksburg that in "this garrisoned town, upon which the hopes of a whole people are set, and which is liable at any time to be cut off from its interior lines of communication, there is not now subsistence for one week. The meat ration has already been virtually discontinued, the quality being such that the men utterly refuse to eat it." When alerted to the need for provisions, commissary agents immediately brought in 500,000 pounds of hog meat, some molasses, corn, salted beef, and salt.[20] Additional provisions were hastily acquired, but they would not be nearly enough.

When the Federal army turned from Jackson and headed west to Vicksburg, Pemberton directed that there should be no provisions left in the area around Vicksburg. The Confederates evacuated Snyder's Bluff, along with an estimated 25,000 to 30,000 bushels of corn that had to be burned because there were no available transports to move it into the city. The Confederate troops filled what wagons they had with chickens, turkeys, peas, corn, rice, and sugar, and brought them into the city. Beef cattle, dairy cows, sheep, hogs, and mules were rounded up and driven ahead of the retreating Confederate forces. As the Confederate army retreated into Vicksburg on May 17, they brought everything they could into the city. Vicksburg resident Emma Balfour observed: "From 12 o'clock until late in the night the streets and roads were jammed with wagons, cannons, horses, men, mules, stock, sheep, everything you can imagine that appertains to an army—being brought hurriedly within the entrenchment." She also noted the chaos: "Nothing like order prevailed."[21]

With what had already been stockpiled in the city, Pemberton believed that Vicksburg "had ample supplies of ammunition as well as of subsistence to stand a siege" for at least six weeks.[22] He believed that before the city starved, Johnston's army outside the city would lift the siege and free the encircled city, or at least that was his plan. Johnston was shocked that Pemberton allowed his army to be trapped in Vicksburg, and he had no rescue plan for the garrison.

Grant's forces twice stormed the city's fortifications, but failed to break through. When additional reinforcements arrived, the Union army settled into trench warfare. While the siege was underway, on May 26, Grant directed Major General Francis Blair to raid the rich agricultural area around the Yazoo River. Verbally, Grant gave "special instructions" to Blair to take or destroy all the food and forage that he found. Blair spent a week going forty-five miles up the river, burning or confiscating crops, cattle, and anything edible. Many of the cattle were herded back to Grant's army besieging Vicksburg. Northern soldiers secured additional provisions from Southern planters outside the city who, much to the dismay of those sealed up in Vicksburg, readily sold produce and other foodstuffs to the Union army during the siege.[23]

Throughout the siege, artillery and mortars regularly lobbed shells into the city and both soldiers and civilians had a rough time. To protect themselves from the bombardments, civilians dug caves into the hills in the city, cooking outside the entrances to their caves when the shelling was light. Foods commonly eaten in these makeshift shelters included rice and "coffee" brewed from sweet potatoes.[24]

As the siege continued, diminishing food supplies become critical. Daily rations for Confederate soldiers consisted of fourteen ounces of food per man. This included "four ounces each of bacon, flour, or meal, the rest comprising peas, rice, and sugar. It was less than half the rations normally issued and led, some believed, to sharply increased sickness among the debilitated troops." By May 30, the Confederate meat ration was cut in half. On June 4, Sergeant William Tunnard, of the 3rd Louisiana Infantry, wrote that "all surplus provisions in the city were seized, and rations issued to civilians and soldiers alike. To the perils of the siege began now to be added the prospect of famine." By June 12, the meat ration was exhausted.[25]

A plentiful supply of cowpeas (also called black-eyed peas), grown by local farmers for animal feed, had been stockpiled in the city before the siege. These were ground into flour that was used to make bread of sorts. Not every Confederate soldier was thankful for this blessing. Ephraim Anderson of the 1st Missouri Brigade wrote that cowpea bread was a "novel species of the hardest of 'hard tack.'" The cowpea meal "was ground at a large mill in the city, and sent to the cooks in camp to be prepared. It was accordingly mixed with cold water and put through the form of baking; but the nature of it was such, that it never got done, and the longer it was cooked, the harder it became on the outside, which was natural, but, at the same time, it grew relatively softer on the inside, and, upon breaking it, you were sure to find raw pea-meal in the centre. The cooks protested that it had been on the fire two good hours, but it was all to no purpose; yet, on the outside it was so hard, that one might have knocked down a full-grown steer with a chunk of it." After being fed to the troops for three days and making soldiers sick, cowpea bread was taken off the menu. Boiled cowpeas, however, continued to be about one half of their total subsistence. When the Union soldiers outside the city heard about the cowpea bread, presumably from deserters, a Southerner reported that they "hallooed over for several nights afterwards, enquiring how long the pea-bread would hold out; if it was not about time to lower our colors; and asking us to come over and take a good cup of coffee and eat a biscuit with them. Some of the boys replied that they need not be uneasy about rations, as we had plenty of mules to fall back upon."[26]

And it did come to mule meat. Alexander St. Clair Abrams, who worked for the *Vicksburg Whig*, reported that "mules were soon brought in requisition, and their meat sold readily at one dollar per pound, the citizens being as anxious to get it as they were before the investment to purchase the delicacies of the season." Mule meat "was also distributed among the soldiers, to those who desired it, although it was not given out under the name of rations. A great many of them, however, accepted it in preference to doing without any meat, and the flesh of the mules was equal to the best venison." Abrams "found the flesh tender and nutritious, and, under the *peculiar circumstances*, a most desirable description of food." Ephraim Anderson arrived at one dinner one evening to find that mule meat was the main course: "The appetites of some of the boys were so good, that they partook of it even with a relish." Anderson himself only tasted it, finding it "not very pleasant and by no means palatable." The *Vicksburg Daily Citizen* pronounced mule flesh "very palatable" and "decidedly preferable to the poor beef which has been dealt out to the soldiers for months past, and that a willingness was expressed among those who tried the meat to receive it as regular rations."[27]

For its part, the Northern press had a field day when reporters heard about Vicksburg's mules. The Chicago *Tribune* fabricated a bill of fare for a fictitious "Hôtel de Vicksburg":

SOUP.
Mule Tail.

BOILED.
Mule Bacon, with poke greens.
Mule Ham, canvassed.

ROAST.

Mule Sirloin.

Mule Bump, stuffed with rice.

VEGETABLES.

Peas and Rice.

ENTREES.

Mule Head, stuffed a la mode.

Mule Ears, fricasseed a la got'ch.

Mule Side, stewed, new style, hair on.

Mule Beef, jerked, a la Mexicana.

Mule Spare Ribs, plain.

Mule Salad.

Mule Tongue, cold, a la Bray.

Mule Liver, hashed.

Mule Brains, a la omelette.

Mule Hoof, soused.

Mule Kidneys, stuffed with peas.

Mule Tripe, fried in pea-meal batter.

JELLIES.

Mule Foot.

PASTRY.

Cottonwood Berry Pies.

Chinaberry Tarts.

DESSERT.

White Oak Acorns.

Blackberry Leaf Tea.

Beech Nuts.

Genuine Confederate Coffee.

LIQUORS.

Mississippi Water, vintage of 1492. Superior, $3

Limestone Water, late importation. Very fine, $2.75.

Spring Water, Vicksburg brand, $1.50.

at all hours.

Gentlemen to wait on themselves. Any inattention on the
part of servants to be promptly reported at the office.

JEFF. DAVIS & Co., Proprietors.

CARD. The proprietors of the justly celebrated Hôtel de Vicksburg, having enlarged and refitted the same, are now prepared to accommodate all who favor them with a call. Parties arriving by the River or Grant's inland route, will find Grape, Cannister & Co.'s carriages at the landing, or at any depot on the line of entrenchments. Buck, Ball & Co. take charge of all baggage. No effort will be spared to make the visit of all as interesting as possible.

J. D. & Co.[28]

Mule meat was not all that was consumed in Vicksburg. According to Confederate Major S. H. Lockett, Confederate soldiers ate rats "with the relish of epicures dining on the finest delicacies of the table." A resident noted in her diary: "rats are hanging dressed in the market for sale with mule meat,—there is nothing else. The officer at the battery told me he had eaten one yesterday." The price for rats was $2.50. *The Daily Citizen* reported that they had "not as yet learned of any one experimenting with the flesh of the canine species," although there were reports of a paucity of dogs and cats on the streets of the city.[29]

During the last few weeks of June, conditions in Vicksburg worsened. "Many families of wealth had eaten the last mouthful of food in their possession, and the poor class of non-combatants were on the verge of starvation," according to a report.[30] As soldiers' rations were reduced, malnutrition set in, and many soldiers ended up in the hospital (or remained ill at their posts), suffering from diseases exacerbated by hunger. Colonel Ashbel Smith of the 2nd Texas Infantry reported:

> Our rations were reduced to little more than sufficient to sustain life. Five ounces of musty corn-meal and pea flour were nominally issued daily. In point of fact, this allowance did not exceed three ounces. All the unripe, half brown peaches, the green berries growing on the briars, all were carefully gathered and simmered in a little sugar and water, and used for food. Every eatable vegetable around the works was hunted up for greens. Some two or three men approached to succumb and die from inanition for want of food, but the health of the men did not seem to suffer immediately from want of rations, but all gradually emaciated and became weak, and toward the close of the siege many were found with swollen ankles and symptoms of incipient scurvy.

Captain Ferdinand O. Claiborne, of the 3rd Maryland Battery, recorded in his diary: "Our rations are growing more scarce every day and we must eventually come to mule meat. We have a quantity of bacon yet on hand, but breadstuff is the great desideratum. The men receive only one-quarter rations of breadstuffs such as rice, pea meal and rice flour—the corn has given out long since, rations of sugar, lard, molasses and tobacco are issued but this does not make amends for the want of bread, and the men are growing weaker every day."[31]

On June 28, Pemberton received an anonymous letter signed "many soldiers." It read, in part: "Our rations have been cut down to one biscuit and a small bit of bacon per day, not enough scarcely to keep soul and body together, much less to stand the hardships we are called upon to stand. If you can't feed us, you had better surrender us, horrible as the idea is . . . This army is now ripe to mutiny unless it can be fed."[32] Deserters reported the same thing. Charles A. Dana wrote on June 29, to Secretary of War Edwin Stanton: "Two separate parties of deserters from Vicksburg agree in the statement that the provisions of the place are near the point of total exhaustion; that rations have now been reduced lower than ever; that extreme dissatisfaction exists among the garrison, and that it is agreed on all hands that the city will be surrendered on Saturday, July 4, if, indeed, it can hold on so long as that."[33]

The Father of Waters Goes Unvexed to the Sea

The deserters were right. General Pemberton, along with more than 27,000 Confederate soldiers, surrendered on the Fourth of July. The Confederates had received no rations on July 3, and the victorious Union soldiers empathized with them. Since the Federal army had ample supplies, many soldiers gave Confederate soldiers bread and other food, which "was accepted with avidity and thanks." A Federal soldier named Isaac Jackson found that the Confederate soldiers "were nearly starved. I was talking with one who had been eating mule meat for four days & but one biscuit a day for over a week. It looked hard to see the poor fellow pitch into our 'hard tack' which our boys gave them. We had plenty, and they carried them off by armloads. Poor fellows, they needed them." According to a Confederate soldier, Union soldiers "aided us greatly by many acts of kindness. They would go out to their sutler's tent with the greenbacks we had borrowed from their dead comrades and purchase food for us, and doubtless many a starving 'Reb' felt that his life was thus saved."[34]

A Confederate officer named J. H. Jones approached a Union lieutenant and requested permission to buy food. The lieutenant responded that he needed to ask permission through military channels for that to happen. Jones replied that

> he must know, from my appearance, I would be dead some days before its return, to which he laughingly assented. He suddenly remembered that he had some "trash" in his haversack and offered it. The "trash" consisted of about two pounds of ginger snaps and butter crackers; luxuries I had not seen for three years. I was struck dumb with amazement. "Trash," quoth he? . . . I fell upon that "trash" like a hungry wolf and devoured it. A bystander afterwards declared that it disappeared in my mouth like grains of rice before a Chinaman's chop stick. Be that as it may, the memory of that sumptuous feast still lingers, and my heart yet warms with gratitude towards that good officer for the blessing he bestowed."[35]

Vicksburg merchants who had hoarded supplies during the siege began selling food to civilians at extortionate prices: "$200 for a barrel of flour, $30 for the same amount of sugar, corn $100 a bushel and $5 for a pound of flour." Other merchants brought out "wines for which the sick had pined in vain" and "luxuries of various kinds were found in profusion." A great deal of food collected by the Confederate government was also in Vicksburg. When located, it was "rolled out into the streets" and given to the Confederate soldiers and the civilians of the city. William H. Tunnard of the 3rd Louisiana reported that the Union troops threw the provisions into the streets and shouted, "'Here rebs, help yourselves, you are naked and starving and need them.'" Tunnard observed, "What a strange spectacle of war between those who were recently deadly foes."[36]

Within a few days, the Confederate soldiers were paroled—sent home to await official exchange. As for wounded and ill soldiers, they remained in Vicksburg, while medical professionals tried to cure their illnesses and treat their wounds. Weeks after the surrender, many still had not recovered. A Northern reporter described them in this way: "Their emaciated appearance made them look like a weak, tottering procession of skeletons, while their dirty white uniforms assisted materially in adding to the ghastliness of the pallor that overspread each countenance."[37]

Nine days after Vicksburg fell, Grant sent Sherman back to Jackson, Mississippi, which Johnston had reoccupied. Sherman was ordered to break up Johnston's army and "destroy the rolling stock and everything valuable for carrying on war, or placing it beyond the reach of the rebel enemy."[38] Sherman reported back to Grant: "We are absolutely stripping the country of corn, cattle, hogs, sheep, poultry, everything, and the new-growing corn is being thrown open as pasture fields or hauled for the use of our animals." Sherman considered this "wholesale destruction" to be the scourge of war. As a reporter for the *Chicago Times* wrote: "The country between Vicksburg and Jackson was completely devastated. No subsistence of any kind remained. Every growing crop had been destroyed when possible. Wheat was burned in the barn and stack whenever found. Provisions of every kind were brought away or destroyed. Livestock was slaughtered for use, or driven back on foot."[39]

As for Pemberton, Grant released him and sent him to report back to Johnston. Pemberton was roundly criticized in Southern newspapers for placing the garrison in the position of being starved out. On August 3, 1863, he wrote his official report of the surrender. In it, he claimed that the lack of food played no part in his decision to surrender the city: "The assertion that the surrender of Vicksburg was compelled by the want of subsistence, or that the garrison was starved out, is one entirely destitute of truth. There was at no time any absolute suffering for want of food among the garrison. That the men were put upon greatly reduced rations is undeniably true; but, in the opinion of many medical officers, it is at least questionable whether under all the circumstances this was at all injurious to their health."[40]

To support his assertion, Pemberton defiantly pointed out that, at the time of surrender, Vicksburg had "about 40,000 pounds of pork and bacon, which had been reserved for the subsistence of my troops in the event of attempting to cut my way out of the city; also, 51,241 pounds of rice, 5,000 bushels of peas, 92,234 pounds of sugar, 3,240 pounds of soap, 527 pounds of tallow candles, 27 pounds of Star candles, and 428,000 pounds of salt." This looks impressive, but is not. Soap, candles, and salt are not edible, and the quality of the meat and rice was highly questionable, and even if it had been distributed, would have run out in a few days. That just left a large sugar reserve, which is hardly sustenance.[41]

The availability of food was contradicted by virtually every other report—Confederate and Federal—that emerged from Vicksburg. Confederate soldiers and civilians might have been able to hold out for a few more days, but without food the city and its garrison would have starved. According to all accounts, Confederate soldiers had no food. According to the surrender accord, Grant was required to supply the Confederate army with food. Most likely such statements were Pemberton's way of avoiding responsibility for his failure to store enough food in the city for a long siege or, possibly, for his failure to avoid entrapment in Vicksburg in the first place, a view that Johnston maintained at the time. Pemberton's assertion that there were insufficient means of transportation to move food into the city is also questionable, as Grant proved when he landed at Bruinsberg and confiscated all the transport vehicles he needed from surrounding plantations.

When it was suggested to Jefferson Davis that Vicksburg fell for want of provisions, he responded, "Yes, from want of provisions inside and a general outside who wouldn't fight." Davis's swipe at Johnston's failure to relieve Vicksburg may have been unjustified. His forces were located east of Jackson, and they were also without provisions, which was one reason Johnston gave for his failure to come to the aid of Vicksburg. Independent observers reported that his army "had been subsisting almost wholly on green corn for several weeks, and half his troops were probably unfit for duty. They were found sick at almost every house, and languishing or dead in hundreds of fence-corners. The utter impossibility of supplying his army with necessary food had been a sufficient reason for Johnston's not falling upon Grant's rear and attempting to raise the siege."[42]

The final conquest of the Mississippi River occurred five days after the fall of Vicksburg, when Port Hudson in Louisiana fell to the besieging army directed by Nathaniel Banks. Like Grant at Vicksburg, Banks tried to assault the Confederate fortifications at Port Hudson, and when direct assault failed, he settled down into a long siege. Port Hudson was also under the nominal command of Pemberton, who had been responsible for supplying the town with enough food to survive a siege. For the next forty-eight days, Banks tried to starve out the Confederate garrison. Like the Confederate forces in Vicksburg, the defenders of Port Hudson suffered from malnutrition and then starvation. One Confederate soldier reported in his diary that he and fellow soldiers had eaten "all the beef—all the mules—all the dogs—and all the rats." After news of Vicksburg's fall reached the garrison and their food and supplies were exhausted, the Confederates surrendered Port Hudson on July 9. For the first time in two years, the Mississippi River was open for ships to travel unimpeded from the Midwest to the mouth of the river. In Abraham Lincoln's immortal phrase, "The Father of Waters goes unvexed to the sea."[43]

In late November 1863, General Grant, flush from his victory at Vicksburg, took charge of the stalled and starving Federal army at Chattanooga, where he defeated the Confederates. Grant's victories at Vicksburg and Chattanooga made him a national hero in the North.

His aggressiveness and military successes impressed President Abraham Lincoln, who appointed him General-in-Chief of all armies in March 1864.

Vicksburg Effects

During the Mississippi River campaign, food was used as both a strategic and tactical weapon. As a tactical weapon, the sieges prevented food from entering the cities, which directly contributed to their surrender. Strategically, the victories at Vicksburg and Port Hudson prevented food and supplies from Texas from reaching the Southern states. As a result of the loss of beef from Texas, the South had to reduce its meat rations for Confederate soldiers east of the Mississippi River.[44] Just as important was the strategic value of the Mississippi River for Northern commerce. After these Union victories, Midwestern farmers could once again send provisions down the Mississippi River to New Orleans. Southern farmers and plantation owners with access to the Mississippi began selling molasses, cotton, and other commodities to Union traders, and this sapped Confederate morale.

Most important, the Vicksburg campaign represented a sea change in the Federal strategy to end the war. At the beginning of the war, Northerners believed that there was strong support for the Union in the South, and that Southerners would eventually come to their senses, reject the firebrand secessionists, and rejoin the Union willingly. However, after occupying large sections of the Confederacy in Arkansas, Tennessee, Mississippi, and Virginia, it became clear that Northern forces were viewed as conquerors and not as liberators, and that whatever support existed for the Union in the South before the war had largely vanished once the conflict began. The activities of Southern guerrillas and cavalry raids proved that it would be impossible to supply the Federal troops who would have to garrison the South, which led Grant, Sherman, Lincoln, and many other Northern leaders to conclude that it would be impossible to win the war by traditional military means. What emerged was a new strategy that focused on the use of raiding armies to disrupt the Southern food supply, making it harder for Confederate guerrillas and armies to operate. As this new policy would directly affect civilians, it would also sap the South's morale and its willingness to continue the war, or so it was hoped.

6

Traders or Traitors?

General Robert E. Lee's campaign in Pennsylvania ended in defeat at Gettysburg in July 1863; it had consumed tremendous amounts of supplies that just could not be replaced. The Army of Northern Virginia once again suffered from shortages of food, particularly beef. Beef was available in Texas, but after the fall of Vicksburg, it became almost impossible to move the cattle and other goods from the trans-Mississippi region to the lower South. Florida was another potential source of cattle, and Confederate agents traversed the state "buying up all the cattle obtainable, paying any price so they can get the animals." By late 1863, however, few cattle remained in Florida that could survive the long drives to the slaughterhouses in Georgia or the Carolinas.[1]

Weather again had played havoc with Southern crops in 1863. In July and August, it rained forty-five days out of fifty, and Virginia's wheat crop was a total loss. Josiah Gorgas, the Confederate Chief of Ordinance, wrote in his diary in mid-July: "All the crops in this part of the country have been lost." By the end of October the *Richmond Examiner* reported that much of northern Virginia was devoid of crops, and Gorgas concluded that there was not enough food to sustain Richmond's population. The *Richmond Whig* worried about an approaching famine and urged residents to leave the city for regions of Virginia that had plenty of food.[2] If Richmond and the Army of Northern Virginia were to survive the upcoming winter, they had to acquire food somewhere very soon.

The solution appeared, not via blockade-runners, foreign intervention, or mobilizing their own agricultural strengths, but from the North, which had an abundance of food coupled with an insatiable appetite for cotton. In January 1864, the Confederate-controlled Weldon Railroad sent several hundred bales of cotton to the Federal lines in North Carolina. In return, the Confederates picked up 120,000 pounds of beef. The beef was then partly transported to Richmond. At first, this exchange with the North occurred occasionally, but as the war dragged on and the Confederacy became more desperate for food, the exchange became a regular event. According to historian Ludwell Johnson, during the last months of the war Union sources supplied more meat to the Confederate armies in Virginia and North Carolina than was provided by all Southern sources. During the first few months of 1865, the North daily exchanged 10,000 pounds of bacon and other supplies, such as sugar, coffee, molasses, and codfish, for fifty bales of cotton, and this transaction was just one trading scheme.[3]

Trading between the Lines

Many Northerners and Southerners viewed trading with the enemy as unpatriotic; others considered it treason. In reality, official policies regarding trading between the lines were ambiguous from the beginning and continued to be so throughout the war. The Confederate Congress never directly outlawed importing goods from the United States, although it did try to regulate and control exports. In May 1861, for instance, the Confederate Congress outlawed trading cotton, molasses, rice, sugar, tobacco, and other goods except through designated Southern seaports and through Mexico. In the following year, the Confederacy outlawed shipping these products to Southern cities controlled by the North. The United States Congress did not prohibit trading between the lines until

July 13, 1861, and even then, the law provided for exceptions licensed by the president and controlled by the Treasury Department. It took another month for President Abraham Lincoln to declare that "all commercial intercourse" with the Confederacy was "unlawful, and will remain unlawful until such insurrection shall cease or has been suppressed."[4]

The opposition to trading between the lines is understandable. As previously discussed, Southerners believed that the Union would recognize their independence just as soon as it was deprived of cotton: New England's textile mills would languish, and since cotton was the major export of the United States, when the North was no longer able to export it, the outflow of the North's gold reserves might make it impossible to prosecute the war. So the South did not want to barter cotton for the goods it needed. However, Northern traders would not accept Confederate currency for their goods, so all sales had to be transacted in greenbacks or specie, and Southern leaders believed that this harmed their financial system. Finally, trading with the enemy was bad for Southern morale, as it demonstrated that the agrarian South could not provide for its basic needs.[5]

Many Northern leaders also believed that trading between the lines was embarrassing and would harm public support for the war if it were public. Those who profited from these trades were often those with political connections and there was always a whiff of graft and corruption associated with them. Trading between the lines was strongly opposed by the military, who complained bitterly that virtually all transactions helped the Confederate military.

Despite strong public opposition to trade between the North and South, there were significant reasons why it made sense. For the South, such trade became necessary as the blockade became effective and food-producing areas of the South were occupied or destroyed. The South had an abundant supply of cotton, which was in great demand by textile manufacturers in New England, Britain, and France, and it desperately needed food. For the North, there was a legitimate concern at the beginning of the war that the lack of cotton would throw Northern textile mills, the largest single industry in the nation, into a tailspin, with tens of thousands of workers unemployed. While these problems never materialized, the cotton trade did generate handsome profits for many influential Northern manufacturers as well as for traders who sold the cotton abroad. For the U.S. government, cotton exports helped protect the nation's gold reserves and they discouraged intervention in the war by France and Great Britain on behalf of the Confederacy.[6]

Sub-rosa trading between the lines had gone on since the beginning of the war. During the first year of the war, trade flourished between the Confederacy and the border states. Kentucky, for example, became a "veritable highway" between the United States and the Confederacy. This trade was a very profitable business, justifying Kentucky's efforts to remain neutral during the first months of the war. As once common items, such as coffee, sugar, and salt, became rare and prices shot up, Virginia residents also began an extensive trade—some legal and much illicit—with traders in Maryland and Pennsylvania.[7] As the borders between the South and the North were long, porous, and often ill-defined, small-scale illegal trading between the lines was virtually impossible to stop. Likewise, Confederate and Union soldiers often exchanged goods—usually food for tobacco—despite repeated efforts by their superior officers to prevent fraternization.

Safe-Conduct, Open Market, and Prompt Shipment

Beginning in 1861, Northern contractors with the Union army expressed willingness to supply the Confederate army as well. They wanted half the payment in cotton, half in Confederate bonds. Evidently, the Federal government approved the proposals; the Confederate government turned them down. When Robert Garlick Hill Kean, the Head of the Confederate Bureau of War, found out about the proposals and the rejections, he concluded that the turndown was a mistake: "The question is simply whether they suffer more for the comparatively small quantity of cotton, say 100,000 bales, or we for the indispensable articles of salt, meat, clothing, medicines."[8]

When the United States captured New Orleans, Nashville, and Memphis, trading between the lines picked up.[9] The Federal government tried to woo local residents over to the Union cause by offering trade permits that made it possible for them to export cotton and to import provisions and other goods they needed. Technically, this trade was only conducted with loyal Unionists in areas controlled by the North, but many goods ended up with the Confederate military.

Benjamin F. Butler, the Federal military governor in New Orleans, went one step further. Butler hailed from Lowell, Massachusetts, a major textile manufacturing center, and was particularly enthusiastic about acquiring cotton for his friends and relatives in the textile business back home. Butler was more than willing to exchange salt and other provisions for cotton. Butler did not care at all where the cotton came from or where the bartered supplies ended up. Three months after the Union occupied New Orleans, Butler assured a commissioner from the U.S. State Department that he would guarantee "safe-conduct, open market, and prompt shipment" of all cotton sent to New Orleans.[10] When an Englishman proposed to Butler that cotton be sent from Confederate-controlled Mobile to Union-controlled New Orleans and thence to England, Butler wrote directly to the Confederate commander in Mobile, offering to trade salt for cotton. The commander sent the proposal to Confederate officials in Richmond, who turned it down.

Butler wasn't rebuffed by this turn of events. He redoubled his efforts to promote trade with the Confederacy by establishing stores ostensibly intended to sell provisions to Southern families living within Union lines. In fact, these stores served as meeting places for Northern merchants wishing to acquire cotton and Confederate purchasing agents interested in acquiring provisions for the military. Additional trading between Northern merchants and Confederate agents were conducted outside the stores. Butler was relieved of his command in November 1862, but because he was well connected politically, he was reassigned to the Army of the James in southeastern Virginia.[11]

Even after Butler's departure, trade increased between New Orleans and the Confederacy. In 1864 the Union General E. R. S. Canby, commander of western Mississippi, concluded that New Orleans, since its occupation, had done more "to the support of the rebel armies, more to the purchasing and equipment of privateers that are preying upon our commerce, and more to maintain the credit of the rebel Government in Europe than any other port in the country," with the single exception of Wilmington, North Carolina, which was one of the few remaining ports still controlled by the Confederacy.[12]

To Feed, Clothe, Arm, and Equip Our Enemies

Memphis may have surpassed New Orleans in trading between the lines. It started innocently enough. While in control of Memphis, Major General William T. Sherman permitted exchanging clothing intended for Southern farmers and their families for locally grown cotton. Then this trade was expanded to include those Southerners who expressed "loyal sentiment" to the United States. Lots of Southerners were willing to express such sentiment, and the trade expanded exponentially. Sherman noted in his *Memoirs* that the profits on this trade were enormous. Thousands of barrels of salt and millions of dollars were exchanged for cotton, and Sherman had "no doubt" that the Confederate armies had "received enough salt to make bacon, without which they could not have moved their armies in mass; and that from ten to twenty thousand fresh arms, and a due supply of cartridges have also been got."[13]

In October 1862, a trader in Memphis proposed trading cotton from behind Confederate lines for "ten thousand hogsheads of bacon certainly, and probably twenty thousand hogsheads more." The proposal was sent to the Confederate Secretary of War, George Randolph, who believed that the Confederacy faced the alternative of either violating the policy "of withholding cotton from the enemy or of risking the starvation of our armies." Randolph believed that the Confederate army's need for food far outweighed the benefits of the North receiving Southern cotton. He endorsed the proposal and forwarded it to Jefferson Davis, who agreed to the arrangement. When Davis changed his mind and postponed the deal, Randolph resigned as Secretary of War.[14] His replacement, James A. Seddon, made an agreement with the trader in Memphis, but this exchange was later cancelled after Davis intervened.

Lucius Northrop, the Confederate Commissary General, also urged that trade be commenced with Union-controlled Southern cities, such as Nashville, Memphis, and New Orleans. He proposed that Confederates barter cotton for meat and salt. This proposal was supported by Seddon, who diplomatically noted that "illicit dealing with persons of doubtful position or mercenary natures might be encouraged to the extent of procuring supplies, particularly of meat."[15] This too was eventually turned down by Davis. The message was clear: Don't ask, don't tell. Just trade quietly behind the scenes.

Private individuals who engaged in major cross-border trade were considered traitors. They often bribed army officers on both sides to approve exchanges or to look the other way, and both traders and military officers were occasionally arrested for their actions in this illegal trade. Sherman arrested an officer for "aiding and abetting the public enemy by furnishing them salt wherewith to cure bacon, a contraband article; also for trafficking on the river without license or permit." Sherman strongly opposed the "nefarious practice" of trading with the enemy and once asked Grant, "What use in carrying on war while our people are supplying arms and the sinews of war?" Grant agreed with Sherman and he tried to stop the exchanges, but he was overruled by officials in Washington.[16]

Speculators, including a number of leading industrialists and members of the U.S. Congress, flocked to cotton-growing areas under Federal control. Some were willing to trade virtually anything for cotton, including military hardware and war supplies, and many of these transactions included the payment of bribes and smuggling. In December 1862, Grant had had enough of the extensive black market activities in his department, which consisted of Kentucky, Tennessee, and Mississippi. He blamed Jews for such trading. Grant summarily issued the notorious General Orders No. 11, which expelled all "Jews and other Vagrants" from the areas under his control. Specifically, he wrote, "The Jews, as a class, violating every regulation of trade established by the Treasury Department and also Department orders, are hereby expelled from the Department." Jewish residents were required to leave within twenty-four hours, and those who refused were to be imprisoned.[17] Grant's anti-Semitic views were shared by many others in the North and the South. In the South, for instance, Jews were identified as speculators and hoarders; in the North they were the ones identified as engaged in illegal trade between the lines, despite the fact that most between-the-line traders were not Jews. Many Jews, however, were recently arrived immigrants from Germany, and they were easily identifiable by their clothing and accents, so Union and Confederate leaders frequently used them as scapegoats.

Grant's order caused an uproar and the War Department directed him to rescind it, which he did. Nevertheless, Grant never changed his opinion of trading between the lines. In July 1863, he wrote a letter to Secretary of the Treasury Salmon P. Chase, who was responsible for licensing trade between the lines, concluding that "any trade whatever with the rebellious States is weakening to us of at least thirty-three per cent of our force. No matter what the restriction thrown around trade, if any whatever is allowed it will be made the means of supplying to the enemy all they want. Restrictions, if lived up to, make trade unprofitable and hence none but dishonest men go into it. I will venture that no honest man has made money in West Tennessee in the last year, whilst many fortunes have been made there during the time." A copy of the letter mysteriously appeared in the *New York Times* a few months after it was written, presumably leaked by someone, possibly Grant himself, who wanted to pressure the Lincoln Administration to stop the trade.[18]

Major General Cadwallader C. Washburn, serving as the Federal administrative commander of Memphis, concluded that trading activities in the city had prolonged the war by helping "largely to feed, clothe, arm and equip our enemies." He believed that Memphis was of more value to the Confederacy "since it fell into Federal hands than Nassau," the center for blockade-running in the Bahamas. He believed that this trade "has given strength to the rebel army, while it has demoralized and weakened our own. It has invited the enemy to hover around Memphis as his best base of supply, when otherwise he would have abandoned the country. It renders of practical non-effect the blockade upon the ocean, which has cost and is costing so many millions." During an eight-month period in 1864, an estimated $12 million worth of supplies passed through Memphis to the Confederate armies. After numerous complaints from the military, Lincoln declared Memphis and west Tennessee to be in "a state of insurrection," and greatly restricted further trading in this area.[19]

The Necessities of Loyal Persons

Benjamin Butler, while commander of the Army of the James, actively permitted his brother-in-law and various friends from Massachusetts to engage in massive trading between the lines. This exchange included food, farm equipment, and all sorts of other goods, which were shipped from Union-controlled Norfolk directly into ports in North Carolina controlled by the Confederacy. When Union blockade squadrons stopped the ships, the captains and crews claimed that they had legal permission to make the transactions. When men were jailed for such activities, Butler freed them. When cargoes were confiscated, the owners of the ships demanded and received compensation for their losses.[20]

In early 1864, Federal regulations were changed to permit supplying "the necessities of loyal persons residing in insurrectionary States within the lines of actual occupation by the military." Since military lines were fluid, the regulations also authorized U.S. Treasury agents to buy cotton from within Confederate-held territory, provided that the grower took an oath of allegiance to the United States. Growers were given three quarters of the then-current market value of cotton at the New York commodity exchange. They would receive one quarter of the money up front, and the remainder when the war ended. Although hundreds of thousands of bales of cotton had already been traded to the North, the Confederate Congress did not officially authorize military commanders to do so until November 1864. This policy was liberalized in February 1865 to permit the government to export cotton free of restrictions through the lines. The commissary in Petersburg did business "night and day" and he had booked the bartering of 6,000 bales in just one month. Under discussion with the Union were an additional 20,000 bales. One pound of cotton was exchanged for one pound of bacon, or two pounds of sugar and coffee. As bales weighed five hundred pounds, these trades provided the potential infusion of tons of provisions just when the Confederate army needed it the most.[21]

In North Carolina, Southern hog producers, who did not grow cotton themselves, acquired cotton from their Southern neighbors and traded it to Northern merchants for salt and sugar. They used the salt to preserve pork, which was then sold to the Confederate commissary. With the money from these sales, the North Carolinians bought more cotton, creating a very lucrative trade that helped Confederate armies survive near-famine conditions during the last year of the war. By 1865 this trade in North Carolina bartered fifty bales of cotton a day in exchange for 10,000 pounds of bacon and codfish. These provisions were sent to Lee's army, which was at the time besieged by Grant at the Petersburg-Richmond front. As historian Ludwell H. Johnson has pointed out, Grant was in the unenviable position "of trying to defeat the Confederates by cutting supply lines over which food was flowing from Union territory in the rear of his own army." Grant opposed this trade so strenuously that in February of 1865 President Lincoln finally agreed to stop all trade with the Confederacy—but only southeast of the Alleghenies.[22]

A Piece of the Rancid Stuff

Trade between the North and South was also conducted around the blockade. Legally, Union ships could enter Canadian ports and unload goods. By this action, these goods were now Canadian. The same ships then reloaded the same goods, now identified as Canadian, and sailed to Bermuda or the Bahamas. On the return trip, the ships picked up cotton and proceeded back to Canadian ports, where they offloaded, then reloaded the cotton. Then, loaded with "Canadian" cotton, American ships sailed to American ports and sold their cargoes to textile mill owners. This subterfuge was proper under U.S. law, but it was cumbersome.

As the war progressed, American ships forgot about the offloading and lading of goods in Canada, and using fake papers saying that they picked up the goods in Canada, just proceeded directly to Bermuda, the Bahamas, or Cuba, where they exchanged their cargoes for cotton and returned directly back to American ports. Direct trade between northeastern American ports and Bermuda, the Bahamas, and Cuba doubled during the Civil War years, and trade with Matamoros, Mexico, on the Texas border, virtually nonexistent before the war, mushroomed during the war. Virtually all cargo coming into these places from the United States ended up in the Confederacy. As the war progressed, Northern companies established agents in the Bahamas and Bermuda to facilitate this lucrative trade, and the American consul in Nassau reported that there were "enormous quantities of American provisions" arriving in the Bahamas. Richmond diarist John B. Jones noted that one ship per day was entering or clearing Southern ports and most of the goods on the ships originated in the United States.[23]

Not all trades went smoothly. In May 1863, Confederate agents bought three million pounds of bacon from the United States and it was dutifully shipped to Bermuda and Nassau. The bacon remained on the docks for a year, waiting for a blockade-runner to pick it up, and much of the meat spoiled. Even so, it was eventually sent through the blockade to Wilmington. As James Sprunt later wrote, Northrop ordered the "rotten, putrid bacon called 'Nassau'" to be distributed to Confederate soldiers and Union prisoners. Sprunt continued: "Many a time have we imprecated curses both loud and deep on poor old Northrop's devoted head as we forced down a piece of the rancid stuff." Northrop himself ate none of it, for he was a vegetarian.[24]

By mid-1864, the Confederate commissary department concluded that the army needed to acquire large quantities of imported meat. "If the Army is to be kept up to its present numbers, it will require at full rations 81 million pounds of meat. Of this a very large part must come from abroad, and much of it, of necessary and in common prudence, is wanted instantly." The Confederate government began offering exorbitant profits to those who could import meat through the blockade and between the lines. During the second half of 1864, blockade-runners brought in an estimated 3.5 million pounds of meat. One of these entrepreneurs, an Englishman named Thomas Taylor, was offered a contract with a 350 percent profit on any provisions he could bring in within three weeks. Taylor left Wilmington, North Carolina, for Nassau in the Bahamas, and eighteen days later he returned with enough beef to generate a profit of £27,000.[25]

The foodstuff generated by this trade was intended for the Southern armies, but much of it never reached the soldiers. Some supplies rotted in warehouses waiting for railroads. The Confederacy was unable or unwilling to assign soldiers to guard supply deports or supply trains, so many foodstuffs were heisted and ended up in the stomachs of railroad workers and their families. Other heisted meat ended up in the hands of speculators who sold it to the highest bidder. The well-to-do in the Confederacy ate well, and many did so right up to the end of the war.

Trading Effects

During the war, the North ended up with an estimated total of 900,000 bales of cotton from the South, which the U.S. Treasury Department greatly appreciated, since much of it was sold abroad. This trade protected the gold reserve of the Federal government and prevented inflation from soaring out of control, as it did in the Confederacy.[26] The South, for its part, acquired much needed food and war material in exchange for cotton. Some historians believe that this trade prolonged the life of the Confederacy for months longer than it would otherwise have survived.

At the beginning of the war, there was a legitimate concern in the North about a possible economic crisis due to the lack of cotton. Such a crisis never materialized. After mills used up their stockpiles of cotton accumulated before the war, textile workers easily found other jobs or joined the army. As the war progressed, United States mills acquired cotton from India—an estimated two fifths of all the cotton used in the North during the Civil War.[27] Thanks to these imports and trading between the lines, many textile mills in the border states and New England were able to keep their factories open throughout much of the war. But what were the consequences of this trade?

The United States Congress held hearings on trading between the lines in the summer of 1864 and reported: "Under the permission to trade, supplies have not only gone in, but bullets and powder, instruments of death which our heroic soldiers have been compelled to face and meet upon almost every field of battle in which they have been engaged in the South." In the Mississippi valley, Northern cotton speculators disrupted any movement of Federal forces that might affect the cotton trade. Canby believed that the Southern armies "both east and west of the Mississippi had been almost completely provisioned by this trade, and that it added strength to the confederates equal at least to 50,000 men."[28]

A U.S. Congressional committee examining trading between the lines in 1865 agreed with Canby. Trade with the Confederacy prolonged the war and "cost the country thousands of lives and millions upon millions of treasure." The historian James Ford Rhodes concluded that trading between the lines was "of greater advantage to the Confederacy than to the Union. For the South it was a necessary evil; for the North it was an evil and not a necessary one."[29]

7

The Confederacy's Breadbasket

*I*n June 1864, a Union army commanded by Major General David Hunter moved rapidly down the Shenandoah Valley, torching crops and threatening some of Richmond's vital supply lines. General Robert E. Lee sent Lieutenant General Jubal Early's corps to push Hunter out of the valley. Early's wildly successful venture did just that and more: After he forced the Union army out of the valley, he then headed into Maryland, threatening Washington, D.C., on July 11. Early was unable to take the well-fortified city, so he returned to the Shenandoah, where he continued to harass and defeat Union forces.

Ulysses S. Grant, the newly appointed General-in-Chief of the Union armies, had had enough of Early and the Shenandoah Valley. On August 7, he sent Major General Philip Sheridan and his cavalry to the valley with simple orders: "Give the enemy no rest, and if it is possible to follow to the Virginia Central road, follow that far. Do all the damage to railroads and crops you can. Carry off stock of all descriptions, and negroes, so as to prevent further planting. If the war is to last another year, we want the Shenandoah valley to remain a barren waste."[1]

Within two months of his arrival in the Shenandoah, Sheridan had devastated four hundred square miles of the valley. In a report to Grant, he boasted: "I have destroyed over 2,000 barns, filled with wheat, hay, and farming implements; over 70 mills, filled with flour and wheat;

have driven in front of the army over 4,000 head of stock, and have killed and issued to the troops not less than 3,000 sheep. This destruction embraces the Luray Valley and Little Fort Valley, as well as the main valley." When the destruction was completed, Sheridan proclaimed that "the Valley, from Winchester up to Staunton, ninety-two miles, will have but little in it for man or beast."[2]

Their Hoarded Stores

The Shenandoah Valley extends almost two hundred miles southwest from Harper's Ferry on the Potomac River to Roanoke, Virginia. Twenty to forty miles wide, the valley is bordered by the Blue Ridge Mountains to the east and the Allegheny Mountains to the west. The Shenandoah Valley was one of the richest agricultural areas in the nation and Virginia's most abundant wheat-growing region, where farmers annually produced 2.45 million bushels of wheat, 3.56 million bushels of corn, and considerable oats, rye, and hay. In 1860, valley farmers possessed 41,000 horses, 80,000 sheep, 89,000 oxen, 96,000 cattle, and thousands of hogs and chickens. Farmers also grew potatoes as a field crop, and in their kitchen gardens they grew a wide range of fruits and vegetables. During the first two years of the Civil War, the Shenandoah was the "granary of the Confederacy," and provisions for the Army of Northern Virginia as well as food for the civilians in Richmond came from there.[3]

In addition to the Shenandoah's fertile land, there were two other reasons for the valley's great productivity. The first was slavery: 18 percent of the valley's population was enslaved, and virtually all those slaves worked on farms. The second reason was mechanization: The Shenandoah Valley was one of the few places in the South that had mechanized agriculture. Cyrus McCormick, the inventor of the most popular mechanical reaper, was born in the Shenandoah Valley and developed his invention in Steele's Tavern, about halfway between Lexington and Staunton. For business reasons, McCormick had moved to Chicago in 1848, but he retained his farm in the Shenandoah Valley and continued to sell reapers and other farm machinery in the valley until the outbreak of the war.

In 1862, agricultural production in the Shenandoah Valley began to decline. Federal cavalry regularly raided the northern end of the valley, reaching as far south as Winchester, Strasburg, and Woodstock.[4] Military actions also disrupted the area's crops, and both Union and Confederate armies confiscated or impressed livestock as well as grain and other provisions. Some destruction in the region also resulted from conflicts between valley residents who supported the Confederacy and those who supported the Union; the two groups often burned each others' homes and crops, whenever they got the chance.

Another reason for the Shenandoah Valley's agricultural decline was due to farm machinery that had worn out or broken down and could not be replaced. This meant that more laborers were needed to plant and harvest crops, and since many Shenandoah Valley men had volunteered or were conscripted into the Confederate army or militia, there was no manpower to be had. Local communities and the soldiers themselves petitioned the governor of Virginia and Confederate President Jefferson Davis to release the men in the militia so they could help with seasonal farming duties. The farmers of the valley reported that they "would be unable to raise supplies sufficient for our own subsistence."[5] Their pleas were ignored.

Agriculture in the Shenandoah Valley was also dependent on slaves, who fled en masse as soon as they thought they could make it to Union lines. Escaped slaves told Union forces where their former masters had stashed their food. This information was passed on to foragers who then went out and liberated these goods.[6] Some slave owners took their slaves to regions that were less likely to be raided. Either way, the result was an ever-diminishing workforce in the valley as the war progressed. Since it was almost impossible to hire labor or acquire slaves during the war, women and children were often left to work farms by themselves, and many farms simply fell into disuse.

From the beginning of the war, the Army of Northern Virginia acquired much of its food from farms in the Shenandoah Valley. Even as the farms began to produce less, government agents impressed more provisions, including 62,000 bushels of wheat, 20,000 bushels of oats, and 1.48 million pounds of hay. The Confederate military also impressed horses, mules, and wagons, leaving fewer draft animals for use in planting and harvesting and fewer wagons for farmers to transport their goods to market. Inevitably, the "granary of the Confederacy" began to run dry.[7]

To make matters worse, a drought hit the Shenandoah Valley in 1862 and continued into the following year. A local woman wrote in her diary in October 1862: "Not rain enough yet to enable the farmers to seed; consequently they cannot sow half crops. What is to become of the country? The fear is that there is not enough food in it to keep the people from starving." Another valley farmer recorded that "the people are seeding with much difficulty, the ground is so dry." In 1863, the corn crop had been reduced to an estimated 41 percent of the previous year's crop, wheat had been reduced by an estimated 50 percent, and oat production was down by almost 70 percent.[8]

But compared to other agricultural areas in northern Virginia, the Shenandoah Valley remained relatively productive. Some farmers resisted selling their produce to impressment agents, hiding their commodities to avoid selling them. Others hoarded what they had because the Confederate economic system was in shambles. Their behavior was no secret: When Richmond again faced famine in the spring of 1864, the *Richmond Examiner* declared: "There are many farmers in Western Virginia who could spare largely from their hoarded stores for the general want." The editor of the *Staunton Spectator* denied that any hoarding was under way, but Federal armies would soon prove that the *Richmond Examiner* was right.[9]

A Waste Barren Land

In 1862, Major General Nathaniel Banks was charged with the task of capturing the Shenandoah Valley and preventing Confederate forces under General Stonewall Jackson from joining with the Confederate army protecting the city of Richmond. If Banks could reach Staunton, he could cut the Virginia and Tennessee Railroad, one of Richmond's most important supply lines. Banks did march down the Shenandoah Valley, and the Union cavalry conducted raids thirty miles below Winchester, burning crops and confiscating cattle, sheep, horses, oxen, and other farm animals. One valley resident described the situation in the area from Woodstock to Winchester: "Now began the devastation of war; that beautiful and fertile valley laid waste, trees all cut down, fences destroyed and houses looking desolate, for miles as we journey no signs of fences or of thrift." Before the war it had been a beautiful valley, she continued, "but now marred by the hands of contending armies, was a waste barren land."[10]

Conditions sent valley refugees south to Charlottesville, where the road was "thronged from morning until night with people running horses, wagons, carriages, cattle, sheep & everything from the Yankees." Lieutenant General Thomas "Stonewall" Jackson defeated the numerically superior Federal army by using lightning raids.[11] He was able to conduct such raids because he had no supply trains. Instead, his army lived off the bounty of the valley's farms.

Not every resident of the Shenandoah supported the Confederacy; there were also many Union supporters, particularly at the northern end. Bitter partisan combat commenced at the beginning of the war and continued until its end. Confederate guerrilla units and rangers also operated in and around the Shenandoah, the most famous being the 43rd Virginia Battalion under the command of Captain John S. Mosby. Mosby's Rangers regularly assaulted Union forces in the valley, and burned out the homes of Union supporters there. The Rangers lived almost entirely off the land, and when not engaged in military activities, most lived in their homes. The area just east of the Shenandoah Valley was so supportive of Mosby that it was called "Mosby's Confederacy."[12]

Grand Union Strategy

In early 1864, Abraham Lincoln and General Ulysses Grant developed a grand strategy to end the war. Major General William T. Sherman would move from Chattanooga to Atlanta and disrupt the supply lines to Richmond. General Nathaniel Banks, stationed in Louisiana, was to take Mobile, Alabama. The Army of the Potomac would move directly south from Fredericksburg and capture Richmond. Major General Benjamin Butler and the Army of the James would advance against Petersburg and cut off Richmond's supply lines to the south. Major General Franz Sigel's army was to proceed down the Shenandoah Valley and cut the Virginia Central Railroad, which supplied the Army of Northern Virginia from the west and, if possible, move eastward toward Confederate supply bases at Gordonsville and Charlottesville.[13]

By June 1864, the grand strategy was in shambles. Sherman was mired in northern Georgia. Banks had been defeated in the Red River campaign in Arkansas and never moved toward Mobile. Butler was stalled before Petersburg. After several costly battles, Grant brought the Union armies to the doorstep of Richmond, but was unable to take the city by storm. Things weren't going well in the Shenandoah Valley, either. Sigel had followed orders and marched south through the valley, but his troops were defeated at New Market on May 15, 1864, by a numerically inferior Confederate force that included cadets from the Virginia Military Institute.

Grant replaced Sigel with Major General David Hunter, who was ordered to march down the Shenandoah Valley burning crops, warehouses, mills, and anything else of potential military or economic value as he went. Hunter's troops also burned private homes in the vicinity where Northern soldiers had been "assassinated" by "bush-wackers." Hunter was then supposed to push on "to Charlottesville and Lynchburg, and destroy the railroad and canal beyond possibility of repair for weeks." On June 6, he made it to Staunton, about halfway down the valley. Along the way he demolished mills, storehouses, furnaces, factories, foundries, and farm equipment, and confiscated any supplies that could be helpful to the Confederacy. The Virginia Central railroad, which ran the length of the Shenandoah Valley, was one of Richmond's most important supply lines. Hunter's men severed the railroad for miles around Staunton and then proceeded south along the railroad to Lexington, where he disabled more of the railroad and burned the Virginia Military Institute and the home of John Letcher, the ex-governor of Virginia. Hunter continued along the railroad line to Lynchburg, a major supply depot and another connection point for the Virginia Central. Northern newspapers exulted over Hunter's success and predicted that Lee would soon be "cut off from Lynchburg to complete the cordon of famine."[14] The newspapers turned out to be wrong in their prediction.

Jubal Early

To avoid losing the Shenandoah Valley and prevent supply lines from being cut off, Lee ordered Jubal Early and his army corps to leave the

Petersburg trenches and go to the Shenandoah Valley. Early had graduated from West Point in 1837 and became a successful lawyer in Virginia after leaving the army. When the Civil War commenced, Early
voted against secession, but when Virginia left the Union, he joined the
Confederate army, serving first under Stonewall Jackson and then under Robert E. Lee in the Army of Northern Virginia. Early became the
commander of the Second Corps after the battle of Cold Harbor in
June 1864.

Jubal Early arrived at Lynchburg on June 17, 1864. With Early's
army arrayed before him, David Hunter retreated down the Shenandoah Valley. When pursued by Confederate forces, Hunter retreated to
West Virginia, leaving the valley open for Early to march his army of
fourteen thousand men into Maryland and to the gates of Washington,
D.C. As a result, Grant was forced to transfer two army corps from
Petersburg to protect the nation's capital.

Early's troops did little more than engage in an artillery duel with
two forts protecting Washington, before he broke it off and returned to
the Shenandoah Valley. Subsequently, he sent a raiding party to Chambersburg, Pennsylvania, where the Confederates stocked up on supplies and, under Early's orders, burned the city, in retaliation for
Hunter's destruction of private property in the Shenandoah Valley.
Soon, "Remember Chambersburg" became a war cry of the Army of
the Potomac.[15]

Early planned to stay in the Shenandoah Valley until the autumn
grain harvest, which would then be used to supply the Army of Northern Virginia during the winter ahead. To counter this plan, Grant ordered Hunter to reform his army at Harper's Ferry and follow the
Confederates as closely as possible and "to eat out Virginia clear and
clean as far as they go, so that crows flying over it for the balance of this
season will have to carry their provender with them." Grant continued
that it was "desirable that nothing should be left to invite the enemy to

return. Take all provisions, forage, and stock wanted for the use of your command; such as cannot be consumed, destroy."[16] When Hunter proved unequal to the task, Grant looked around for a replacement.

Give the Enemy No Rest

Philip Sheridan and his roommate, George Crook, graduated from West Point in 1853. Before the Civil War, Sheridan was stationed in the Pacific Northwest. When the war began, he served for a few months as a staff officer to Henry Halleck, who later became General-in-Chief of the army. In December 1861, Sheridan became the commissary officer for the Union's Army of Southwest Missouri. He then met Sherman, who appointed Sheridan colonel of a cavalry regiment, even though Sheridan had had no previous cavalry experience. After success in the battle at Boonville, Mississippi, Sheridan was appointed commander of a division in the Army of the Ohio. During the battle of Chattanooga, Sheridan's division participated in the action that took Missionary Ridge. This brought Sheridan to Grant's attention, and when Grant became General-in-Chief of all Federal armies, he selected Sheridan to command the Army of the Potomac's cavalry.

Within a month of Sheridan's appointment, he launched a major raid on Richmond's supply lines, in May 1864. Serving under Sheridan were two young stars—Brigadier Generals George Armstrong Custer and Wesley Merritt. On May 9, 1864, Sheridan's cavalry was assigned to raid Richmond. His troops passed around the left flank of the Confederate army, crossed the North Anna River, tore up tracks on the Virginia Central Railroad, one of Richmond's most important supply routes, and captured a supply train carrying an estimated 1.5 million rations, including 200,000 pounds of bacon. Sheridan's cavalry circled completely around the Confederate army, ending up at Malvern Hill, where they joined the lines of the Army of the James under the command of Benjamin Butler. Although Sheridan's raid did not achieve all that had been hoped, the commander of the Confederate cavalry, Major General J. E. B. Stuart, was wounded at the battle of Yellow Tavern. Stuart, who had led the Confederate cavalry to victory for two years, died of his injuries on May 12.

In August 1864, Grant selected Sheridan to replace Hunter. Grant reiterated the orders given to Hunter: "Give the enemy no rest, and if it is possible to follow to the Virginia Central road, follow that far. Do all the damage to railroads and crops you can. Carry off stock of all descriptions, and negroes, so as to prevent further planting. If the war is to last another year, we want the Shenandoah valley to remain a barren waste."[17]

Sheridan marched south from Harper's Ferry down the Shenandoah Valley, defeating Early's forces at Opequon Creek (Winchester) and Fisher's Hill. Major General George Crook's force in West Virginia also was placed under Sheridan's command, and Crook was directed to join forces with Sheridan. While in the valley, Crook was ordered to destroy as much as possible of the crops, provisions, mills, and anything else of military value. According to one soldier, Crook was quite successful at this. Using imagery from Grant, the soldier reported: "A crow passing over the country would be obliged to carry his rations with him."[18]

After these victories, Sheridan believed that the Army of the Shenandoah was worn out, and that they didn't have enough provisions or adequate means of transportation to make it to Charlottesville or Lynchburg. Nevertheless, his army continued the "destruction of the crops in the valley and the means of planting," and they burned barns, mills, warehouses, crops, and public buildings. Horace Greeley, editor of the influential *New York Tribune*, reported that Sheridan had executed his orders to the letter. "Whatever of grain and forage had escaped appropriation by one or another of the armies which had so frequently chased each other up and down this narrow but fertile and productive vale, was now given to the torch."[19]

On August 17, 1864, the First Cavalry Division under the command of Brigadier General Wesley Merritt ravaged everything in the valley of potential value to the Confederate army and guerillas. A woman living in Berryville gave a Dantesque description of the situation: "Fires of barns, stockyards, etc. soon burst forth and by eleven, from a high elevation, fifty could be seen blazing forth. The whole country was enveloped with smoke and fire. The sky was lurid and but for the green trees one might have imagined the shades of Hades had descended suddenly." She continued, "In almost every instance every head of stock was driven off. Those young animals that refused to go were shot down." During a ten-day period General Merritt noted the destruction of 515 acres of corn, 630 barns, 410,000 bushels of wheat, 1,347 cattle, 1,231 sheep, 725 pigs, and many other agricultural items. Merritt estimated the goods to have a value of $3,304,672.[20]

Black with Smoke

A Confederate soldier in the Shenandoah Valley described the scene to his wife: "Just think of Sheridan's proceedings in the Valley of Virginia, burning every house, barn, mill, and every stack of hay, and killing or driving off every negro, horse, mule, ox, cow, and every other animated thing, leaving the entire white population without shelter or food." Another soldier reported that Sheridan's army "had burned every barn and nearly every dwelling house from Staunton to Strasburg," a distance of seventy miles. Another soldier who watched the valley burn reported: "Immediately in my view were burnt not less than one hundred hay stacks and barns. Nearly every farm large or small has been visited by the torch." He believed that these same tactics would be employed in the rest of the Confederacy.[21]

Northern observers confirmed these eyewitness accounts. One reporter who traveled sixty miles with Sheridan wrote that "language would fail me to describe the terrible desolation which marked his path. Dwelling-houses and other buildings were almost universally burned; fences, implements of husbandry, and everything available for the sustenance of human life, so far as he could do so, were everywhere destroyed." Another newspaper writer accompanying Sheridan was more graphic: "The atmosphere, from horizon to horizon, has been black with the smoke of a hundred conflagrations, and at night a gleam, brighter and more lurid than sunset, has shot from every verge. The orders have been to destroy all forage in stacks and barns, and to drive the stock before for the subsistence of the army. The execution of these orders has been thorough." He continued, "Few barns and stables have escaped. The gardens and cornfields have been desolated. The cattle, hogs, sheep, cows, oxen, nearly five thousand in all, have been driven from every farm. The poor, alike with the rich, have suffered. Some have lost their all . . . Hundreds of nearly starving people are going north. Our trains are crowded with them. They line the wayside. Hundreds more are coming—not half the inhabitants of the valley can subsist on it in its present condition. Absolute want is in mansions used in other days to extravagant luxury."[22]

A committee of Shenandoah Valley residents assessed the damage done in their county: 30 dwelling houses, 450 barns, 31 mills, and 3 factories were burned, and 100 miles of fencing, 100,000 bushels of wheat, 50,000 bushels of corn, and 6,233 tons of hay were demolished. Thousands of cattle, horses, sheep, and hogs were carried off and "an immense amount of Farming Utensils of every description were destroyed, many of great value, such as McCormick's Reapers, Threshing Machines." The losses in the one county alone were valued at $25.5 million.[23]

After stripping the upper Shenandoah Valley of most of its supplies and provisions, Sheridan returned to Strasburg, Virginia, and his army took up a position on the north side of Cedar Creek. He then detached one corps and returned it to Grant in Petersburg. Sheridan left the valley to consult with the War Department in Washington. Meanwhile, Jubal Early had moved swiftly up the valley and returned to Fisher's Hill on October 13. Two days later he attacked a gap in the Union lines. The Army of the Shenandoah was not prepared for it, and the Union lines broke and fled to the rear. With victory within his grasp, Early ordered his troops to pursue the fleeing Union soldiers. Instead, many hungry Confederates plundered the food supplies in the Union encampment.[24] Sheridan, who was returning from the meeting in Washington, heard the gunfire. He rode swiftly onto the battlefield, rallied the Union fleeing soldiers, and routed the Confederates. Although fighting would continue in the Shenandoah Valley almost to the end of the war, it would never again provide provisions for the Army of Northern Virginia.

Burning Raid

This success emboldened Sheridan to try to put a halt to the activities of Mosby's Rangers, who lived off the land or off captured Union supplies. On November 27, Sheridan sent a division over the Blue Ridge into "Mosby's Confederacy" with the following orders: "To clear the country of these parties that are bringing destruction upon the innocent as well as their guilty supporters by their cowardly acts, you will consume and destroy all forage and subsistence, burn all barns and mills and their contents, and drive off all stock in the region the boundaries of which are above described. This order must be literally executed, bearing in mind, however, that no dwellings are to be burned and that no personal violence be offered to the citizens. The ultimate result of the guerrilla system of warfare is the total destruction of all private rights in the country occupied by such parties. This destruction may as well commence at once, and the responsibility of it must rest upon the authorities at Richmond, who have acknowledged the legitimacy of guerrilla bands." In four days, the "Burning Raid," as it was later called, torched barns, flour mills, sawmills, hay stacks, and grain, and Union troops confiscated or slaughtered horses, cattle, and sheep. Officials estimated the value of the destruction at one million dollars. Unofficially, the toll was much higher. Sheridan told an officer that "should complaints come in from the citizens of Loudoun County tell them that they have furnished too many meals to guerrillas to expect much sympathy."[25]

By December 1864, the remaining residents of the Shenandoah Valley were in desperate shape. A local newspaper asked the rest of Virginia to send supplies into the valley, but there was little to send. At the same time, Halleck ordered Sheridan to refuse rations to "disloyal" Southerners within his lines. Instead, they should be "sent South to feed upon the enemy," while "loyal refugees should be temporarily assisted and sent North, where they can earn a livelihood. While the men of Virginia are either serving in the rebel ranks, or as bushwhackers are waylaying or murdering our soldiers, our Government must decline to support their wives and children." Northern soldiers believed that the hungrier the Confederacy got, the sooner the war would be over.[26]

Shenandoah Effects

The Shenandoah Valley campaign was fought mainly for strategic reasons. Lee wanted to distract Grant from his siege of Richmond; Grant wanted to remove the valley as a source of subsistence for the Army of

Northern Virginia and he wanted to destroy railroads running through the valley that were Richmond's lifelines. Most historians have concluded that the Shenandoah Valley had been an important source of provisions for Confederate armies and that its destruction in 1864 hastened the end of the war. Whatever crops might have been harvested in the valley in the summer and fall of 1864 were destroyed by Sheridan.

Southerners condemned Sheridan's actions. A. L. Long, an artillery commander and Lee's military secretary, wrote in his memoirs: "The Valley campaign above described was attended with a series of barbarities happily without parallel in the history of the war. General Hunter had gone in his depredations far beyond any warrant in the exigencies of war. The destruction of agricultural products, and even of mills and factories, might have been defended as a warrantable military measure, but the burning of private habitations was an instance of pure vandalism utterly devoid of excuse, and sure to instigate retaliatory measures of the same barbarous character." Barbarous as they were, the Federal victories in the Shenandoah Valley caused morale to sink in the South. Confederate resistance in the valley collapsed and desertions among Southern soldiers climbed sharply. Conversely, Sheridan's victories greatly improved the morale of Union soldiers and his work was welcomed by many Northerners. Coupled with Sherman's victory in Atlanta, the Shenandoah campaign contributed to Lincoln's reelection in November 1864.[27]

Sheridan had no difficulty defending his actions in the Shenandoah Valley. He explained to the Joint-Congressional Committee on the Conduct of the War, "we were obliged to live to a great extent on the country. Forage had to be thus obtained for our horses, and provisions for our men, consequently many hardships were necessarily brought on the people, but no outrages were tolerated." He did not regret this: "These men and women did not care how many were killed or maimed, so long as war did not come to their doors, but as soon as it did come in the shape of loss of property, they earnestly prayed for its termination. As war is a punishment, and death the maximum punishment, if we can, by reducing its advocates to poverty, end it quicker, we are on the side of humanity."[28] The Shenandoah campaign reflected a change in Union strategy from wooing Southerners back into the United States to "uncivilized war," "total war," "scorched earth," or "hard war." This new strategy destroyed everything of potential value to guerrillas, military units, and Southern sympathizers.

8

Giving Thanks and No Thanks

W hen President Abraham Lincoln issued a proclamation declaring that Thanksgiving would be celebrated on November 24, 1864, George W. Blunt, a New Yorker, proposed to lift the spirits of Union soldiers and sailors in Virginia by supplying them "with poultry and pies, or puddings, all cooked, ready for use." While he admitted it would be "a big undertaking," Blunt thought it "would be a grand sight to see that army of brave men, loyal to the flag, feeding on the good things of the land they have fought for, whilst the miserable traitors, if they still hold out, are crouched behind their defences hungry and starving." Blunt wrote to Lincoln about his proposal and asked: "Will not all who feel that we have a country worth defending and preserving do something to show those who are fighting our battles that they are remembered and honored?"[1]

Blunt was a member of the Union League Club of New York, founded in 1863 by well-to-do citizens who supported the Union cause. One of its founding members was Theodore Roosevelt, Sr., a descendant of Dutch immigrants. His family's business—importing plate glass—had made him a wealthy man, and he spent much time supporting philanthropic causes. His wife was born in Georgia, and when the Civil War began, her family supported the Confederacy, as did she. To avoid familial conflict, Roosevelt chose not to enlist in the Union army and paid a substitute to fight for him—a common practice among the nation's wealthy during the Civil War.

Roosevelt and others at the Union League Club liked Blunt's idea, and they immediately appealed to New Yorkers to help make the 1864 Thanksgiving a strong show of support for the nation's armies: "We desire that on the twenty-fourth day of November there shall be no soldier in the Army of the Potomac, the James, the Shenandoah, and no sailor in the North Atlantic Squadron who does not receive tangible evidence that those for whom he is periling his life, remember him." They requested "donations of cooked poultry and other proper meats, as well as for mince pies, sausages, and fruits," but all contributions were welcome.[2] Thus began one of the most unusual morale boosters of the Civil War.

Feasting Background

During the early nineteenth century, the United States celebrated only two national holidays: Washington's Birthday and Independence Day. Sarah Josepha Hale, a poet, novelist, and editor, believed that Thanksgiving should become the third national holiday. From her position as editor of the influential *Godey's Lady's Book*, she commenced a campaign to make it so in 1846. For the next seventeen years, Hale wrote annually to members of Congress, prominent individuals, and the governors of every state and territory, requesting each to proclaim the fourth Thursday in November as Thanksgiving Day.

Southerners remained less enthusiastic than New Englanders about Thanksgiving. Some governors had declined to proclaim days of thanksgiving for various reasons. Virginia Governor Henry H. Wise had objected to the "theatrical national claptrap of Thanksgiving"; specifically he objected to the clergy using Thanksgiving sermons to preach against slavery. Northern clergy had indeed used Thanksgiving services to preach against slavery, and when these sermons were published, Southerners began associating abolitionism with Thanksgiving. Thus, when the Civil War broke out, Southern states refused to celebrate Thanksgiving at the end of November, although Jefferson Davis, the president of the Confederacy, did proclaim several days of thanksgiving after specific Southern military victories.

In the North, Thanksgiving was observed throughout the Civil War. Lincoln ordered government departments to be closed for Thanksgiving on November 28, 1861, but such great losses had been suffered during that year that Northerners saw little to be thankful for. In September 1862, after the Union victory at Antietam, the mood in the country became more sanguine: Thanksgiving was publicly celebrated, and civilians sent food to the Northern armies to help them celebrate Thanksgiving. Newspapers and magazines published accounts of the foods—and beverages—consumed by Union troops at Thanksgiving. The proclamations and celebrations were nice, but Hale still wanted to make Thanksgiving Day a national holiday and she wanted it celebrated on the fourth Thursday of November. She wrote to U.S. Secretary of State, William H. Seward, who was also a former governor and senator from New York. New York had been the first state outside New England to make Thanksgiving a holiday, and Seward supported Hale's efforts. On September 28, 1863, two months after the North's military victories at Gettysburg and Vicksburg, Hale wrote directly to Lincoln, who forwarded the letter to Seward. Seward promptly prepared a Thanksgiving Day proclamation for Lincoln to sign.[3] Hale had finally achieved her goal, but the greatest Thanksgiving celebration was still to come.

Gratefully Remembered

In early May 1864, the Union's Army of the Potomac broke camp in northern Virginia and marched south. After a month of battles—several of them tactical defeats with tens of thousands of casualties—the Union army finally arrived at the gates of Richmond, Virginia, a city with formidable defenses. The Union commander, General Ulysses S. Grant, attempted a frontal assault on the fortifications, but failed. He then tried to cut off Richmond's supply lines by moving south toward Petersburg, which controlled two railroads that brought supplies into Richmond and the Confederate Army of Northern Virginia. The two opposing armies built fortifications and dug trenches, and for the next nine months they engaged in brutal trench warfare that in many ways prefigured the terrors of World War I.

George Blunt's idea of giving Union soldiers and sailors a lavish Thanksgiving feast was picked up in New Jersey. The *Trenton Gazette and Republican* called it "the duty of every male civilian to buy a chicken or turkey for the troops, indicating where [they] might get it cooked if they were without family or could not do it themselves." The women of Trenton gave C Company of the 21st Regiment a "sumptuous dinner," which they themselves attended. A local newspaper reported that, "with their lovely and smiling faces," the ladies added much to the event by "doing their utmost to cause us to realize to the fullest extent, the importance of the occasion, fully succeeded in their efforts, causing our minds to wander to our homes, where perchance our wives, mothers and sisters, were doing a similar Christian duty toward faithful Union soldiers that may be encamped in the vicinity." In Jersey City, citizens contributed $1,500 for the purchase of cigars and tobacco for the troops. The residents of Orange sent bags of tomatoes for sauces.[4]

And then the idea spread to other states. In Connecticut, the "Soldier's Aid" of Norwich collected "five hundred and seventy-four dollars, two hundred and fifteen turkeys, one hundred and ninety-nine pies, thirty-three chickens, ninety-six cans of tomatoes, four and three-quarters barrels of apples, twelve tongues, forty-five bottles of pickles. Also, divers roast geese, spare-ribs, beef á la mode, corned beef, roast veal, brown bread, sugar, cheese, oranges, crackers, gingerbread, cake, crullers, doughnuts, cookies, ginger-snaps, nuts, raisins, plum-puddings, tobacco." This was sent to Connecticut regiments in the Armies of the James and Shenandoah.[5]

Massachusetts civilians furnished Thanksgiving dinners to Union troops stationed in Boston, contributed funds to the national Thanksgiving effort, and fed wounded soldiers in hospitals in Washington, D.C. The Adams Express Company of Boston transported sixty tons of Thanksgiving supplies to the soldiers for free. The citizens of Maine sent 1,300 food packages to their cavalry regiment stationed at Pensacola, Florida. Subsistence Committees and branches of the Christian Commission throughout the North prepared food for camps and hospitals in their areas. In Pittsburgh, soldiers were given "two hundred barrels of apples, ten barrels of canned fruit, and mince-meat for six thousand pies." Pittsburgh also sent dinners to Union troops stationed at Nashville, Tennessee. In Philadelphia, a "Mrs. Dr. Egbert" contributed $5,000 for holiday foods to be given to hospitalized soldiers. Marylanders sent 260 barrels of comestibles to Union troops at New Bern, North Carolina, and eleven boxes to sailors on the ironclad ship *Dictator*.[6]

In Indianapolis, women brought an "abundant dinner" to the 17th Regiment at the state arsenal. As the *Indianapolis Daily Journal* noted, "Such kindnesses are bright spots in a soldier's life, and coming as they did on this occasion, from those to whom they are comparatively strangers, are fully appreciated and will be gratefully remembered." Citizens throughout New England, New York, Pennsylvania, New Jersey, Michigan, and Ohio participated in sending food to local military units.[7]

In New York, the Union League Club requested that New York's hoteliers, restaurateurs, bakers, and private individuals (with the means to do so) roast twenty or more turkeys and chickens and send them to a central location so they could be shipped south. New Yorkers didn't need to be asked twice. Delmonico's, the city's most fashionable restaurant, contributed the services of its chefs to stuff and roast thousands of turkeys. These goodies were packed up and sent by train, ship, and wagon all the way to Virginia.[8]

In just three weeks, the Union League Club collected more than $56,500 towards the purchase of 146,586 pounds of poultry. New York's Fulton Market supplied much of the poultry and donated a $3,386 profit back to the fund. An additional 225,000 pounds of poultry were received as contributions, along with enormous quantities of other Thanksgiving dinner ingredients. Express shipping companies agreed to transport the food free of charge, and Union supply steamers delivered food to sailors in the blockade squadron and on gunboats along the Virginia rivers. Four steamers left New York on the Sunday before Thanksgiving carrying 400,000 boxes and barrels headed for City Point in Virginia, which served as the supply depot for the Union army around Richmond and Petersburg.[9]

Soldiers received word—via newspapers, letters, and rumors—that this feast was on the way, but there was considerable skepticism regarding its arrival. As George Williams, a correspondent covering the Army of the Potomac for the *New York Times*, wrote on the night before Thanksgiving, "I am afraid that the bounty of the Northern people will be sadly diverted from those for whom it is especially intended. My past experience has taught me a sad lesson."[10]

A Continuous Thanksgiving

The cooked turkeys and other edibles sent to the soldiers were distributed by various means, often by government transport in the war zone. This meant disrupting the normal supply system for the Union armies. Ohio General Rutherford B. Hayes grumbled that the "overcoats, stockings, shirts, etc.," which were greatly needed, "couldn't come because all the transportation was required to haul up the turkeys and

Thanksgiving dinner!" However, when the food arrived, he proclaimed, "The turkeys, etc., sent from the Christian land [have arrived] and everyone is happy and jolly."[11]

Most Union troops in the East in the field and many on ships at sea were furnished with dinners on Thanksgiving Day in 1864. One soldier related that they were sent a "large store box, which, when opened, was found to contain six turkeys, a boiled ham, four cans of peaches and the same number of stewed green corn; about two bushels of apples, cakes galore, and several fine clusters of fresh Catawba grapes." A *New York Times* reporter with Sheridan's army wrote: "About one pound of turkey, goose or duck was the allowance for each man, and with plenty of potatoes and bread for stuffing, the quantity of which was quite sufficient for a good, hearty meal, and right well did the men enjoy it, not because such food is so much a rarity in this army—far from it—but because every mouthful that the soldiers took was a reminder of friends back home—many of them unknown but nevertheless connected by a mysterious bond of sympathy—were thinking of them and enjoying the satisfaction of having contributed to the turkey fund."[12]

Aldace Freeman Walker, serving with a Vermont Brigade in the Shenandoah Valley of Virginia, celebrated the day in camp. Drilling and working were suspended, and "barrels of turkeys and other good things had been forwarded from the north, which were faithfully distributed among the men." Captain George F. Noys, the purveyor of the Army of the Shenandoah, supplied the soldiers with fifty thousand uncooked turkeys on Thanksgiving eve. A shortage of roasting spits and "tin kitchens" (reflecting ovens used with an open fire) did not stop the preparation of the feast: turkeys were boiled or stewed instead, and the soldiers relished them nonetheless. A Sergeant Walker in an Ohio regiment serving with Sheridan wrote in his diary on November 24, 1864, "The train stopped at our depot to-day and put off 1,000 pounds of turkeys for this brigade, our share of 36,000 pounds sent to the Army of the Shenandoah by the citizens of New York City. All honor to the noble State that could thus remember the soldiers in the field. I will venture to say this is the first instance on record of turkeys being furnished to an entire army."[13]

Not everyone received their promised dinner on Thanksgiving Day itself. The 48th Pennsylvania Regiment, for one, did not receive any food on November 24: "The promised goodies failed to materialize, but next day they all came to hand, lots of 'em, with doughnuts and crullers and other 'fixin's,' and a good time was had in putting them out of sight." The 13th Regiment of Ohio Cavalry didn't receive their dinner until two days after Thanksgiving, but even late it was still welcomed: "The good people of the North have sent us chickens, turkey, cakes, onions, apples, pickles and saur kraut. They had been put up in good shape but reached us very mouldy, but the boys did not mind that, they have been eating hard tack and sow belly too long to mind a little mould on such delicacies as came to them. There is many a smiling face behind a turkey bone today," one soldier wrote.[14]

Some Union soldiers lost patience waiting for their holiday feast. Robert Tilney of the Army of the Potomac noted in his diary on November 25 that "Thanksgiving Day was an utter failure" for they had not "received one particle of any of the 'dinner' that we were promised," except for 138 barrels of apples. He concluded that "the Commissary Sergeant has confiscated them for his own use." He also noted bitterly, "Scarcely a negro was to be seen who did not have a turkey under his arm, while men were seen carrying boxes off by the dozen, carrying them to a stone and splitting them open, taking just what suited them, and no one interfered." He hoped that in the future the "good friends at the North" would "keep their dollars in their pockets, for they will derive much more benefit from them than the army will from the proceeds." Tilney felt that the food shipments represented "money thrown away; for by the time they have passed through the hands of a dozen or more commissaries and others of that genus there is apt to be little left for the men." Tilney was soon to change his mind. On the Saturday after Thanksgiving, a clerk "brought a 'drumstick' and eight apples for each man . . . and one small chicken, among twenty men, of which only the drumstick remains. So much for the great Thanksgiving movement." Then more arrived later: "Four small chickens," which were dismembered and "divided into piles, fresh and mouldy." This small allotment of meat "and two mince pies," he sarcastically proclaimed, was "a big dinner for twenty hungry men." Finally, on the Sunday following Thanksgiving, Tilney wrote of "the arrival of a large load of poultry, so we shall dine to-morrow on turkey and chicken. We have fared better than we expected to in our Thanksgiving dinner, on the installment plan!"[15]

Most soldiers in the armies of the James, Shenandoah, and Potomac received a delightful dinner, but in some cases the food did not arrive in good condition, and in a few cases the quantity was insufficient. One New York artillery regiment compensated for the shortcomings of the food that they received by consuming "unlimited quantities of liquids, to the extent that the evening brigade dress-parade was said to have been quite a *spirited* affair."[16]

Thanksgiving dinners were not just enjoyed by the Northern armies in Virginia. A *New York Times* reporter in Nashville, Tennessee, proudly announced that Union soldiers enjoyed "a sumptuous dinner. Thus, the liberal provisions made for the soldiers by the enterprising home folk reached even there. Memories of home and absent friends deepened the pleasure with which thousands of war-worn and suffering soldiers enjoyed the good things provided for them. How slight is the trouble, how trifling the outlay to procure a feast like this, compared with the amount of pleasure given, of gratitude awakened, of strength for the present suffering and future toils, and sacrifices imparted. The country owes the soldier more than ever it can repay him. All kindly acts, showing him to have a warm place in the hearts of the people, make him wear his harness lightly, and nerve his arm for the blows that bring success."[17]

Major General William T. Sherman's army, which had left Atlanta in early November, received no Thanksgiving delicacies from the North because Sherman had cut his supply lines when he headed into the rich farmland of Georgia. Nevertheless, his men did attempt a makeshift Thanksgiving feast. One officer under Sherman stated that Thanksgiving Day "was very generally observed in the army; the troops scorning chickens in the plentitude of turkeys with which they had supplied themselves." Another observer reported that Sherman's troops had liberated chickens, turkeys, and "vegetables of all kinds, and in unlimited quantities . . . as the gratification of the stomach goes, the troops are pursuing a continuous thanksgiving." One report calculated that Sherman's army stole an estimated 25,000 turkeys and chickens from Southern farms for their Thanksgiving celebrations.[18] When Sherman's army emerged in the vicinity of Savannah on December 10, Union ships resupplied the troops—including the dinners they had supposedly missed at Thanksgiving.

Turkeys Hot and Turkeys Cold

Along with the Thanksgiving provisions, generous Northerners sent Union troops thousands of signed or anonymous notes of encouragement. A Mrs. R. Scott, of Oswego, New York, wrote, "Thanksgiving offerings to the brave defenders of our country."[19] Another unit received a note with "a cake with a pretty name and Jersey City address and 'Tell me how you like my cake' on the bottom of it." Another Jersey City note came from "loyal supporters of the flag, and warm friends of the men at the front."[20]

Soldiers, in turn, responded to many of the missives. A Pennsylvanian cavalryman wrote to a New York contributor saying that the food had restored "new vigor to the hearts and lives of the soldiers, knowing that part of the human sex (the ladies) are for the preservation of the Union and our glorious country, which braces us up to fight our foe and enemies of the Southern Confederacy." A Connecticut woman tucked a note into her contribution addressed "to any soldier or sailor who may receive this Thanksgiving gift." She received a prompt response thanking her for her "kind and sympathising letter, which added good sauce, making a kind gift the better from feeling how truly you felt for us who are in the field, facing the common foe. It is not in the power of my pen to describe the feeling of satisfaction and pleasure, and of gratitude, we all feel that those at home could think of the poor soldier." Thanksgiving dinner was "a repast which, if not dainty enough for Lucullus, was of dimensions that would have satisfied Gargantua."[21]

The events of the November 24, 1864, moved some Northerners to write poetry. One contributor of food to the troops wrote:

Please find enclosed
My little mite
To give the soldiers
An extra bite.
Be it turkey,
Goose or hen.
I don't care which,
If it suits them.[22]

A soldier replied:

Turkeys hot and turkeys cold,
Ditto young and ditto old,

Ditto tender and ditto tough,
And, thank the Lord, we had enough.[23]

The officers of a New York regiment in the Army of the Shenandoah sent a letter to the *New York Times* thanking "Mrs. Hazen and other kind ladies" who sent the "rich feast consisting of turkeys, chickens, cakes and fruits." It was "just one more evidence that we are not forgotten, nor can we ever forget those who, while they are enjoying all the comforts of home and plenty, still think of, and by their noble deeds testify that they remember the soldier."[24]

Held in Grateful Remembrance at Home

It wasn't the food so much as the idea that counted. The correspondent wrote: "The want of proper appliances compelled most men to broil or stew their turkeys, but every one seemed fully satisfied and appreciated the significance of this sympathetic thank-offering from the loyal North. One soldier said to me, 'It isn't the turkey, but the idea that we care for,' and he thus struck the key note of the whole festival. Could the donors of this Thanksgiving gift have been with us on this ride they would have felt satisfied that, whether as a token of grateful appreciation of past valor or as the inspiration of future effort in the good cause, it had not been made in vain." Another correspondent to the *New York Times* wrote: "The friends who so liberally contributed towards the purchase of this welcome gift will be pleased to know that their worthy effort has already been productive of the most cheering results. Both officers and men have repeatedly testified their appreciation of the generous motive which prompted this consideration of their comfort and happiness on Thanksgiving day, and look upon the act as one not to be forgotten."[25]

Abram P. Smith, a soldier with the 67th Regiment New York Volunteers, declared, "Nothing could have been devised more encouraging than this manifestation. The avalanche of 'good things,' fresh from the hands of loyalty and affection was intensely enjoyed by rank and file. Not only did the begrimed soldiers relish these delicious viands for the physical gratification afforded, but for the associations accompanying them." These offerings "proved to the soldier that he was held in grateful remembrance at home—that place where the true soldier cares most to be remembered, and this thanksgiving dinner strengthened the armies more morally, if not physically, than the addition of thousands of men."[26]

Another Union soldier exclaimed, "God bless those dear friends for their kindness in not forgetting us. All will remember with gratitude the donors of the good things sent us on that ever to be remembered thanksgiving day." Another wrote in his diary: "We will thank the women and thank Him who put it into their hearts to thus remember us." An officer on General Grant's staff noted that "this remembrance of them by their friends at home is truly encouraging." Another diarist named Thomas Edwin Vassar wrote, "The turkeys and pies arrived. Many thanks to all who so remembered our brave men." A correspondent for the *New York Herald* who was with the Army of the Shenandoah proclaimed that "the soldier in the field appreciates fully such evidence of his being remembered kindly by those at home."[27]

Giving No Thanks

The Thanksgiving extravaganza received wide coverage in Northern newspapers and magazines, but Confederate newspapers said little about it. The *Richmond Dispatch* dryly noted: "Yesterday was observed as a day of thanksgiving in Grant's army, who, no doubt, devoured the several thousand turkeys sent them from the North, and about which the Yankee newspapers have been talking so much of late."[28]

Yet, some Southerners, inspired by the North's support of the Union army at Thanksgiving, resolved to do the same for the Army of Northern Virginia. The dinner was first proposed for the day after the Northern Thanksgiving feast, but then it shifted to Christmas dinner for Virginia regiments. Then the idea expanded to include all the military units stationed around Richmond-Petersburg. This was a more ambitious plan, and the organizers concluded that they needed more time and a dinner on New Year's would be better. In 1865, New Year's Day fell on a Sunday, so its celebration was shifted to Monday, January 2. Southern newspapers jumped on the bandwagon for such an effort and published a barrage of articles and letters encouraging every citizen in Richmond and the surrounding countryside to assist in this mammoth undertaking. According to the newspapers, citizens were busy preparing food for what was to be called "the soldier's dinner."[29]

Others made financial contributions to fund the event. The Confederate Secretary of the Treasury, George Trenholm, gave $2,000 of his own money. The Richmond Theatre raised $15,000 with a benefit performance. The Southern Express Company volunteered to transport the provisions for free. One bakery claimed to have made 36,000 loaves of bread. The Virginia legislature voted a day's pay to help ensure the success of the dinner. Rev. Charles B. Dana, a close friend of Robert E. Lee and his wife, helped organize the effort.[30]

The *Richmond Examiner* declared, "Let the soldiers, while reminded of home and all its enjoyments, be admonished that, though cut off from these home festivities, there are those who appreciate their valour and devotion, and are willing to make their absence a pleasurable reminiscence." A broadside was circulated describing the event's intention: "As a slight token of gratitude to the Army of Gen. Lee, the citizens propose to give them a New Year's Dinner." Everyone was asked to send their money and food to Richmond by December 29. Henry Young, a Major on Lee's staff, hoped that this would come to fruition, "for if ever men deserved the good things of the citizens these poor fellows do."[31]

The *Richmond Examiner* directed readers to send their contributions to John P. Ballard, who gave up the unoccupied portion of his hotel, the Ballard House, and provided "unrestricted and unlimited use of his cooking range, boilers of great capacity, and all the other appurtenances and conveniences attached thereto, and not to be found elsewhere in the city." A local caterer named Thompson Tyler supervised the cooking, which began on December 27 and continued day and night until the morning of January 2. Giving the citizens of Richmond and their armed forces a preview of the upcoming feast, newspapers listed the types of food that were on their way to the army: " 'rounds of beef,' saddles of mutton, venisons, white shoats, hams, sausage of country make, rich with sage and redolent with pepper; turkies, ducks, chickens, with vegetables, such as potatoes, turnips, large as cannon balls, and beets like oblong shells." The provisions were packed in barrels and shipped to the army. Unfortunately, by December 30 only five barrels had been filled; but much more food was in the process of being cooked. The *Richmond Examiner* bragged that "the Thanksgiving dinner of the North to Grant's Ghouls was an eleven o'clock lunch to what the people propose to do for their sons, brothers, fathers and kindred in Gen. Lee's host of veterans."[32]

On December 31, 1864, the *Richmond Examiner* reported even better news: "Already there are rumors of the hospitals being depopulated, the laggards and skulkers returning, all hastening to Gen. Lee's lines, to the end that they may partake of a nation's gratitude and a nation's pride in the dinner to the whole army, in which the commonest private will be entitled to the first helping and the best." Lee's wife, Mary Custis Lee, wrote that the soldiers' dinner "has exhausted the markets here of everything but we are very willing to relinquish in their favor."[33]

Since the Confederates had given the Union army an informal cease-fire at Thanksgiving, the Union army returned the courtesy and agreed to an informal peace on January 2, 1865. The *Richmond Examiner* regaled its readers with a prediction that "the biggest barbecue ever gotten up on this continent," would be served to the troops on "a table twenty miles long."[34]

Despite the planning, prepared food, contributions, good intentions, optimistic projections, and positive reports, the New Year's Day dinner was a bust. Little food reached the troops, and those who did receive some of the holiday menu found it very disappointing. One soldier wrote that the "citizens of Richmond and surrounding country made up a great New Year's dinner for the army and when it was sent out to us it consisted of 3 or 4 bites of bread and 3 bites of meat and it was quite a snack for a feast." Another, who received one third of a loaf of bread and one third the usual ration of meat, sourly noted that it was "rather a poor treat the troops thought after the extensive preparations the papers led them to believe were being made." Others called the dinner "a complete fizzle," a "grand farce," and a "complete failure." Still others complained that only Virginia troops received goodies, while non-Virginians were lucky just to get some leftovers.[35]

Even the lucky Virginia soldiers who received food were unimpressed with the "bounty." Harry Townsend, a corporal in the Richmond Howitzers, sadly wrote in his diary: "Our expected dinner was delayed until patience was exhausted, and then when it came it was of such meagre dimensions that we concluded to give our portion to the other companies of the battalion. We bore our disappointment quite well however under the circumstances."[36]

Another Virginia soldier reported to the *Richmond Dispatch* that everyone "expected really a good treat to the inner man, and plenty of it, basing their expectations upon the colossal preparations in Richmond, the great number of Confederate dollars contributed by worthy and patriotic citizens, the glaring articles in the newspapers, and the names of the gentlemen who composed the committee, satisfied all of them that it would be a good thing; and, laboring under these impressions, we prepared accordingly, setting our incisors." For the regiment of 260 men and officers, the contents consisted of two barrels filled with "thirty-two ordinary-size loaves of bread; two turkeys, one of them a very diminutive specimen of that species of fowl (some swore that it was a chicken); a quarter of lamb and a horse-bucketful of apple butter. Well, of course this immense weight of provender had to be divided out to the various companies. After our company had received its due proportion, the whole lot was, by unanimous consent of the company, (numbering thirty men,) condensed into six parts, and by a species of lottery, all thirty participating, the six "piles" fell to six men; so twenty-four received nothing, and six all." The soldier who reported this was one of the lucky six. He received a leg of a turkey and a half-pound of mutton. He pointedly recorded that "the New Year's dinner had come and gone, or rather, gone, without coming."[37]

The *Richmond Enquirer*, which had advocated strongly for the New Year's dinner, published an apology of sorts: Its publisher desired "to state to his friends in the army that he had nothing to do with the distribution of the New Year's dinner." Two days later, the *Richmond Examiner* claimed that speculators had ended up with much of the money that had been donated for the meal.[38]

Thanking Effects

The Thanksgiving Dinner organized in the North was a visible manifestation of civilian support for the Union military. In addition to private mailings of food and other treats, Northern civilians gave $70 million dollars for the welfare of their fighting men. Much of this was contributed through churches, religious organizations, subsistence committees, relief associations, Christian commissions, and sanitary commissions that ministered especially to wounded soldiers.[39]

The massive effort of Northerners to supply their soldiers with a good Thanksgiving dinner in November 1864 was a tremendous boost to the troops' morale. While the food itself was just a token, Union soldiers and sailors believed that this gesture showed that the North was behind them, and their spirits soared. Northern newspapers crowed about the feast. The *New York Herald* proudly announced: "A people in the midst of a bloody war, having tens of thousands of soldiers in the field, and war ships studding every sea, yet every day expanding into greater commercial importance, and celebrates its national elections, feasts, and holidays with peace and harmony. Our soldiers' Thanksgiving dinner shows what we are capable of doing. It takes a republic to do it."[40]

The Thanksgiving feast made little difference to the physical ability of Union soldiers to fight the war. The psychological impact, however, was enormous. The Thanksgiving event demonstrated the vast abundance of food in the North, efficient organization on a vast scale, and popular civilian support for the army and the war. In contrast, the New Year's dinner in the South demonstrated scarcity, devious speculation and fraud, and wavering public support for the army and the war. As historian J. Tracy Power concluded in *Lee's Miserables*, the soldiers' disappointment at the dinner "could not help but increase the misery felt throughout the army."[41] Confederate desertions grew, gathering into a flood after New Year's Day.

9

Hard War

*M*ajor General William T. Sherman captured Atlanta in September 1864, and debate raged where his army should head next. Abraham Lincoln wanted him to return to Chattanooga and defend the city against possible attack by Confederate forces under the command of John B. Hood. General Ulysses Grant wanted Sherman to head toward Mobile, Alabama, one of the few remaining Confederate-controlled ports on the Gulf Coast. Sherman himself wanted to cut his communications and supply lines and have his army live off the land as it marched east toward the Atlantic. He planned to demolish one of the richest agricultural areas of the South and cut off the supplies from Florida and Georgia that were provisioning Lee's army in Virginia.

Before leaving Atlanta in November, Sherman evacuated the city and set fire to government buildings, hospitals, foundries, mills, factories, railroad depots, roundhouses, rolling stock, machine shops, and all private buildings that could be turned into machine shops. The engineer responsible for the destruction concluded that "for military purposes the city of Atlanta has ceased to exist." With an army of sixty-two thousand men, Sherman headed off into the Georgian countryside, intent on devastating the Southern supply system and making "Georgia howl."[1]

Every Living Animal Killed and Eaten

Sherman was born in Ohio in 1820 and entered West Point at the age of sixteen in 1836. Upon graduation, he served in the army in Florida, Georgia, and South Carolina. When war between Mexico and the United States commenced in 1847, Sherman was assigned administrative duties in California. As a result, he was one of the few senior Civil War generals not to have served in combat during the Mexican-American War. Sherman left the military in 1853 and after several moves, he finally settled in Pineville, Louisiana, where he was superintendent of the Louisiana State Seminary of Learning & Military Academy (later renamed Louisiana State University). Just before the Civil War broke out, Sherman resigned his superintendency and moved north. In May 1861, Sherman was appointed a colonel in the U.S. Army; he served with distinction during the Union defeat at Bull Run in July 1861. He was then promoted to brigadier general and sent to Kentucky, where he took command of the Department of the Cumberland. After complaining bitterly to the War Department about conditions in Kentucky, and offering exaggerated estimates of Confederate strength, Sherman suffered a nervous breakdown and contemplated suicide. In November 1861, at his own request, he was removed from his post. A month later, he resumed service as a logistical officer. In this capacity he supported Grant's efforts to capture Fort Donelson in Kentucky. After the battle, Sherman was assigned to the Army of West Tennessee as commander of a division. On the first day at Shiloh, Sherman conducted an orderly retreat and saved the Union army from a complete rout. The following day, reinforcements arrived and the Federals won the battle, although with heavy casualties.

During the first two years of the war, Sherman tried to follow the rules he had been taught at West Point about provisioning an army in the field. He established supply bases and stockpiled goods shipped in from northern depots. Strongly opposed to living off the land, Sherman complained early in the war about Union soldiers who "preyed" on civilians. He also was strongly opposed to "plundering" and harming "cornfields, orchards, potato-patches" or any private property owned by "friend or foe." In January 1863, Sherman bemoaned the destruction caused by the Union army: "Farms disappear, houses are burned and plundered, and every living animal killed and eaten."[2]

By the time Sherman arrived at Grand Gulf, near Vicksburg, in May 1863, he had changed his views about provisioning troops and had come to support Grant's ideas about the army living off the land. Specifically, he expected to take all the "corn, bacon, ham, mules and everything to support the army," but he still opposed "universal burning and wanton destruction of private property," which he considered "not justified in war." By September, his views had evolved once again: he now considered it his duty to "destroy both the rebel army and whatever of wealth or property it has founded its boasted strength upon."[3]

Since the beginning of the war, long-range cavalry raids launched by both the North and South tore up railroads and destroyed military supplies. Despite the widespread publicity and fear these raids generated, they were of limited usefulness. The cavalries could not linger in one place for long because they were usually pursued by vastly superior forces. Damage to the railroads was easily repaired and supplies were promptly replaced. Sherman had a different idea for conducting a raid—it would be much larger and would involve infantry who would live off the land and take their time destroying railroads, bridges, warehouses, machinery, and military depots as thoroughly as possible.

The idea of troops living off the land was not a new tactic. Southern forces had done so in many campaigns when they lacked the supplies or transportation needed to support their armies in the field. Living off the land offered a decided military advantage: military units not encumbered by large wagon trains filled with supplies could move faster, and in war, speed often meant the difference between victory and defeat.

By January 1864, Sherman's views toward destruction of property in the South had again shifted. In a letter to an officer trying to deal with Confederate guerrillas in northern Alabama, Sherman expounded upon the treatment of "inhabitants known or suspected to be hostile." He now believed that the Union armies fighting in the South had "any and all rights which they choose to enforce in war, to take their lives, their homes, their lands, their every thing, because they cannot deny that war does exist there; and war is simply power unrestrained by constitution or compact. If they want eternal war, well and good—we will accept the issue." Specifically, he believed: "When provisions, forage, horses, mules, wagons, etc., are used by our enemy, it is clearly our duty and right to take them, because otherwise they might be used against us. In like manner, all houses left vacant by an inimical people are clearly our right, or such as are needed as storehouses, hospitals, and quarters." Sherman's views were implemented by Union military in northern Alabama, which suffered widespread destruction. Postwar visitors found northern Alabama desolate and deserted.[4]

Sherman decided to test an army's ability to conduct large-scale raids. He returned to Vicksburg to launch a large raid against Meridian, Mississippi, which lay 150 miles away, near the Alabama border. This was to be a dress rehearsal for his planned invasion of Georgia, scheduled for May. On February 3, 1864, Sherman left Vicksburg with 21,000 men and headed for the third time to Jackson, Mississippi. An Illinois infantryman with Sherman's forces declared that by the time they left, Jackson was "a heap of ruins." Its citizens referred to it as "Chimneyville," in reference to "the great number of standing chimneys from which the buildings had been burned." A Confederate soldier who was in the area a month later wrote to his wife that it was "a dreary spectacle indeed. The largest plantations are thinning out, grown up in weeds & pastured upon by a few scattering cattle; fences are pulled down & destroyed; houses burned; Negroes run off. A general gloom pervades everything and the people appear to be in a listless spirit, perfectly impassable, subjugated, in some instances, by prospective want and suffering, and utterly devoid of any disposition to continue longer the struggle for Independence."[5]

Sherman then headed eastward toward Meridian, where he arrived eleven days after leaving Vicksburg. Union forces remained there for five days. During that time, Sherman announced that "ten thousand of our men worked hard and with a will, in that work of destruction, with axes, sledges, crowbars, clawbars, and with fire, and I have no hesitation in pronouncing the work well done. Meridian with its Depots, Storehouses, Arsenals, offices, Hospitals, Hotels, and Cantonments, no longer exists." Throughout the campaign, Sherman's soldiers had "lived off the country and made a swath of desolation fifty miles broad across the state of Mississippi." In all, Sherman's army burned or confiscated an estimated two million bushels of corn and other provisions that could not be removed before the Union army arrived.[6]

Meanwhile, Confederate guerrillas continued to harass Union forces. Perhaps based on Sherman's experience in the Meridian campaign, the Union War Department issued on April 30, 1864, an "instruction" that was "not to be printed." It authorized commanders to "take the proper measures to supply, so far as may be possible, the wants of their troops, in animals and provisions, from the territory through which military operations are conducted. Special care will be taken to remove horses, mules, live stock, and all means of transportation from hostile districts infested or liable to be infested by guerrilla bands of rebels."[7] These two principles—armies living off the land and depriving enemy forces of supplies—became central to Sherman's—and the Union's—thinking.

Cripple Their Military Resources

When Lincoln appointed Grant to the position of General-in-Chief of the Union armies, Sherman succeeded Grant as commander of the Military Division of the Mississippi. Sherman promptly left Chattanooga with a hundred thousand men, the maximum number he estimated could be supplied by a single-track railway that passed through 350 miles of hostile territory—a feat some considered unprecedented in military history.[8] To help supply Sherman's army, secondary supply depots were established at Marietta and Allatoona, Georgia, and local farms and plantations were raided for horse and mule fodder, as well as whatever supplies were needed. Confederate forces had no supply line, and they sought fodder and food in the same area.

Within fifteen miles of the path of the Confederate and Union armies, rural areas were stripped of provisions, but it was not enough. Confederate soldiers suffered from malnutrition and scurvy. Refugees, fearing famine, flooded into Atlanta. Between May 1860 and June 1864, the city's population jumped from 15,000 to 35,000. With a steeply rising demand for food, and a sharply diminished supply, food prices in Atlanta escalated—a pound of butter cost $15, a bushel of potatoes sold for $24, a barrel of flour went for $250, and one hundred pounds of bacon cost $500.[9]

From May to August 1864, Sherman's army plodded through northern Georgia with their focus on Atlanta. Sherman took time out from the campaign to write a letter blaming the Confederates for being first to introduce terror into the war and also first to force civilians to contribute provisions "to diminish their wagon trains and thereby increase the mobility and efficiency of their columns." As a consequence of living off the land, Southern armies traveled faster than Union armies, which were slowed down by their long wagon trains, laden with supplies and provisions, and the need to protect their supply lines from Confederate cavalry and guerrilla groups. Sherman continued, "No military mind could endure this long, and we are forced in self-defense to imitate their example." That is precisely what Sherman did, and it looked as if his strategy would succeed: His troops found plenty of food in Georgia. In a letter to U.S. Secretary of War Edwin Stanton, Sherman threw in a sarcastic directive: "Convey to Jeff. Davis my personal and official thanks for abolishing cotton and substituting corn and sweet potatoes in the South. These facilitate our military plans much, for food and forage are abundant."[10]

Atlanta was an important railroad hub with both east-west and north-south railroads traversing the city. After the fall of Nashville to the Union army in 1862, Atlanta became the supply depot for the Confederate armies in the west. From and through Atlanta, railroads carried supplies for Confederate armies, including those in northern Virginia. Atlanta was also one of the few manufacturing centers still functioning in the Confederacy. In addition to railroad repair shops, machine shops, and foundries, the city's factories produced military hardware, armaments, and ammunition, although by the time Union forces arrived in the Atlanta area, many factories had been moved to safer locations farther south. After two months of battles around Atlanta, the Union armies were finally in position to sever all the railroad lines into the city. Rather than remain in Atlanta and suffer a fate like that of Vicksburg, the Confederates, now under the command of Lieutenant General John Bell Hood, abandoned the city on September 2, and the Union army marched in.

Desperately in need of provisions, Hood assaulted the Union supply depot at Allatoona in early October 1864. The surprise Confederate attack captured more than a million rations of hardtack, many of which were later reacquired by counterattacking Union soldiers. Captured supplies hardly solved the Confederate army's supply problem, however. As historian Lee Kennett, author of *Marching Through Georgia*, writes, "both men and horses would be called upon to subsist much of the time on the same fare—hard corn—and sometimes the officers would have to 'stand guard over their horses, when fed, to keep the corn from being stolen.'"[11]

Hoping to find more supplies for his troops, Hood decided to head northwest into Alabama and then he planned to move into Tennessee. From northern Alabama, Hood could disrupt Sherman's supply line and force Sherman to withdraw from Atlanta to protect Chattanooga. His plan had two flaws—northern Alabama had already been burned over by Union raids and there weren't many supplies to be had. His troops were paralyzed for three weeks due to supply problems.

The second flaw was that Sherman had no intention of staying in Atlanta or protecting his supply line. Holding Atlanta would require a large military force to protect the supply lines to Chattanooga. Sherman had telegraphed Grant: "Until we can repopulate Georgia it is useless to occupy it but the utter destruction of its roads, houses and people will cripple their military resources. By attempting to hold the roads we will lose 1,000 men monthly, and will gain no result." When Sherman was told that Hood was headed northward, he was delighted: "If he will go to the Ohio River I will give him rations; my business is down South."[12]

War Is Barbarity

Grant gave his final approval for Sherman's march to Savannah on November 2. Sherman moved all wounded soldiers out of Atlanta and directed his commissary to stockpile thirty days' rations and return all surplus supplies to Chattanooga. Without releasing his destination, Sherman issued orders to the Union army in Atlanta on November 6.

These portions of those orders make clear Sherman's intent to have his troops leave nothing viable in their wake. His orders included the following:

> The army will forage liberally on the country during the march. To this end each brigade commander will organize a good and sufficient foraging party under the command of one or more discreet officers, who will gather, near the route of travel, corn or forage of any kind, meat of any kind, vegetables, corn meal, or whatever is needed by the command, aiming at all times to keep in the wagons at least ten days' provisions for his command and three days' forage. Soldiers must not enter the dwellings of the inhabitants or commit any trespass, but during the halt or camp they may be permitted to gather turnips, potatoes, and other vegetables, and to drive in stock in sight of their camp. To regular foraging parties must be intrusted the gathering of provisions and forage at any distance from the roads traveled.
>
> As for horses, mules, wagons, etc., belonging to the inhabitants, the cavalry and artillery may appropriate freely and without limit; discriminating, however, between the rich, who are usually hostile, and the poor and industrious, usually neutral or friendly. Foraging parties may also take mules or horses to replace the jaded animals of their trains, or to serve as pack mules for the regiments or brigades. In all foraging, of whatever kind, the parties engaged will refrain from abusive or threatening language, and may, where the officer in command thinks proper, give written certificates of the facts, but no receipts, and they will endeavor to leave with each family a reasonable portion for their maintenance.[13]

These orders were legitimate under the rules of engagement at the time, and Sherman did specifically order his soldiers to treat civilians respectfully and not to harm personal property. But Sherman knew perfectly well that with his army spread out over sixty miles and with foragers operating independently, often without officers, his orders would be difficult to enforce and there would be theft and needless destruction of personal property. In addition, stragglers following behind the army would likely destroy more and commit other crimes.

Wherever the local populace attempted to hinder the progress of the Union army by sabotaging equipment, burning bridges, or destroying provisions, Sherman's forces planned to lay waste to the entire surrounding area. By November 1864, the three-year-old war had already cost more than half a million lives. Sherman believed that bringing hard war to Southern civilians would help end the conflict. The destruction of food, property, industry, railroads, and bridges would also make it difficult for Confederate guerrillas or cavalry forces to operate around Sherman's army.

Despite reports to the contrary, Sherman's troops did not depart Atlanta empty-handed. Even before Sherman occupied the city, Union commissaries had been oversupplying his army with provisions. When Union troops left Atlanta, the army had 5,500 cattle and 2,500 wagons. In all, the army departed with an estimated 1.2 million rations, of which each man carried five days' worth. Among the provisions were a twenty-day supply of bread and a forty-day supply of sugar, coffee, and salt. After the war, the Union Commissary of Subsistence, who had arranged for the shipments to Sherman, asked, "Can it be wondered that, with such a power-generating commissariat, they were enabled to triumph over a hungry foe?"[14]

On November 16, Sherman and 62,000 men marched out of Atlanta and headed eastward into the Georgian countryside. In his *Memoirs*, Sherman described this "foraging" operation in jaunty style: "Each brigade commander had authority to detail a company of foragers, usually about fifty men, with one or two commissioned officers selected for their boldness and enterprise. This party would be dispatched before daylight with a knowledge of the intended day's march and camp; would proceed on foot five or six miles from the route traveled by their brigade, and then visit every plantation and farm within range. They would usually procure a wagon or family carriage, load it with bacon, corn-meal, turkeys, chickens, ducks, and every thing that could be used as food or forage, and would then regain the main road, usually in advance of their train. When this came up, they would deliver to the brigade commissary the supplies thus gathered by the way." While on the march, Sherman passed foraging parties at the roadside. He was "amused at their strange collections—mules, horses, even cattle, packed with old saddles and loaded with hams, bacon, bags of corn-meal, and poultry of every character and description. Although this foraging was attended with great danger and hard work, there seemed to be a charm about it that attracted the soldiers, and it was a privilege to be detailed on such a party. Daily they returned mounted on all sorts of beasts, which were at once taken from them and appropriated to the general use."[15]

A *New York Herald* correspondent described the work of "bummers," as foragers were derisively called: "A planter's house stands by the wayside; without a halt the whole premises are overrun as if by ants, the heads of sorghum barrels are knocked in and the tin cupsfulls scooped out; beehives are knocked in pieces, and wild grabs are made for the last vestiges of 'comb,' sweet potato catches are broken in, and the contents packed in pockets, in handkerchiefs, in anything that will hold that esculent; hogs are bayoneted, quartered with the hair on and hung on the ends of muskets to bleed; chickens, geese, turkeys &c., knocked over with sticks, and strung in garlands around the necks of sweaty warriors." The correspondent concluded that "General Sherman's army has so far lived off the country, and lived well, as soldiers should live if the land produces."[16]

Many foragers were delighted with their assignment. Some were genuinely hungry, of course, and foraging met their needs. Others enjoyed the adventure. Most blamed the South for the Civil War and wanted to punish it. Only a small percentage of the bummers, who were under loose supervision or were stragglers, engaged in theft of property unrelated to supplying the army with provisions. As soldiers had to carry their own booty, many of the stolen valuables were subsequently discarded along the march.[17]

Burn All Bridges

After the fall of Atlanta, Jefferson Davis called for all Georgian men to join the army. If just half the men currently absent without leave from the army reported for duty, he announced, "we can defeat the enemy." Georgia's governor Joseph Brown also tried to mobilize all the able-bodied men in the state to fend off Sherman's army. Confederate General P. G. T. Beauregard urged Georgians: "Arise for the defense of your native soil!"[18]

Despite such stirring calls to action, few Georgians enlisted in the Confederate army or returned to duty if they were on leave or absent without leave. One soldier said that "the men of Georgia staid at home or at least a large portion of them, trying to save what they had left." Georgian men simply refused to enlist, most likely because the Union army might be headed in their direction and they would not abandon their families. Historians have surmised that the failure to heed the calls of their leaders demonstrated a lack of enthusiasm for the war among the greater part of the white population.[19]

Southern leaders anticipated that Sherman would try to live off the land. Hood directed the Confederate forces in Georgia to "destroy all things that would be useful to them and to drive out of the country into which they may advance all the live stock you can." Hood also directed Confederates to burn "all the mills within ten miles of their line of march, retarding them as much as possible." Confederate newspapers advised Georgians to move all supplies out of Sherman's way, hide all their machinery, and to destroy all supplies, crops, and animals, as the Russians did when Napoleon invaded their country in 1812. Like Napoleon's forces, Sherman's army could be defeated, they claimed, when it ran out of food. The *Augusta Constitutionalist* proclaimed that if Sherman's army survived, it would be due to "the mean and cowardly selfishness of the people" as well as "the inertness and indifference of Confederate officers." They called on Georgians to burn their own food supplies rather than let the enemy eat them.[20]

Georgian Congressmen, safely ensconced in Richmond, issued a proclamation of their own: "Let every man fly to arms. Remove your negroes, horses, cattle, and provisions from Sherman's army, and burn what you cannot carry. Burn all bridges, and block up the roads in his route. Assail the invader in front, flank, and rear, by night and by day." Georgia Senator B. H. Hill urged Georgians to "remove all provisions from the path of the invaders, and put all the obstructions you can in his way. Every citizen with his gun, and every negro with his spade, can do the work of a good soldier. You can destroy the enemy by retarding his march."[21]

The calls for Georgians to destroy their own property, like the calls urging enlistment, went unheeded. Union soldiers found a large bounty on plantations. Sherman wrote in his *Memoirs* that "we found abundance of corn, molasses, meal, bacon, and sweet-potatoes. We also took a good many cows and oxen, and a large number of mules . . . the country was quite rich, never before having been visited by a hostile army; the recent crop had been excellent, had been just gathered and laid by for the winter." Sherman also noted that "our men were well supplied with all the essentials of life and health, while the wagons retained enough in case of unexpected delay, and our animals were well fed.

Indeed, when we reached Savannah, the trains were pronounced by experts to be the finest in flesh and appearance ever seen with any army." One reason for the healthy condition of the animals was that soldiers expropriated thoroughbred horses from the surrounding plantations. Officers who did not usually have mounts acquired horses, which they rode with the permission of their superior officers. As for the cattle, their numbers actually climbed for a while as the army marched through rural Georgia.[22]

W. D. Tyrell, a plantation owner in Putnam County, Georgia, chronicled that Union troops demolished his gin house, broke his wheat thresher, and hacked to pieces his carriage. They shot or confiscated all his sheep, cows, pigs, fowl and all but two of his horses and mules. All his flour, corn, oats, and fodder was either burned or confiscated, and his six slaves fled. At another plantation, Union troops found chickens under the house and pulled them out. A Southern woman pleaded with the soldiers to leave a few chickens for her children. A Union soldier responded, "Madam, we're going to suppress this rebellion if it takes every last chicken in the Confederacy."[23]

To live off the land, Sherman's troops had to keep moving. The army averaged ten to fifteen miles per day, ensuring fresh supplies for the taking from plantations, farms, and supply depots. Flankers protecting the army from Confederate cavalry and the foragers averaged about twenty miles per day. To keep up this pace, supply wagons had to be replenished during the march. Quartermasters constantly shifted the loads on their wagons so that several always stood empty, ready to be refilled as foragers returned. Riding well ahead of the wagons, the foragers located fodder or corn, moved the empty wagons out of the column, filled them with supplies, and then hurried back to the column of march. On at least one occasion, wagons were loaded without even stopping: When Sherman's soldiers found a large, full corn crib, they hoisted it up a couple of feet, and as the wagons drew up alongside, they pulled a lever, releasing the corn into the wagons as they passed by.[24]

Foragers brought back a wide variety of goods. One vehicle was "loaded down with pumpkins, chickens, cabbages, guinea fowls, carrots, turkeys, onions, squashes, a shoat, sorghum, a looking-glass, an Italian harp, sweetmeats, a peacock, a rocking chair, a gourd, a bass viol, sweet potatoes, a cradle, dried peaches, honey, a baby carriage, peach brandy and every other imaginable thing under the sun a lot of fool soldiers could take in their heads to bring away."[25] Another account proclaimed, "In truth, so far as the gratification of the stomach goes, the troops are pursuing a continuous thanksgiving." Another soldier noted that the march through Georgia was "a delightful gastronomic" experience: "The cattle trains are getting so large that we find difficulty in driving them along." As another soldier said, "Few of the 'boys in blue' made the march on empty stomachs."[26]

The Federal Quartermaster's Department had assembled a large fleet of vessels that had been sent to various locations on the Southern coast as they were not completely sure where Sherman would emerge. When Sherman reached the Atlantic Ocean on December 13, 1864, supplies poured in from this fleet and from the Union supply base on Port Royal Island. Sherman offered the Confederate forces in Savannah the opportunity to surrender, be assaulted, or suffer "the slower and surer process of starvation." On December 22, Confederate forces withdrew from Savannah and Sherman and his army marched in. Once in the city, Sherman's troops were fed by the navy as well as by enterprising African-Americans.[27]

Sherman's army had been thorough in its destruction of the countryside it traversed. During the "march to the sea," Georgia suffered devastation in a swath thirty to sixty miles wide and 265 miles long. While reports vary on the amount of provisions confiscated or destroyed by Sherman's army, best estimates include 10,000 horses and mules,

13,000 cattle, half a million tons of fodder, and 13 million tons of corn, plus untold numbers of hogs, sheep, chickens, and vast quantities of sweet potatoes and other produce. Sherman's troops had demolished an estimated three hundred miles of railroad tracks, numerous bridges, mills, gin houses, warehouses, cotton gins, tons of cotton, public buildings, barns, and many homes.[28]

As one Union soldier wrote, "No one without being here, can form a proper idea of the devastation that will be found in our track. Thousands of families will have their homes laid in ashes, and they themselves will be turned beggars into the streets. We have literally carried fire and sword into this once proud and defiant State." Another reported, "I think a katydid, following our rear, would starve." A Georgian woman complained to Sherman about the conduct of his men, saying: "General, this is barbarity." Sherman quipped back, "Madam, war is barbarity."[29]

Sherman believed that his campaign should serve as an example for future Federal armies operating in the Confederacy. He urged the highest priority on "deep incisions into the enemy's country because this war differs from European wars in this particular: we are not only fighting hostile armies but a hostile people, and must make old and young, rich and poor, feel the hard hand of war, as well as their organized armies. I know that this recent movement of mine through Georgia has had a wonderful effect in this respect."[30]

A Heap of Smoldering Ashes

After Sherman's capture of Savannah, Northern leaders again debated what his next steps should be. Grant wanted Sherman to leave Savannah by boat and assist him in Virginia. Sherman himself proposed heading straight to Charleston, where he could "starve out" the city.

Henry Halleck, the Union army Chief of Staff, also hoped that Sherman would proceed to Charleston: "I hope that by some accident the place may be destroyed; and if a little salt should be sown upon its site, it may prevent the growth of future crops of nullification and secession." Six days later Sherman replied, "I will bear in mind your hint as to Charleston, and do not think 'salt' will be necessary." Sherman went on, "The truth is, the whole army is burning with an insatiable desire to work vengeance upon South Carolina. I almost tremble for her, but feel she deserves all that seems in store for her."[31]

As emotionally gratifying as burning Charleston might have been, it was the strategic decision to interdict Lee's supply lines in Goldsboro, North Carolina, that won the debate. On the last day of January 1865, Sherman and his army marched out of Savannah, heading toward Columbia. On his way, he planned to devastate the rich agricultural lands in the interior of the state. Once Sherman's intentions were known, Confederate forces abandoned Charleston and hastened after Sherman's army.

Sherman's army was traveling even lighter than when it had left Atlanta. On the way to Columbia, one officer wrote that where "the rich, aristocratic, chivalrous, slave-holding South Carolinian lived, was now a heap of smoldering ashes." A South Carolinian described it differently: "Along the sixty-mile-wide path of the invading army as it leisurely took its course through South Carolina on its march from Savannah, blackened chimneys marked the sites of once happy homes; iron rails brought to a white heat in fires made from the wooden ties that had supported them, and twisted into grotesque shapes, showed where the railroads had been; and the absence of the voices of poultry, sheep, or kine from the desolated fields and ruins along the roadside proclaimed the reign of famine and despair. The country was swept as clean of food as is a man's face of his beard by a well-plied razor."[32]

When Sherman marched into Columbia, his soldiers stripped

warehouses, demolished the railroad machine shops, and burned cotton mills and government buildings. Private dwellings were also burned, but no one in the Union army particularly cared. Columbia residents asked Union soldiers if they thought they could beat the Confederate army. According to diarist Emma LeConte, "The Yankees replied that they did not expect to whip our armies, but meant to starve us out."[33]

With much of Columbia in ashes, Sherman marched northward to Winnsboro, South Carolina. Foragers came into town, and a minister reported that the " 'Boys in Blue' played snowball along the fire-lit streets with precious flour; made bonfires of hams and sides of bacon that were worth almost fabulous sums in a time of such dearth; set boxes and barrels of crackers afloat on streams of vinegar and molasses that were sent flowing down the gutters from headless barrels; and fed their horses from hats filled with sugar, throwing what remained into the flames or the mud. In this wanton horse-play enough foodstuff was destroyed to have nourished the community abundantly for at least a year." While the army was in the city, a quartermaster issued "an army ration of 'hardtack' crackers and pickled pork" every day to each head of household, provided that "the male adults of such households should take the oath of allegiance to the United States government." Those who refused to do so, were not given rations.[34]

Sherman's army continued northward toward the supply depots and railroad lines in North Carolina. Jefferson Davis worried that if the supplies around Raleigh and Goldsboro were lost, it would be impossible to maintain the Confederate armies in Virginia and North Carolina. Lee concurred. If the Army of Northern Virginia were "deprived of the supplies from east North Carolina," it could not be supported.[35]

Sherman reached Goldsboro on March 23. As in previous campaigns through Georgia, Sherman's troops had lived off the land for much of the seven weeks since they had left Savannah. One officer wrote that since, for most of the time, he had "not drawn from the commissariat a single government ration, you can understand how entirely we have lived on the country. There have been times of great anxiety, when it seemed as if the country could yield nothing, but we have always had great herds of cattle to fall back on, so that there was never much danger of suffering." When Union troops marched into Goldsboro, a correspondent for the New York *Daily News* reported that many of the soldiers were mounted on "farm wagons and buggies, hacks, chaises, rockaways, aristocratic and family carriages, all filled with plunder. There was bacon, hams, potatoes, flour, pork, sorghum and freshly slaughtered pigs, sheep, and poultry dangling from saddle tree and wagon, enough one would suppose, to feed the army for a fortnight."[36]

From Goldsboro, the Federal army then headed toward Raleigh, which it occupied on April 13—four days after Lee's surrender to Grant at Appomattox. General Joseph E. Johnston, the Southern commander opposing Sherman, requested a truce and, after conferring with officials, he surrendered all Confederate forces in the Carolinas, Georgia, and Florida on April 26, 1865.

Producing a Bad Effect

Sherman's conquest of Atlanta and his subsequent marches through Georgia and the Carolinas sapped the morale of even ardent Confederates. That his army could traverse several hundred miles of Confederate territory without serious resistance—virtually no civilian guerrillas emerged, and few bridges were razed by nonmilitary forces to slow Sherman's advance—shocked many Southerners. Indeed, even the Confederate army mounted little effective action to delay the advance of Sherman's army. In February 1865, Robert E. Lee wrote to the Governor of North Carolina, "The state of despondency that now prevails among our people is producing a bad effect upon the troops. Desertions are becoming very frequent, and there is good reason to believe that they are occasioned to a considerable extent by letters written to the soldiers by their friends at home."[37]

Sherman's destruction of railroads in Georgia made it more difficult for the Confederates to send grain and beef from southern Georgia and Florida to Lee's army in northern Virginia. Sherman's subsequent march of destruction in the Carolinas further disrupted the Confederate supply system and also reduced civilian food caches. This left Richmond and the Army of Northern Virginia critically short of supplies and sapped the morale of Southern civilians and soldiers. Reports of the devastation caused by Sherman's army reached Confederate soldiers fighting in northern Virginia, and many soldiers deserted. One Georgia newspaper later concluded that the news of Sherman's march had shattered the morale of Lee's army, and named Sherman, not Grant, as "the victorious general who really subdued the Confederacy."[38]

Sherman's march through Georgia was long remembered. It was immortalized by the character Scarlett O'Hara in Margaret Mitchell's *Gone with the Wind*, who vowed, "As God is my witness, I'll never be hungry again!"

10

Capital Hunger

From the beginning of the war, Union armies had targeted Richmond, the capital of the Confederacy. Until May 1864, the generals commanding the Army of the Potomac had followed a predictable pattern: They developed a strategy, executed it, lost a battle, and then retreated to northern Virginia to prepare for the next round. In April 1864, General Ulysses S. Grant started on the same path, but after his defeat in the Battle of the Wilderness on May 5–7, he did something unusual. Rather than retreat, as previous Union armies had done, Grant flanked the Confederate army and headed southeast, only to be defeated again at Spotsylvania Court House. Rather than retreat, Grant moved again to the southeast, but was stopped at Cold Harbor.

After failing to dislodge Lee's troops from their positions, Grant flanked Lee yet again, crossed the James River, and arrived at Petersburg, where he connected with Major General Benjamin Butler and the Army of the James. Despite Union infantry assaults and cavalry raids behind their lines, the Confederates could not be budged from their strong fortifications around Richmond and Petersburg. Grant decided on a war of attrition—he would keep Lee holed up protecting Richmond while the Union cavalry cut as many Confederate supply lines as possible, and eventually the Army of Northern Virginia would be starved out. Commenting on Grant's strategy, Edmund Ruffin, a firebrand Confederate leader living in Richmond, foresaw accurately that "the result will be the reduction of Richmond & of Va, not by arms, but by starvation of the country & destitution of our armies."[1]

Verge of Famine

As the war dragged on, food production in the Confederacy continually declined. This was due to many factors: the destruction caused by fighting on the ground, diminishing agricultural land as the Confederacy shrunk, the loss of slave labor, the policies of both the Confederate and Union government, and—always a factor in farming—the weather. By 1864, the production of corn and wheat were down by an estimated 60 percent.[2] As corn was the main feed for livestock, herds of cattle, swine, and sheep also dwindled. As many Southerners left their homes rather than live under Union control, the greatly reduced food system needed to feed almost the same number of people. As many railroads wore down or were destroyed by war, the ability to transport food from where it was plentiful to where it was needed diminished.

Southern newspapers regularly wrote about the food crunch. "The cry in the army and out of the army is 'more food,'" read one article, which continued, "If we do not produce, we must starve." Another editor suggested that the solution to the food crisis was to look at unusual alternatives to traditional fare. His potential list of foods for those who were desperate included cats, crows, dogs, earthworms, frogs, locusts, rats, snails, and snakes. Other voices suggested that the war had to end: "Peace alone can prevent starvation!" declared the *Raleigh Daily Progress*. The author believed that it was "folly to talk to us about there being enough supplies in the country. Such is not the fact, and those who adhere to such a proposition will find out, when it is too late, that they have been mistaken." The *Franklin Repository* took a strong position against the wealthy who had plenty of food: "The rich may house their meat and bread, but we tell them it will not remain with them unless the poor can be provided for. The muscle of the country will not starve while there is bread in the land."[3] And there were many more such articles as malnutrition and hunger stalked the Confederacy, particularly in the last two years of the war.

While hunger was a problem throughout most cities in the Confederacy, it reached truly critical levels in Richmond. The war had devastated the region between that city and the Potomac River, an area that was "eaten out," as the *New York Herald* phrased it, adding, "Three years of wasting war have reduced its inhabitants to the verge of famine." Worsening the crisis was the fact that farmland in the Shenandoah Valley, which had supplied Richmond with provisions earlier in the war, had been rendered unproductive by war and drought. The paucity of food in Richmond was especially hard on government workers and the poor. John B. Jones, a clerk in the war department, was unable to "subsist and clothe his family." Judith MacGuire, a clerk in the commissary department, asked, "How are the poor to live?"[4]

The scarcity of foodstuffs greatly affected the Army of Northern Virginia. In January 1864, Lee wrote the Secretary of War, "Short rations are having a bad effect upon the men, both morally and physically. Desertions to the enemy are becoming more frequent, and the men cannot continue healthy and vigorous if confined to this spare diet for any length of time." To feed the army, supplies were sought from Georgia and South Carolina. This much longer supply line caused even more wear and tear on the Southern railroad system, which was already faltering. Southern locomotives and rolling stock were going out of commission one by one, and there were no replacements for them.

When James Longstreet advised Lee to take the offensive and move toward Washington before the expected Union spring offensive in 1864, Lee rejected the idea: "You know how exhausted the country is between here and the Potomac; there is nothing for man or horse." Lee believed that "the great obstacle everywhere is scarcity of supplies. That is the controlling element to which everything has to yield." Lee sent out expeditions to acquire more supplies, but they failed to bring back much.[5]

Richmond Must Starve

Throughout Grant's campaign to capture the capital of the Confederacy, one of his major objectives was to disrupt the supply lines to Richmond and Petersburg. A series of cavalry raids in May and June 1864, two led by Major General Philip Sheridan, tore up tracks on the Virginia Central Railroad, but the damage was repaired. Union cavalry occupied the Jerusalem Plank Road to the south of Petersburg, another supply line, on June 21. Between June 22 and July 1, Major General James H. Wilson and Brigadier General August Kautz led a cavalry raid that destroyed thirty miles of the South Side Railroad. On August 14, Grant sent a corps led by Major General Gouverneur K. Warren on a raid to Globe Tavern south of Petersburg to cut the Weldon Railroad. Warren's forces succeeded in wresting a portion of the railroad. Rather than retreat back to Union lines, Grant decided that Warren's troops should dig in and force the Confederates to attack them; when reinforcements arrived, the raid became a permanent part of the siege lines around Petersburg. Northern control of this section of the railroad forced the Confederates to transport supplies from Wilmington to Stony Creek, about sixteen miles south of Petersburg. The supplies were then offloaded from the train cars and hauled by wagon up Boydton Plank Road to Petersburg.

These raids pressured the Confederate supply system. In August 1864, the army ran out of corn. Lee still hoped for the best. "If we can get through the next month or six weeks the corn crop will begin to be available in Virginia, and afford us great relief," he told the Confederate

Secretary of War James A. Seddon. One soldier at Richmond wrote: "My comrades know how we were put to it for something to eat. Sometimes we had bread (such as it was), and sometimes meat, sometimes neither."[6] Simultaneously with these raids, Major General William T. Sherman's army disrupted rail traffic in Georgia that would have brought supplies from Alabama, Mississippi, southern Georgia, and Florida.[7]

Southerners believed that Grant's attempt to cut off Lee's supplies was a deliberate "starvation policy." The *Richmond Dispatch* agreed, proclaiming that the North "has sought, by the destruction of provisions, and the burning of mills and agricultural implements," to starve the South into submission. Northern newspapers happily reported the same: "While the soldiers and people of the loyal states are luxuriating upon the fat of the land, the soldiers and people of the rebellious States are reduced to the verge of general famine." The *New York Herald* reported in November 1864 that "the simple truth is that the rebellion is already beginning to feel the pangs of a famine, and the winter has not yet set in." The Virginian John Tyler, the son of the former president of the United States, feared starvation "more than the muskets and cannon of the enemy." In Richmond, the price of flour rose to "$400 per barrel and everything else in proportion. Many in and out of Richmond must starve to death this coming winter," as an observer reported. Completely oblivious to the growing food catastrophe, Jefferson Davis—proclaimed that there really wasn't a problem—the army would be fed and the abundant crops coming in would end "the inhumane attempt of the enemy to produce by devastation famine among the people."[8]

In December 1864, the Governor of Virginia, William Smith, complained that "hoarding, hiding, and other disreputable shifts and evasions, to avoid their contribution to the support of our own gallant Army" were "very demoralizing." The residents of Richmond met their supply problems as best they could. Sara Agnes Rice Pryor, the wife of a prominent Confederate official, reminisced: "With all our starvation we never ate rats, mice, or mule meat" in the waning days of the Confederacy, but she and her children survived on a little milk, peas, bread, sorghum, and ground corn. Many residents had even less. A common joke at the time was that Richmonders carried their money in baskets on the way to the market and carried their beef in their pocketbooks on the way home.[9]

The Greatest Beefsteak Feast Ever

Trench warfare continued around Richmond and Petersburg throughout the summer and fall of 1864. South of Petersburg, Confederate cavalry guarded the approaches to the southern end of Lee's right flank. They also guarded the Weldon railroad, which connected Petersburg with Wilmington, North Carolina, one of the South's most important ports for blockade-runners, as well as the Boydton Plank Road, which controlled access to the South Side Railroad, connecting Petersburg with Lynchburg, Virginia. Both railroads were vital lifelines carrying supplies from the south and southwest to the Confederate army and civilians in Petersburg and Richmond.

The Confederate cavalry guarding these approaches to Petersburg and Richmond was under the command of Charleston-born Lieutenant General Wade Hampton, a wealthy plantation owner who was reputed to own more slaves than anyone else in the South. Although Hampton had no military experience, he paid for the outfitting of this cavalry unit, which came to be called Hampton's Legion. He served with distinction and he was selected to command Lee's cavalry on May 11, 1864, when the legendary Confederate leader J. E. B. Stuart was killed at the battle of Yellow Tavern.

On September 3, 1864, Robert E. Lee asked Hampton to deliver a "sudden blow" behind Federal lines, should an opportunity emerge.[10] Hampton sent scouts around the lightly defended southern flank of the Union line near Petersburg. Dressed in a Union uniform, George D. Shadburne, a sergeant in the Jeff Davis Legion, mapped out the southern end and eastern rear of the Federal army. Shadburne wrote to Hampton and mentioned that there were three thousand cattle on the James River at Coggin's Point. To Hampton, three thousand cattle seemed like a worthy target—as they did to Lee.

Coggin's Point was only eight miles northeast of Petersburg, but between the Confederate lines and the cattle were entrenched the majority of Grant's army of 80,000 men. Shadburne offered Hampton a solution: If the raiding force went far to the south of the Union lines and came in behind them, they would find few Northern troops all the way to the cattle, which were lightly defended by only about 150 men. Hampton liked the plan and requested Lee's permission to capture the cattle and herd them back to Confederate lines. On September 14, Hampton took off with 2,500 cavalry and four pieces of artillery and sped around the southern flank of the Union line. The troops then rode to the James River, caught the Union guards by surprise, captured the cattle, and drove them southward. At times, the cattle herd stretched from four to seven miles. Despite Union pursuit, almost all cattle safely made it behind Confederate lines.[11]

Upon returning from the raid, Captain Chiswell Dabney delightedly exclaimed, "We then proceeded to have the greatest beefsteak feast ever known in the Army of Northern Virginia. As one of our men described it, we snatched the victory right out of their mouths." The butchered cattle were distributed to "General Lee's starving army, many of whom had not tasted fresh meat for months." It was enjoyed even more because the soldiers knew it came from far behind Union lines, and Hampton's raid was greatly appreciated. The grateful Confederates who received the fresh beef came to call it "Hampton Steaks."[12] In addition to providing several weeks' supply of meat, the most important effect of the raid was as a morale booster—one of the few enjoyed by the Confederate army around the Richmond-Petersburg front. In a season filled with bad news, the so-called Beefsteak Raid gave a decided boost to Southern morale.

Of the raid, Grant later wrote in his *Memoirs*, "It was a fair capture, and they were sufficiently needed by the Confederates." Grant, however, was none too pleased at the time with the ineffective Union response to the Confederate raid; asked when he expected to starve out Lee and take Richmond, Grant quipped, "Never, if our armies continue to supply him with beef-cattle."[13]

Starvation Parties

During the first year of the conflict, Richmonders "very freely and very liberally" hosted entertainments where "wine and suppers were generously furnished, but as the war progressed all this was of necessity given up." Those with money ate the finest oysters and terrapins and "revelled" in canvasback and greenback ducks from the Chesapeake Bay. As the war progressed, the fare at dinner parties declined. By the time of the Richmond bread riot in April 1863, "starvation parties" became common. These were social events at which young men and women danced and made merry, parties where they did everything they would have done before the war except eat.[14]

For starvation parties, young ladies and their escorts (usually Confederate officers) assembled at fashionable residences and enjoyed music and dancing, reported one participant, "but not a morsel of food or a drop of drink was seen." Diarist Mary Chesnut remarked that starvation parties cost "thirty dollars for the music and not a cent for a morsel to eat." Basil L. Gildersleeve, a Confederate officer who attended the parties, reported a bit more sustenance: "apples were the chief refreshment," although "strange streaks of luxury varied this dead level of scant and plain fare. The stock of fine wines, notably madeiras, for which the South was famous, did not all go to the hospitals."[15]

Those who wanted to invite friends over for dinner, "but who could not afford to call in the costly aid of a confectioner, resorted to various expedients. Calves' foot jelly was made without wine or lemons, peach brandy and vinegar being the substitutes, and was not an unpalatable dish. Milk was always procurable, and ice cream, in consequence, not unknown. Such desserts as could be made with sorghum molasses were those most frequent. Indeed, there was a surfeit of sorghum to those who used it in lieu of something better, and the word became a slang term for flattery—the equivalent of the Yankee 'soft sawder.' Preserves put up with sorghum molasses had always a twang which betrayed their origin—a twang barely mitigated by the use of soda. Yet few people could afford the use of sugar for the purpose, and those who could not, gladly availed themselves of the cheaper makeshift."[16]

Some Richmonders sought culinary luxuries (and necessities) outside the city. Whenever the wife of Senator Clement Clay faced starvation in the city, she visited her uncle's plantation in Warrenton, North Carolina, where she found a "sumptuous board" with "only the bona fide stuff! We had sugar in abundance, and pyramids of the richest butter, bowls of thick cream, and a marvellous plenitude of incomparable 'clabber.'" She returned from Richmond "laden with hampers of sweets and meats and bread made of the finest 'Number One' flour, which proved a fine relief to the 'seconds' to which the bread-eaters of the Confederate capital were now reduced. In the course of a year molasses and 'seconds' (brown flour with the bran still in it) came to be regarded as luxuries by many who but a short time ago had feasted capriciously upon the dainties of a limitless market."[17]

Barrels of Flour, Sacks of Coffee

Despite the starvation parties and widespread hunger in Richmond, those with money could acquire virtually anything in the way of food or beverage. Even as food became scarcer, the elite continued to entertain, although not as sumptuously as in the past. Whenever Chesnut or her friends acquired a "large jug of sorghum, had a pretense of some real flour or acquired a tiny sack of 'true-and-true' coffee," a summons went forth to share in the bounty. In January 1864, Chesnut wrote of the many "dinners, suppers, breakfasts we have been to. People have no variety in war times, but they make up for that lack in exquisite cooking." Evidently, these meals that had "no variety," according to Chesnut, only served terrapin stew, gumbo, fish, oysters, lobster, venison, mutton, lamb, ham, veal, turkey, goose, chicken, game, woodcock, partridge, robin, plover, snipe, homemade bread, butter, jelly cake, chocolate, a variety of vegetables, eggs served a variety of ways, butter, fresh fruit, milk, coffee, and tea.[18]

An English military observer, Fitzgerald Ross, visited the Confederacy for several months in 1863 and 1864. He had access to leaders of the Confederacy and he was sympathetic to the Southern cause. While visiting Richmond, he reported that the bill of fare at the Oriental Saloon in Richmond consisted of roast beef, beefsteaks, oysters, roast mutton, lamb, veal, venison, turkey, goose, chickens, egg dishes, woodcock, partridge, robin, plover, snipe, lobster, assorted vegetables, milk, coffee, tea, cake, and a large assortment of wines, porter, spirits, brandies, and liquors. Ross confessed that he "never saw such universal profusion and . . . waste. Hot meats and cold meats, venison pies, fish, oysters (prepared in half-a-dozen different ways), eggs, boiled, poached, 'scrambled,' and in omelettes, hot rolls and cakes, several kinds of bread, fruit in the season, &c., &c., are served up for breakfast, with 'confederate' (*i.e.,* artificial) coffee and tea, at hotels and boarding-houses, in quantities sufficient to satisfy an army of hungry soldiers." On the question of starvation in the Confederacy, Ross wrote that "I have no opportunity of seeing much of what goes on in the private houses of the poorer people, and can only judge from what I see at hotels, and eating and boarding houses. Here, not hundreds, but thousands upon thousands of people take their meals, and one may fairly conclude that what is set before them is what they are accustomed to expect at their own homes."[19]

Ross's estimate of the number of Richmonders enjoying such opulent meals is farfetched, but other observers reported the same general types of fare in Richmond—right up to the last days of the Confederacy. The English blockade-runner Thomas Taylor "managed to live in comparative comfort and at times even fared sumptuously" in Richmond. In late 1864, Taylor gave a dinner for fourteen Confederate department heads. This lavish meal, complete with champagne, sherry, and Madeira, cost Taylor five thousand Confederate dollars, but "it was a great success, and well worth the cost." Unlike Ross, Taylor recognized that "the privations of the regular residents in Richmond in those days were very great, as food of all kinds was very expensive."[20]

A few months before the war's end, the menu for a wedding reception in Richmond consisted of "turkeys and hams and delicious breads, and most beautifully stuffed eggs, and great piles of smoking sausages, and dishes of unsurpassed domestic pickles," but there was no oil for salad or sugar for the preserves. Someone gave the bride a wedding present of coffee, which was immediately put to good use, and the rooms were filled with its delightful aroma. This was consumed without sugar, but "with great gusto. Great bowls of apple toddy, hot and cold, filled with roasted pippins, stood on the tables, and furnished all needful warmth and cheerfulness for any wedding feast." Less than six weeks before the evacuation of Richmond in April 1865, a Colonel Richard

Maury dined on "oysters, venison, mutton and all of the delicacies of the season."[21]

In addition to eating well in public, many wealthy people in Richmond stockpiled commodities intended for future use. A Southern businessman who traveled frequently to Richmond during the war later reminisced about one experience in early 1865: "The host simply took me to his bed-room, and raising the coverlet, showed several barrels of flour, sacks of coffee, sugar and other groceries snugly stowed away. This, he said, I would find to be the case in nearly every household in the city."[22]

Thousands of Their Own Men Starved

For the first two years of the war, the North and South exchanged prisoners on a regular basis (although the Confederacy refused to exchange African-American prisoners, many of whom were shot when captured, while others were sent into slavery). As a result, most captured soldiers did not have to spend much time in temporary prisoner-of-war camps situated near front lines. Rather than wait for official prisoner exchanges, captured soldiers occasionally were paroled with the understanding that they would return home and wait till they were officially exchanged before they could rejoin the army. When Vicksburg surrendered in July 1863, for instance, the entire 27,000-man Confederate garrison was paroled pending an official exchange. A few months later, some of these paroled soldiers who had not been officially exchanged were captured again while fighting against the Union army at Chattanooga. This upset Northern leaders, as did the refusal of the South to exchange African-American prisoners of war.

Union Secretary of War Edward Stanton made the decision to suspend all prisoner exchanges in late 1863. As cruel as this new policy might be, Grant supported it.[23] The North had plenty of men to fill its ranks, while the South was being drained of its manpower. Why exchange prisoners just to have them return to the enemy's army?

Declining prisoner exchanges made it harder for the Confederacy to fill its military ranks; in a grim corollary, Southern prisoner-of-war camps were soon filled to overflowing and the South had to find a way to feed prisoners. In theory, Union prisoners were to receive the same amount of rations as were given to Southern soldiers. In fact, prisoners usually received less. New camps, such as Camp Sumter near a small railroad junction at Anderson (later renamed Andersonville), Georgia, were built quickly and just as quickly had to be expanded. Beginning in February 1864, tens of thousands of captured Union troops were herded into Camp Sumter. Prisoners were fed "from two to four ounces of bacon, and from four to twelve ounces of corn bread daily; sometimes a half pint to a pint of bean, pea, or sweet potato soup, of doubtful value. Vegetables were unknown. Thus giving a total weight of solid food, per diem, of six to sixteen ounces of solid food. The amount was not constant: some days the prisoners were entirely without food, as was the case at Belle Isle and Salisbury. Neither was the deficiency afterwards made good. The amount given was oftener less than ten ounces than more." Much of the food that was given to the prisoners was indigestible and insufficiently nutritious. The commandant of Camp Sumter, Henry Wirz, requested the Confederate government for more food, supplies, clothes, and shelter for the prisoners, but to no avail. Contemporary Confederate sources reported that ample food was readily available: Feeding prisoners simply was not a priority in the last year of the Confederacy.[24]

One of the Confederate officials responsible for making sure prisoners were properly fed was Commissary General Northrop, who was not sympathetic to Union prisoners. After the first Battle of Bull Run, he was asked how to feed the prisoners, then housed in Richmond. His response was: "I know nothing of Yankee prisoners; throw them all into the James river." Northrop himself claimed that the problems were with his subordinates. Although provisions were readily available in Georgia around Camp Sumter, the Confederacy failed to guarantee that Union prisoners received adequate food. Of the 35,000 Union soldiers at Camp Sumter during its ten months of operation, an estimated 13,000 died, many from starvation or diseases, including scurvy, exacerbated by malnutrition and hunger. An additional 2,000 died on the way home after their release, and many more died shortly thereafter. One former inmate estimated that two thirds of all prisoners at the camp died within two years of its opening.[25]

Southerners believed that the real reason the North stopped exchanging prisoners was to starve the South. Northrop, for instance, noted in February 1865 that "The retention of many thousands of prisoners of war in this city caused the consumption of our reserve of flour." Another Southerner later blamed the barbarity at Anderson on the North for refusing to exchange captured soldiers. He believed that the reason for refusing exchanges was that the North wanted the prisoners to eat "Confederate corn" while thousands of Southerners "starved and rotted with scurvy." As good as this might have sounded to defensive ex-Confederates, the North regularly sent supplies to Union prisoners in the South. Captive soldiers claimed they rarely received these shipments and many believed that these provisions had been siphoned off for use by the Army of Northern Virginia.[26] When the South agreed to exchange all prisoners—including captured African-American soldiers—the exchanges were resumed on a small scale.

Twenty-Four Hours Were Lost

The Army of Northern Virginia's food shortage grew into a full-fledged emergency in early 1865. The country north and east of Richmond and

Petersburg was barren, and occupied by Federal armies. Confederate currency was worthless, forcing commissary officers to impress or barter for any food that was available. The railroad system was in a shambles, and the few large ports—Mobile, Charleston, and Wilmington—still controlled by the Confederacy would soon be captured by Union forces. After Sherman's march from Atlanta to the sea, few supplies could be expected soon from Florida, Alabama, or southern Georgia. Sheridan's destruction of the Shenandoah Valley meant that no food could be expected from that quarter either.

The pressure mounted. By January 1, 1865, the Army of Northern Virginia was on one-quarter rations, and some days the troops had no food at all. The Confederate Chief of Ordinance, Josiah Gorgas, noted in his diary that the army was "almost without bread and quite without meat." Five days later there was still "no food to feed Gen. Lee's army." On January 12, Lee wrote: "There is nothing within reach of this army to be impressed; the country is swept clear. Our only reliance is upon the railroads. We have but two days supplies." On the same day, an order called "on the citizens of Richmond for a part of their supplies."[27] Few Richmonders responded.

The army's morale deteriorated to its lowest level in the war. At the same time, soldiers received letters from their families, who were worried about starvation themselves and begging their men to return home to plant the spring crops. Substantial numbers of Confederate soldiers began to desert their posts—some surrendering to Union forces, but most just trying to return home or find food. Something needed to be done about the food shortage, or the army and the Confederacy itself would soon dissolve.

It wasn't just the soldiers and civilians who were hungry: Animals faced famine as well. The Confederate cavalry was stationed forty miles from Richmond, where there was a better chance that the horses could be fed. As for the mules and horses in the city that were needed to pull wagons and artillery, the fodder famine greatly reduced their numbers and sapped their strength and stamina. When Lee finally retreated from Richmond in April 1865, the Confederate cavalry, riding weakened horses, were unable to keep up with the well-nourished Union mounts, and time and again, the Northerners would beat the Southern cavalry to depots and supply trains sent to feed the Army of Northern Virginia.

By early 1865, the city of Richmond and Lee's army were dependent on two feeble railroads: the South Side Railroad, which headed west from Petersburg to Lynchburg, Virginia, and the Richmond & Danville Railroad, which ran southwest from Richmond to Danville. This railroad connected to the newly completed Piedmont Railroad, which formed a link to the supply areas in central and western North Carolina. Since all Southern railroads were suffering from the loss of rolling stock, engines, equipment, and spare parts, they were subject to frequent delays and accidents.[28]

When floods washed out the Piedmont Railroad in January 1865, the Army of Northern Virginia, as well as the cities of Petersburg and Richmond, were cut off from supply stores in North Carolina. Confederate War clerk John B. Jones reported that there were "not two days' rations for his army!" By January 12 the army had begun to accept "local goods in appraisal," which meant that they had to pay the prevailing price at the place where the goods were impressed, instead of the artificially low prices offered by government agents. Lee asked farmers east of the Blue Ridge Mountains and south of the James River for provisions. He also hoped that more food would be coming from Wilmington, the last major port still in Confederate hands, but Fort Fisher, which guarded the port, surrendered to the Union army and navy on January 15. Lee was desperate for supplies. He had previously opposed trading between the lines with the enemy, but after the fall of Wilmington, Lee asked the Confederate Secretary of War for permission to trade cotton for provisions with the North.[29]

On February 8, Lee informed Secretary of War James A. Seddon that there was "not a pound of meat" at the disposal of the army. Lee projected: "If some change is not made and the commissary department reorganized, I apprehend dire results. The physical strength of the men, if their courage survives, must fail under this treatment" and warned Seddon that he "must not be surprised if calamity befalls us." Seddon sent the letter on to Jefferson Davis, who wrote back, "This is too sad to be patiently considered, and cannot have occurred without criminal neglect or gross incapacity. Let supplies be had by purchase, or borrowing, or other possible mode."[30] It was just like Davis to blame others for the mistakes of his own government, but at least he backhandedly authorized Seddon and Lee to acquire supplies wherever they could, presumably including by trading cotton for foodstuffs with the Union.

General James Longstreet came up with one of the most bizarre suggestions in the Confederacy's long quest for food security. His idea was for the Confederate government to "send out the gold through Virginia and North Carolina and pay liberal prices, and my conviction is that we shall have no more distress for want of food. The winter is about over now, and the families can and will subsist on molasses, bread, and vegetables for the balance of the year, if they can get gold for their supplies. There is a great deal of meat and bread inside the enemy's lines that our people would bring us for gold, but they won't go to that trouble for Confederate money. They can keep gold so much safer than they can meat and bread." Unfortunately, by 1865 the Confederate government had no gold, and it was unwilling or unable to confiscate it from those who had it in order to try Longstreet's suggestion.[31]

The near-famine situation in the Confederacy was well understood by Grant. On February 23, he concluded: "Everything looks like dissolution in the South." To guarantee the Confederacy's collapse, Grant directed Union generals to continue burning crops and factories and disrupting railroads. On March 13, 1865, the *New York Herald* reported that Lee would either evacuate the city or face starvation. Sheridan finally moved out of the Shenandoah Valley and was headed toward Richmond; Sherman was marching up from the South, depriving the Army of Northern Virginia and Richmonders supplies from that direction.[32]

Lee concluded that his troops must break the Union siege before the Northern armies began their expected spring offensive, which his dwindling and starving army would not be able to survive. Lee thus decided to do the unexpected: He would launch a surprise assault on the Union lines at one of their strongest points—Fort Stedman. The fort anchored the northern section of the Union line to the James River. If the Confederates could capture it, the Northern army could be cut off from their supply line, and this might result in the destruction of much of the Union army.

Beginning at 4 a.m. of March 25, General John B. Gordon's soldiers attacked Fort Stedman and they almost succeeded in capturing it, but the Union army regrouped and pushed the Confederates back to their lines. Six days later Grant ordered Sheridan's cavalry to break through the Confederate line. Sheridan succeeded and cut the South Side Railroad, one of Richmond's few remaining supply lines. With the Confederate line flanked and no reserves available to drive back the Union army, Lee made the only decision that he could—it was time to evacuate Petersburg and Richmond.

The Army of Northern Virginia had stockpiled rations in Richmond and there were several supply depots southwest of Richmond. Lee ordered supply trains from Richmond to be sent to Amelia Court House, about forty miles southwest of Richmond. At the same time, Jefferson Davis began extricating the government from Richmond and making plans to destroy anything of military value in the city. The Confederates torched the Tredegar Iron Works as well as the four main food warehouses in Richmond. When the armory was set ablaze, explosions rocked the city, and exploding ammunition set parts of the city on fire. Richmonders watched in disbelief as Confederate soldiers withdrew; others broke into government supply depots and made off with whatever they could. Mobs took control of the streets, and order was not restored until Union soldiers—many of them African-Americans—marched into the city the following day.

After successfully extricating the Army of Northern Virginia from Richmond and Petersburg, Lee headed westward along the Danville Railroad toward Amelia Court House, where he expected provisions to be waiting. When the troops arrived there on April 4, Lee did not find any supplies. During the confusion, the supplies that Lee had ordered to Amelia Court House either were not sent or were destroyed. Lee appealed to local farmers for supplies, but foraging parties returned almost empty-handed. Soldiers ate horses and scant rations of corn. Lee sadly reported that "nearly twenty-four hours were lost in endeavoring to collect in the country the subsistence for men and horses. The delay was fatal and could not be retrieved."[33]

Lee then headed toward Danville, where he knew eighteen days' worth of bread and fifty days' worth of meat were stored. The Confederate commissaries sent supplies to Farmville, only twenty miles from Amelia Court House. As Sheridan's cavalry moved on Farmville, these supplies were hastily packed up and sent by train to meet the oncoming Confederate army. This worked: The army and the supply trains connected on April 7. For many soldiers, this was the first time they had eaten since leaving Richmond and Petersburg. However, this was not enough food to sustain the army. Lee headed toward Lynchburg, hoping to acquire more. Meanwhile, three supply trains that had been sent from Lynchburg were waiting for the army at Appomattox Station. Sheridan sent George Custer's cavalry to Appomattox Junction to cut off further supplies from reaching the beleaguered Army of Northern

Virginia. When Lee arrived at Appomattox Court House on April 8, Custer had already beaten the Confederates to their supply trains. Lee surrendered the following day.[34]

Hungering Effects

When Robert E. Lee surrendered on April 9, 1865, the grand Army of Northern Virginia had an estimated 27,500 men. Yet on April 1, the Confederate army supposedly had 150,000 men on its rolls. Some soldiers were on leave; others were in the hospital, and still others were captured or died along the way to Appomattox. But tens of thousands of soldiers had deserted, and this caused the collapse of the Army of Northern Virginia—and within months the end of the Confederacy.[35]

Soldiers deserted for many reasons, but at the top of the list was hunger. During January 1865, one captured Confederate deserter estimated that two hundred men were separating from Lee's army every day, partly due to the poor and irregular rations. A Confederate commander, J. H. Duncan, reported on January 21 that "desertions are becoming amazingly numerous, and I beg leave to submit for your consideration what I esteem to be the main cause of this dissatisfaction, and is, in my opinion, the controlling influence that prompts our men thus to desert—it is the insufficiency of rations. Our men do not get enough to eat." Duncan predicted that "unless something is done soon to remove this evil, which of all others weighs most heavily on the minds of the troops, I fear that the number of desertions will be greatly increased during the winter."[36]

Others deserted because of hunger back home. According to Joseph E. Johnston, "it was not uncommon for a soldier to be written to by his wife, that so much of the food he had provided for herself and his children had been impressed, that it was necessary that he should return to save them from suffering or starvation. Such a summons, it may well be supposed, was never unheeded." Johnston warned that this "increased desertion from the army, further increasing the likelihood of military defeat."[37]

Lee was well aware of this. In a letter to the Secretary of War, he concluded that the main causes of desertions were "the insufficiency of food, and non-payment of the troops." He continued: "There is suffering for want of food. The ration is too small for men who have to undergo so much exposure and labor." One soldier wrote to his family on January 30, remarking that "I get so hungry that it makes me sick." He continued: "The reason they don't feed us any better may be that thay can not get it. . . . Our men can not and will not stand it much longer."[38]

Thousands of soldiers, many of whom had supported the Confederate cause for four long years, voted with their stomachs and deserted. The Army of Northern Virginia dissolved and within a matter of weeks, the war ended.

From the first shot fired at Fort Sumter on April 12, 1861, until the Confederate armies surrendered four years later, food played a crucial role in the Civil War. While there were many reasons for the Confederacy's defeat, hunger is what tipped the scales in favor of the South's surrender.

Epilogue

When the Civil War ended, the Confederacy was defeated, slaves were emancipated, the Union was restored, and the primacy of the Federal government firmly established in the United States. Large plantations were broken up, and tenant farming became a way of life for many Southerners. These were the most obvious changes wrought by the war; others were closer to home, more personal and individual. The opulent dining habits of plantation life had died with the Confederacy. Freed slaves who were the inventors and practitioners of the antebellum Southern cuisine migrated away from the South. Mrs. Abby Fisher, who had been a cook on a plantation, brought Southern cookery to San Francisco, where her recipes were transcribed and published in a cookbook called *What Mrs. Fisher Knows about Old Southern Cooking*.[1] Other former slaves moved north, where many were employed as professional cooks in restaurants and upperclass households. Writing in 1914, the American historian Gaillard Hunt concluded: "The professional cooks of the country were negroes, and the national cookery came from them."[2]

Those who joined the military traveled—many for the first time—far from their farms, plantations, hometowns, and home states. In farflung camps and ports, they sampled foods that were not part of their culinary heritage. Some Southern foods and dishes, such as fried chicken, barbecue, gumbo, peanuts, jambalaya, rice, and sweet potatoes, became popular throughout the nation.

For many Union soldiers, it was also the first time that they sampled canned food. When they returned home after the war, sales of canned goods soared. With Gail Borden's condensed milk as one of its most notable successes, the American canning industry got a jump-start from the wartime need for field rations. Historian Tom Dicke wrote that the Civil War "stimulated technological change, increased competition, and provided expertise to the next generation of canners, all of which helped bring the cost of canned food down to affordable levels. The war forced hundreds of thousands, who might not otherwise have done so, to try canned food. Once they did, a significant number found canned food had much to offer."[3] Commercial canning made it possible to preserve perishable foods in season and to eat them year-round.

As the cost of producing canned goods declined, fruit, vegetables, milk, and meat were readily available to all but the poorest Americans, and this more varied diet undoubtedly transformed the health of many. During the late nineteenth and early twentieth centuries, Americans grew taller and healthier. Better sanitation, pure food laws, and medical advances no doubt played a part in these improvements, but a reliable supply of year-round canned produce likely contributed as well.

Even as technological innovations made it possible to produce canned goods faster and more cheaply, the equipment necessary for high-speed processing became more expensive. Small and medium-sized canneries that served their local areas could not afford the new machines, and they would be undersold in their markets by national brands. In addition, the Pure Food and Drug Law, passed in 1906, required food processors engaged in interstate trade to adhere strictly to proper health and safety procedures. This added expense made it even harder for smaller companies to survive, and many closed or were bought out. The cost of canned goods declined, and by the 1870s, most urban Americans ate some processed foods. The distinct local foodways once found throughout the nation began to mingle and meld into a homogenous national cuisine.

The westward expansion of the nation accelerated, due in large part to the Homestead Act, passed in 1862, which gave each applicant title to 160 acres of undeveloped Federal land. This made it possible for settlers to establish farms at almost no cost. Few claims were filed under the Homestead Act during the Civil War, but immediately after the war, immigrants streamed into America, and tens of thousands of new homesteads, especially in Iowa, Kansas, Minnesota, and Nebraska, were approved.[4] The Midwest became the center of American agriculture.

Mechanization of America's farms rapidly expanded after the war and farms became much larger. Small farms found it difficult to compete, and tens of thousands of farmers left rural areas and flocked into cities, seeking jobs in rapidly expanding industries. Large farms began to dominate American agricultural production. Mechanization brought the price of food down, making a varied and healthful diet affordable for most Americans.

After the war ended, Southern railroads targeted during the conflict were quickly rebuilt, and new railroad construction commenced across the nation. The construction of a transcontinental railroad began during the Civil War and was completed in 1869. Within a few months, California growers began shipping tomatoes and even bananas to Eastern markets. Within two years, many other agricultural products—apples, pears, plums, vegetables, and salmon, as well as canned goods—were shipped from California. By the century's end large tracts of land in southern California were planted with citrus groves, and soon oranges and lemons from the state were available throughout the country.[5] As railroads crisscrossed the nation, a national food system emerged, making it possible for provisions grown, raised, or processed in a particular region to be shipped anywhere in the country. Grocery store chains, which had begun in New York during the Civil War, expanded rapidly after the war, thus creating a national food distribution system.

Perhaps the longest-lasting culinary effect of the Civil War was related to the passage of two pieces of legislation. One was the Morrill Land-Grant College Act, which allotted each state thirty thousand acres of public land for every senator and representative the state had in Congress. The proceeds on the sale of this land were to be used to create agricultural colleges. This had been under discussion for fifteen years, but the bill had been opposed by Southern legislators.[6] The Morrill Act passed with little dissent on July 2, 1862. During the next few years, agricultural colleges were established in most states. These institutions promoted agricultural education by offering courses in botany, chemistry, zoology, and other subjects related to farming.

The second piece of legislation entailed the creation of the U.S. Department of Agriculture (USDA), which influenced what Americans ate through extensive research, experimentation, and education. Like the Morrill Act, this had been discussed in Congress for years, but had been opposed by Southerners who believed it to be a violation of states' rights. Since its creation, the USDA has promoted agricultural research and dissemination of agricultural information and best practices to farmers. The USDA has assisted farmers in increasing production and lowering the cost of food, and this has led to a more healthful diet for most Americans.

The Civil War wrought great changes in the foods Americans grew, raised, and consumed. Before the war, most people ate what they had grown or raised themselves, or could buy from their neighbors. After the Civil War, Americans began to eat foods that came from hundreds or even thousands of miles away. Thanks to food processing and fast, reliable transportation, fruits and vegetables that had been available only in their high seasons could now be served year round. Americans had traditionally bought the staples they did not grow themselves at general stores or farmers' markets; after the war, they began shopping at grocery stores. Americans increasingly opted for meals that were convenient and easy to prepare. The industrialization of American food, from the farmer's field to the consumer's plate, was in full swing.

Afterword

Charles Adams, the U.S. Ambassador to the United Kingdom, returned to Boston after the Civil War. He was the grandson of President John Adams and the son of President John Quincy Adams. To honor his father, he built the "Stone Library," which some consider the first presidential library in America. Charles Adams died in 1886.

Robert Anderson, the Union commander of Fort Sumter, who surrendered the fort to the Confederates, remained in the Union army, attaining the rank of major general. On April 14, 1865, four years to the day that Anderson lowered the American flag, he raised it over the battered remains of Fort Sumter as part of the Union celebration of victory in the Civil War. President Lincoln had been invited to the ceremony, but he had declined to attend. Instead, he went to Ford's Theatre in Washington, D.C., where he was shot; he died the following day. Anderson died in 1871 in Nice, France.

Nathaniel Banks, the Union General who helped conquer the Mississippi River in 1863, left the army in August 1865 and served as U.S. Congressman for ten additional terms after the war. He died in 1894.

Judah P. Benjamin, the Confederate Secretary of State, was allegedly aware of the plot to assassinate Abraham Lincoln.[1] He burned his papers and escaped from the South in the closing days of the war. Benjamin never returned to the United States. He died and was buried in France in 1884.

Gail Borden, the manufacturer of condensed milk, returned to Texas, where he started several small businesses. He died in 1874, a very wealthy man. Borden's company thrived through the late nineteenth and early twentieth centuries. The company faced financial difficulties during the 1990s, and began to sell off its subsidiaries. Borden, Inc., sold its dairy subsidiary in September 1997; in 2001 it sold the last of its food lines.

Benjamin Butler, the Union general who served as an administrator of New Orleans and later of Norfolk, was relieved by Grant of his command in December 1864. He was undeniably associated with trading with the enemy and other forms of corruption, but was never proven to be directly involved. Butler successfully ran for Congress after the war and served ten years in the U.S. House of Representatives. He was elected governor of Massachusetts and ran unsuccessfully for president under the flag of a minor party in 1884. He died nine years later in Washington, D.C.

E. R. S. Canby was the Union general who accepted the surrender of E. Kirby Smith, leader of the last major Confederate army. Canby remained in the army, where he became involved in Reconstruction and the Indian wars. When the Modoc War broke out in 1873, Canby was sent out to resolve the conflict. While discussing a peace treaty with "Captain Jack," the leader of the Modoc tribe in northern California, Canby was shot twice in the head and his throat was slit.

George Crook, the Union General who helped conquer the Shenandoah Valley, was captured by Confederate partisans in February 1865. Exchanged a month later, he was given a cavalry division that figured prominently in Lee's defeat at Appomattox. After the Civil War, Crook served in the Indian wars on the Western frontier. On June 25, 1876, Crook was involved in the campaign against the Lakota Sioux; his forces were supposed to rendezvous with his Civil War compatriot, George A. Custer, and the Seventh Cavalry. Crook ran into opposition, however, and turned back; Custer and his troops continued on to their deaths at the Battle of the Little Big Horn. Crook died in Chicago in 1898 at age 62.

Jefferson Davis, the Confederate President, was captured in May 1865. He was charged with treason and was held in prison without trial for two years. He was given amnesty in 1869. His two-volume work, *The Rise and Fall of the Confederate Government*, was published in 1881. He died eight years later.

Jubal Early, the Confederate General, refused to give up when Robert E. Lee capitulated at Appomattox in April 1865. Early traveled to Texas in hopes of joining General Kirby Smith's army and continuing the struggle. When Kirby Smith surrendered in May 1865, Early traveled first to Mexico, then to Cuba, and finally to Canada, where he wrote his memoirs, which focused on the Shenandoah campaign of 1864. He returned to Virginia in 1869 and remained there until his death, in Lynchburg, in 1894.

Nathan Bedford Forrest, the Confederate cavalry commander, was defeated several times in battles in 1864 and early 1865. He surrendered in May 1865. After the war, he engaged in several businesses. He is better known for his membership in and leadership of the Ku Klux Klan after the war. He died in 1877. Forrest's life and military tactics have been the subject of numerous books and articles.

Benjamin Grierson, the Union cavalry commander, remained in the army after the war, serving in the Southwest until he retired in 1890. He died twenty-one years later. His cavalry raid from Tennessee through Mississippi was immortalized in the 1959 film, *The Horse Soldiers*, starring John Wayne and William Holden. The raid has also been the subject of several books. Grierson's military career after the Civil War was partially portrayed in the television documentary, "Buffalo Soldiers."

Ulysses S. Grant remained General of the U.S. Army until his election to the presidency in 1868. After leaving office in 1877, he wrote his memoirs, which were completed just before his death in 1885, at age 63.

Sarah Josepha Hale's literary career flourished throughout the mid-1800s. She wrote almost fifty books and continued to serve as editor of *Godey's Lady's Book* until 1877. She died two years later. For her campaign to make Thanksgiving a national holiday, Hale is remembered as the "Mother of Thanksgiving."[2]

Rutherford B. Hayes, a Union division commander in the Shenandoah, would make history in 1876, when he ran for president of the United States. The November election was indecisive and the election was thrown in to the House of Representatives. After many backroom deals, including his agreement to withdraw Union troops from the South and end Reconstruction, he was elected president. He was subsequently referred to as "Rutherfraud" B. Hayes.

David Hunter, the Union General who failed to conquer the Shenandoah in 1864, accompanied the body of President Abraham Lincoln back to Springfield, Illinois, in April 1865. He returned to Washington, D.C., where he presided over the nine-member commission that tried the conspirators who assassinated Lincoln. Hunter resigned from the army in 1866, and published his military memoirs in 1873. He died in Washington in 1886.

Joseph E. Johnston, the Confederate General, had served in several corporate enterprises after the war's end. His memoirs, *Narrative of Military Opera-*

tions Directed During the Late War between the States, were published in 1874. He was a pallbearer at Sherman's funeral in 1891, and died several weeks later.

Robert E. Lee blamed Jefferson Davis for failing to send the supplies for his army at Amelia Station, as Lee had requested. Davis denied ever receiving Lee's request. Had the supplies arrived, Lee believed he would have been able to continue the war. After the Civil War, Lee served as president of Washington College in Lexington, Virginia. After his death in 1870, at age 63, the name of the institution was changed to Washington and Lee College. Lee is buried on the grounds of the university.

John Letcher left the governorship of Virginia in 1864. His home in Lexington, Virginia, was burned by Union troops in June 1864. After the war, Letcher returned to Lexington and took up the practice of law. He served two terms in the Virginia House of Delegates and died in 1871.

Cyrus McCormick, the reaper manufacturer, was a Southerner by birth whose Virginia farm was worked by slaves. He had moved his manufacturing operation to Chicago more than a decade before the Civil War. He opposed the war, but, ironically, became a major contributor to the North's ultimate victory. After the Civil War, McCormick's company continued to thrive. In 1884, the year McCormick died, his company sold 54,841 reapers. Because of his contributions, Cyrus McCormick has been called the "Father of Modern Agriculture."[3]

Edmund McIlhenny, who had worked with his father-in-law Daniel Avery to extract rock salt in Louisiana, returned to Avery Island after the war and began growing chile peppers. He incorporated the McIlhenny Company in 1868, and two years later, began manufacturing Tabasco Sauce.

Joseph Mayo remained the mayor of Richmond until April 2, 1865, when he surrendered the city to General Godfrey Weitzel. Mayo died in Richmond in 1872.

Montgomery C. Meigs, the Georgian who became the Union Quartermaster General, continued in the army. When his son died fighting the Confederacy, he ordered Union dead to be buried in Arlington, Virginia, on the front lawn of the home of Mary Custis Lee, the wife of Robert E. Lee. The Lees never returned to their home. After his retirement from the army in 1882, Meigs was selected as the architect to design the Pension Office building in Washington, D.C. Today, this building houses the National Building Museum. Meigs died in 1892 and is buried in the cemetery he created—Arlington National Cemetery.

John S. Mosby, the Confederate guerrilla leader in northern Virginia, refused to surrender his Rangers at the end of the Civil War. Several weeks after Lee's surrender at Appomattox, Mosby simply disbanded them. During Reconstruction, Mosby became a Republican and befriended Ulysses S. Grant. Mosby supported Grant's bid for reelection in 1872, and in return Grant appointed Mosby to the position of U.S. consul to Hong Kong.[4] Mosby died in Washington, D.C., in 1916.

John C. Pemberton, the Confederate General who surrendered Vicksburg, was vilified in the South for his surrender. Joseph E. Johnston, Pemberton's commanding officer, claimed that Pemberton had caused the disaster at Vicksburg because he had violated orders. Pemberton was not asked to serve again in the Confederate army for a year. At that time he was reduced in rank to lieutenant colonel and served in the artillery defending Richmond against his former foe, Ulysses S. Grant. After the war, Pemberton lived in Warrenton, Virginia, before moving to Pennsylvania, where he died in 1881.

Theodore Roosevelt, Sr., the member of the Union League Club in New York City who had helped organize the effort to give Union military forces a good Thanksgiving dinner in November 1864, died in 1878. His son was President Theodore Roosevelt, Jr., and his granddaughter was Eleanor Roosevelt, wife of President Franklin Delano Roosevelt.

Philip Sheridan, the Union General who conquered the Shenandoah Valley in the fall of 1864, remained in the army after the war and served in the Indian wars on the Western frontier. He used similar tactics against the Indians to those he had used to defeat the Confederates. In 1888, just two months after sending his memoirs to the publisher, he died, at age 57.

William T. Sherman became the Commanding General of the United States Army in 1869. He retired from the army in 1884. Later that year, his name was mentioned as a possible candidate for the Republican nomination for president. Sherman telegraphed his response to the delegates at the convention in Chicago: "I will not accept if nominated, and will not serve if elected." Journalists subsequently corrupted this into the punchier: "If nominated, I will not run; if elected, I will not serve."

John Slidell, the Confederate diplomat in France, had been born in New York. He was among the few Northerners who supported the South, and he was vilified in the North as a traitor. He did not achieve much as a diplomat and his patriotism to the Southern cause was also questioned. He did not return to the United States after the Civil War. He died in 1871 and is buried near Paris.

William Seward, the Union Secretary of State, was wounded by Lewis Powell, who broke into his home as part of the plot to assassinate Abraham Lincoln. Powell was captured and was hanged three months later. Seward recovered and continued as Secretary of State. His main postwar claim to fame was his purchase of Alaska from Russia in 1867, an acquisition many

Americans thought worthless and ridiculed as "Seward's Folly." He left office in 1869 and died three years later in New York.

E. Kirby Smith, the commander of the last large Confederate army, surrendered on May 26, 1865. After a brief time in Mexico, he returned to his home state of Virginia, took the oath of allegiance to the United States, and led a productive life as the president of the University of Nashville and later as a professor of mathematics at the University of the South in Sewanee, Tennessee, where he died in 1893.

Edwin Stanton retained his position as Secretary of War during the presidency of Andrew Johnson. Stanton and Johnson disagreed over how to deal with the South after the war, and Johnson removed Stanton from his position. Radical Republicans believed that Johnson had illegally removed Stanton from office and initiated impeachment proceedings against Johnson. The House of Representatives impeached Johnson, but he escaped conviction in the Senate by a single vote. Stanton was subsequently confirmed by the Senate to serve on the Supreme Court, but he died in 1869 before he was sworn in.

Abel Streight, the Union General who was captured by the Confederates, was held in Libby Prison in Richmond, Virginia. After ten months of confinement, he and 107 other Union officers tunneled their way to freedom. He eventually made it back to the North's lines and was later reinstated as an officer. He resigned from the army in March 1865, served four years in the Indiana State Senate, and died in 1892.

Henry Symonds, the Union Quartermaster, retired from the army in 1865 and worked in New Orleans until 1870, when he moved to Sing Sing, New York, and became a teacher. He published his memoirs in 1888 and lived another twelve years before his death in 1900.

Cadwallader C. Washburn, the Union administrator of Memphis, left the Union army in May 1865, and moved to Minneapolis, where he constructed a large flour mill. He died in 1882, but the company he founded later became General Mills.

Henry Wirz, commandant of the Confederate prisoner-of-war camp at Anderson, Georgia, was court-martialed for murder and conspiracy. He was charged with a number of crimes, including failing to furnish enough food to sustain life. Former prisoners testified that he had committed specific acts of violence against inmates. Wirz presented letters in which he had begged officials in Richmond for food and supplies. Wirz was convicted: he was the only Confederate official to be hanged for his conduct during the war.

Notes

Abbreviations in Endnotes:

O.R.: *The War of the Rebellion of the Official Records of the Union and Confederate Armies*

O.R.N.: *Official Records of the Union and Confederate Navies in the War of the Rebellion*

PROLOGUE

1. Peter D. McClelland, *Sowing Modernity: America's First Agricultural Revolution* (Ithaca and London: Cornell University Press, 1997), 219; Wayne D. Rasmussen, "The Civil War: A Catalyst of Agricultural Revolution," *Agricultural History* 39 (October 1965): 194.

2. William T. Hutchinson, *Cyrus Hall McCormick Seed-Time, 1809–1856*, 2 vols. (New York: The Century Co., 1930), 1, 71.

3. Siegfried Giedion, *Mechanization Takes Command: A Contribution to Anonymous History* (New York: W. W. Norton & Co., 1969), 140.

4. Emerson David Fite, *Social and Industrial Conditions in the North during the Civil War* (New York: Peter Smith, 1930), 1; Barton H. Wise, "Invention and Industry at the South," *The Popular Science Monthly* 44 (1894): 383; James Grant Wilson and John Fiske, eds., *Appletons' Cyclopedia of American Biography*, rev. ed. (New York: D. Appleton and Co., 1900), 4, 95.

5. Arnold Tilden, *The Legislation of the Civil-War Period* (Los Angeles: The University of Southern California Press, 1937), 47.

6. Arnold Tilden, *The Legislation of the Civil-War Period* (Los Angeles: The University of Southern California Press, 1937), 46; T. E. Nichols, Jr., "Transportation and Regional Development in Agriculture," *American Journal of Agricultural Economics* 51 (December 1969): 1457.

7. J. D. B. DeBow, *The Industrial Resources of the Southern and Western States*, 3 vols. (New Orleans: The Office of De Bow's Review, 1852), 2, 484.

8. Louis Bernard Schmidt, "Internal Commerce and the Development of National Economy before 1860," *Journal of Political Economy* 47 (December 1939): 798–801.

9. John S. Otto, *Southern Agriculture during the Civil War Era, 1860–1880* (Westport, CT: Greenwood Press, 1994), 16–17.

10. *Southern Cultivator* 19 (January 1861): 15; "The North American Union," *The Rambler*, New Series 4 (November 1860): 431; "Mr. Dixon's Speech," *Louisville Journal*, April 21, 1861, Frank Moore, *The Rebellion Record*, 8 vols. (New York: G. P. Putnam, 1861), vol. 1, 75; "The North and the South, Their Commercial Relations," *New York Times*, December 11, 1861, p. 4; William Cobden to Charles Sumner, December 12, 1861, in J. A. Hobson, *Richard Cobden: The International Man* (New York: Henry Holt and Co., 1919), 356.

1. Lincoln's Humbug of a Blockade

1. G. W. Snyder to Robert Anderson, April 4, 1861, and Robert Anderson to L. Thomas, April 5, 1861, *O.R.*, ser. 1, vol. 1, 241–42.

2. "The Bombardment of Sumter; Detailed and Graphic Description of the Scene," *The New York Times*, May 5, 1861, 1; Samuel Wylie Crawford, *The History of the Fall of Fort Sumpter* (New York: [F. P. Harper], 1896), 434–48.

3. *New York Herald*, April 28, 1861, 4; *Charleston Mercury*, February 17, 1862, 1; *Louisville Daily Journal*, March 14, 1863.

4. Frank Moore, *The Rebellion Record*, 8 vols. (New York: G. P. Putnam, 1861), 1, 71, 78.

5. Mary Elizabeth Massey, "The Food and Drink Shortage on the Confederate Homefront," *North Carolina Historical Review* 26 (April 1949): 318–21, 333; John Christopher Schwab, *The Confederate States of America, 1861–1865* (New York: C. Scribner's Sons, 1901), 237.

6. Edward A. Pollard, *The Life of Jefferson Davis, with a Secret History of the Confederacy* (Philadelphia: National Publishing Co., 1869), 169; Paul W. Gates, *Agriculture and the Civil War* (New York: Alfred A. Knopf, 1965), 28; S. R. Cockrill to Walker, June 21, 1861, *O.R.*, ser. 1, vol. 52, pt. 2, 114.

7. *Charleston Mercury*, December 10, 1861; February 29, 1964; March 23, 1864; *New York Herald*, June 16, 1862, March 3, 1862, April 13, 1862; *Christian Recorder*, September 28, 1861.

8. J. D. Gladney to Jefferson Davis, August 6, 1862, *O.R.*, ser. 4, vol. 2, 39.

9. James A. Seddon to S. G. French, February 20, 1863, as in *The War of the Rebellion: A Compilation of the Official Records of the Union and Confederate Armies* (Washington: Government Printing Office, 1898), Series 1, Vol. 51, part 2, 682; John Christopher Schwab, *The Confederate States of America, 1861–1865* (New York: C. Scribner's Sons, 1901), 276.

10. Arthur W. Bergeron, ed., *The Civil War in Louisiana* (Lafayette, LA: Center for Louisiana Studies, University of Louisiana at Lafayette, 2002), 92.

11. Mansfield Lovell, "Testimony in the Proceedings of Court of Inquiry," April 4, 1863, *O.R.*, ser. 1, vol. 6, 561.

12. *Harper's Weekly* 6 (June 14, 1862): 380, 383.

13. Robert F. Pace, "'It was Bedlam Let Loose': The Louisiana Sugar Country and the Civil War," *Louisiana History* 39 (Autumn 1998): 391–92, 396–98.

14. Leon F. Litwack, *Been in the Storm so Long: The Aftermath of Slavery* (New York: Alfred A. Knopf, 1979), 51–59; Louis S. Gerteis, *From Contraband to Freedom: Federal Policy toward Southern Blacks* (Westport, CT: Greenwood Press, 1973), 191–93; John S. Otto, *Southern Agriculture during the Civil War Era, 1860–1880* (Westport, CT: Greenwood Press, 1994), 34–35.

15. David G. Surdam, "King Cotton: Monarch or Pretender? The State of the Market for Raw Cotton on the Eve of the American Civil War," *Economic History Review* 51 (1998): 122; *Christian Recorder*, December 14, 1861. *Christian Recorder*, December 20, 1862; *Charleston Mercury*, January 28, 1863, *Charleston Mercury*, February 17, 1863; Lynda Lasswell Crist and Mary Seaton Dix, eds., *The Papers of Jefferson Davis* (Baton Rouge: Louisiana State University Press, 1971), 7, 23.

16. Frank Lawrence Owsley [Harriet Chappell Owsley, ed.], *King Cotton Diplomacy: Foreign Relations of the Confederate States of America*, 2nd ed. (Chicago: The University of Chicago Press, 1959), 24–30; John Christopher Schwab, *The Confederate States of America, 1861–1865* (New York: C. Scribner's Sons, 1901), 251.

17. Ludwell H. Johnson, "Trading with the Union: The Evolution of Confederate Policy," *Virginia Magazine of History and Biography* 78 (July 1970): 535–37, 539.

18. Charles H. Wesley, *The Collapse of the Confederacy* (Columbia: University of South Carolina Press, 2001), 2; Stanley Lebergott, "Why the South Lost: Commercial Purpose in the Confederacy, 1861–1865," *Journal of American History* 70 (June 1983): 66.

19. Richard I. Lester, *Confederate Finance and Purchasing in Great Britain* (Charlottesville: University Press of Virginia, 1975), 150.

20. John Christopher Schwab, *The Confederate States of America, 1861–1865* (New York: C. Scribner's Sons, 1901), 238–39; quote from Ella Lonn, *Salt as a Factor in the Confederacy* (Tuscaloosa: University of Alabama Press, 1965), 35.

21. *Daily Vicksburg Whig*, November 15, 1861.

22. George Goldthwaite to Duff C. Green, March 20, 1862, *O.R.*, ser. 4, vol. 1, 1010; *Southern Confederacy*, May 13, 1862, p. 2; Paul W. Gates, *Agriculture and the Civil War* (New York: Alfred A. Knopf, 1965), 38–39; Jerrold Northrop Moore, *Confederate Commissary General; Lucius Bellinger Northrop and the Subsistence Bureau of the Southern Army* (Shippensburg, PA: White Mane Publishing Co., 1996), 171; David Williams, *Bitterly Divided: The South's Inner Civil War* (New York: New Press, 2008), 90.

23. John Christopher Schwab, *The Confederate States of America, 1861–1865* (New York: Charles Scribner's Sons, 1901), 267–68; Ella Lonn, *Salt as a Factor in the Confederacy* (Tuscaloosa: University of Alabama Press, 1965), 26; Paul W. Gates, *Agriculture and the Civil War* (New York: Alfred A. Knopf, 1965), 122; Robert A. Taylor, *Rebel Storehouse: Florida's Contribution to the Confederacy* (Tuscaloosa: University of Alabama, 2003), 19, 44–65.

24. Ella Lonn, *Salt as a Factor in the Confederacy* (Tuscaloosa: University of Alabama Press, 1965), 29–30; Jerrold Northrop Moore, *Confederate Commissary General: Lucius Bellinger Northrop and the Subsistence Bureau of the Southern Army* (Shippensburg, PA: White Mane Publishing Co., 1996), 161.

25. Paul W. Gates, *Agriculture and the Civil War* (New York: Alfred A. Knopf, 1965), 122; Robert A. Taylor, *Rebel Storehouse: Florida's Contribution to the Confederacy* (Tuscaloosa: University of Alabama, 2003), 19, 44–65.

26. *Confederate Receipt Book* (Richmond: West & Johnson, 1863), 16–17; "Salt from Smoke Houses," *Southern Cultivator* 20 (March-April 1862): 71; Varina Davis, *Jefferson Davis, Ex-President of the Confederate States of America,* 2 vols. (New York: Belford Co., 1890), 2, 588.

27. F. D. Conrad to members of the Confederate Congress, October 5, 1863, *O.R.*, ser. 4, vol. 2, 854–5; Ella Lonn, *Salt as a Factor in the Confederacy* (Tuscaloosa: University of Alabama Press, 1965), 43–45.

28. Wm. M. Wadley to S. Cooper, December 31, 1862, *O.R.*, ser. 4, vol. 2, 272; Jerrold Northrop Moore, *Confederate Commissary General: Lucius Bellinger Northrop and the Subsistence Bureau of the Southern Army* (Shippensburg, PA: White Mane Publishing Co., 1996), 191–92; *Richmond Sentinel*, April 14, 1863, as reprinted in the *New York Herald*, April 15, 1863, 3.

29. George Edgar Turner, *Victory Rode the Rails: The Strategic Place of the Railroads in the Civil War* (Lincoln: University of Nebraska Press, 1992), 267; Charles W. Ramsdell, "The Confederate Government and the Railroads," *American Historical Review* 22 (July 1917): 795, 809–10.

30. Louis Bernard Schmidt, "The Internal Grain Trade of the United States, 1850–1860," *Iowa Journal of History and Politics* 18 (January 1920): 94–124; Emerson David Fite, *Social and Industrial Conditions in the North During the Civil War*

(New York: Peter Smith, 1930), Chapter 1; Louis Bernard Schmidt, "Internal Commerce and the Development of the National Economy before 1860," *Journal of Political Economy* 47 (December 1939): 804; Paul W. Gates, *Agriculture and the Civil War* (New York: Alfred A. Knopf, 1965), 6–7.

31. Charles W. Ramsdell, "General Robert E. Lee's Horse Supply, 1862–1865," *American Historical Review* 35 (July 1930): 763.

32. John Christopher Schwab, *The Confederate States of America, 1861–1865* (New York: C. Scribner's Sons, 1901), 242; Horace Herndon Cunningham, *Doctors in Gray: The Confederate Medical Service* (Baton Rouge: Louisiana State University Press, 1958), 206; Richard D. Goff, *Confederate Supply* (Durham: Duke University Press, 1969), 55.

2. SCARCITY AND HUNGER

1. Robert E. Lee to Jefferson Davis, January 23, 1863, *O.R.*, ser. 1, vol. 21, 1110; Robert E. Lee to James Seddon, January 26, 1863, *O.R.*, ser. 1, vol. 25, pt. 2, 597–98.

2. Charles W. Ramsdell, "General Robert E. Lee's Horse Supply, 1862–1865," *American Historical Review* 35 (July 1930): 761; Ernest B. Furgurson, *Ashes of Glory: Richmond at War* (New York: Vintage Civil War Library, 1996), 192; Douglas Freeman, *R. E. Lee: A Biography,* 4 vols. (New York: C. Scribner's Sons, 1934–35), vols. 3, 6.

3. Jerrold Northrop Moore, *Confederate Commissary General: Lucius Bellinger Northrop and the Subsistence Bureau of the Southern Army* (Shippensburg, PA: White Mane Publishing Co., 1996), 85–93.

4. Jerrold Northrop Moore, *Confederate Commissary General: Lucius Bellinger Northrop and the Subsistence Bureau of the Southern Army* (Shippensburg, PA: White Mane Publishing Co., 1996), 99, 101, 107; George Cary Eggleston, "A Rebel's Recollections II," *Atlantic Magazine* 34 (July 1874): 98; G. T Beauregard to William Miles, July 29, 1861, as in Alfred Roman, *The Military Operations of General Beauregard in the War between the States, 1861 to 1865,* 2 vols. (New York: Harper & Brothers, 1884), 1, 124; G. T. Beauregard to Jefferson Davis, July 29, 1861, *O.R.* ser. 1, vol. 51, pt. 2, 204; G. T Beauregard to Jefferson Davis, August 10, 1861, *O.R.* ser. 1, vol. 51, pt. 2, 1071.

5. Richard D. Goff, *Confederate Supply* (Durham, NC: Duke University Press, 1969), 23.

6. This figure is based on "uninflated" dollars. See John Christopher Schwab, *The Confederate States of America, 1861–1865* (New York: C. Scribner's Sons, 1901), 240; Stanley Lebergott, "Why the South Lost: Commercial Purpose in the Confederacy, 1861–1865," *Journal of American History* 70 (June 1983): 67.

7. Stanley Lebergott, "Why the South Lost: Commercial Purpose in the Confederacy, 1861–1865," *Journal of American History* 70 (June 1983): 62; Jefferson Davis to Joseph E Brown, January 27, 1863, *O.R.*, ser. 4, vol. 2, 376.

8. Frank G. Ruffin to L. B. Northrop, January 1862, *O.R.*, ser. 4, vol. 1, 874.

9. Jerrold Northrop Moore, *Confederate Commissary General: Lucius Bellinger Northrop and the Subsistence Bureau of the Southern Army* (Shippensburg, PA: White Mane Publishing Co., 1996), 59; F. G. Ruffin, "A Chapter in Confederate History," *North American Review* 134 (January 1882): 98–99; L. B. Northrop, as in Edward A. Pollard, *The Lost Cause: A New Southern History of the War of the Confederates,* new and enlarged ed. (New York: E. B. Treat, 1890), 484.

10. L. B. Northrop, "A Comparative View of Commissary Supplies," *O.R.*, ser. 4, vol. 2, 193; R. E. Lee to James A. Seddon, January 12, 1863, *O.R.*, ser. 1, vol. 51, pt. 1, 669; L. B. Northrop, "Subsistence Report," May 4, 1864, *O.R.*, ser. 4, vol. 3, 379; Richard D. Goff, *Confederate Supply* (Durham, NC: Duke University Press, 1969), 22.

11. *Southern Cultivator* 20 (January 1862): 1, as quoted in E. Merton Coulter, "The Movement for Agricultural Reorganization in the Cotton South During the Civil War," *Agricultural History* 1 (January 1927): 10; *Columbus Sun*, as quoted in Paul W. Gates, *Agriculture and the Civil War* (New York: Alfred A. Knopf, 1965), 16; Kenneth Coleman, *Confederate Athens* (Athens: University of Georgia Press, 1968), 92.

12. Samuel Phillips Day, *Down South; Or, an Englishman's Experience at the Seat of the American War,* 2 vols. (London: Hurat and Blackett, 1862), 1, 267.

13. S. B. Buckner, August 11, 1862, *O.R.*, ser. 1, vol. 7, 334; Macon *Telegraph*, as cited in the *New York Herald*, April 21, 1862; L. B. Northrop, April 27, 1862, *O.R.*, ser. 1, vol. 30, 553; L. B. Northrop, "Circular Subsistence Department," April 28, 1862, *O.R.*, ser. 4, vol. 2, 414.

14. *The New York Times*, May 2, 1862, 1.

15. Jerrold Northrop Moore, *Confederate Commissary General: Lucius Bellinger Northrop and the Subsistence Bureau of the Southern Army* (Shippensburg, PA: White Mane Publishing Co., 1996), 127–31; Joseph E. Johnston, *Narrative of Military Operations during the Late War between the States* (New York: D. Appleton and Co., 1874), 98, 103; Steven H. Newton, *Joseph E. Johnston and the Defense of Richmond* (Lawrence: University Press of Kansas, 1998), 53.

16. Jerrold Northrop Moore, *Confederate Commissary General: Lucius Bellinger Northrop and the Subsistence Bureau of the Southern Army* (Shippensburg, PA: White Mane Publishing Co., 1996), 147; quote in Bell Irvin Wiley, *The Life of Johnny Reb: the Common Soldier of the Union* (Baton Rouge: Louisiana State University Press, 1978), 92.

17. Bell Irvin Wiley, *The Life of Johnny Reb: the Common Soldier of the Union* (Baton Rouge: Louisiana State University Press, 1978), 92; Charles W. Ramsdell, "General Robert E. Lee's Horse Supply, 1862–1865," *American Historical Review* 35 (July 1930): 759; Richard D. Goff, *Confederate Supply* (Durham, NC: Duke University Press, 1969), 77–78.

18. Richard D. Goff, *Confederate Supply* (Durham, NC: Duke University Press, 1969), 56–58.

19. Paul W. Gates, *Agriculture and the Civil War* (New York: Alfred A. Knopf, 1965), 26.

20. L. B. Northrop to George W. Randolph, November 3, 1862, *O.R.*, ser. 4, vol. 2, pt. 1, 157–58; Joseph E. Brown to James A. Seddon, February 23, 1863, *O.R.*, ser. 4, vol. 2, pt. 1, 413; Paul W. Gates, *Agriculture and the Civil War* (New York: Alfred A. Knopf, 1965), 119–20; F. G. Ruffin, "A Chapter in Confederate History," *North American Review* 134 (January 1882): 101.

21. Jerrold Northrop Moore, *Confederate Commissary General: Lucius Bellinger Northrop and the Subsistence Bureau of the Southern Army* (Shippensburg, PA: White Mane Publishing Co., 1996), 14; Mary Boykin Miller Chesnut [Isabella D. Martin and Myrta Lockett Avary, eds.], *A Diary from Dixie* (New York: D. Appleton and Co., 1905), 97.

22. George W. Randolph to Jefferson Davis, October 30, 1862, *O.R.*, ser. 4, vol. 2, 151.

23. James A. Seddon to Jefferson Davis, January 3, 1863, *O.R.*, ser. 4, vol. 2, 292; *Daily Southern Crisis*, February 23, 1863, as quoted in Paul W. Gates, *Agriculture and the Civil War* (New York: Alfred A. Knopf, 1965), 120.

24. Charles W. Ramsdell, "Materials for Research in the Agricultural History of the Confederacy," *Agricultural History* 4 (January 1930): 18; Fredonia L. Davis to James L. Davis, June 20, 1862, as quoted in Wayne D. Rasmussen, "The Civil War: A Catalyst of Agricultural Revolution," *Agricultural History* 39 (October 1965): 188.

25. E. Merton Coulter, *The Confederate States of America, 1861–1865* (Baton Rouge: Louisiana State University Press, 1950), 204; Clement Eaton, *A History of the Southern Confederacy* (New York: Free Press 1965), 235–36; John S. Otto, *Southern Agriculture during the Civil War Era, 1860–1880* (Westport, CT: Greenwood Press, 1994), 34.

26. Z. B. Vance's message to the North Carolina General Assembly, November 17, 1862, *O.R.*, ser. 4, vol. 2, pt. 1, 181.

27. *Richmond Dispatch*, February 13, 1863; Jefferson Davis, "Address to the People of the Confederate States," April 10, 1865, *O.R.*, ser. 4, vol. 2, pt. 1, 477; *Richmond Dispatch*, April 15, 1863, as reprinted in *The New York Times*, April 26,

1863, p. 1; Clement Clay, as quoted in Virginia Clay-Clopton [Ada Sterling, ed.], *A Belle of the Fifties: Memoirs of Mrs. Clay of Alabama* (New York: Doubleday, Page & Co., 1904), 194.

28. John Christopher Schwab, *The Confederate States of America, 1861–1865* (New York: C. Scribner's Sons, 1901), 232–33; John B. Jones, *A Rebel War Clerk's Diary,* 2 vols. (Philadelphia: Lippincott, 1866), 1, 261, 288; vols. 2, 3.

29. Mark Thornton and Robert B. Ekelund, Jr., *Tariffs, Blockades, and Inflation: The Economics of the Civil War* (Wilmington, DE: Scholarly Resources, Inc., 2004), 47–48.

30. John B. Jones, *A Rebel War Clerk's Diary at the Confederate States Capital,* 2 vols. (Philadelphia: Lippincott, 1866), vol. 1, 240, 261.

31. J. P. Benjamin to Joseph E. Johnston, December 27, 1861, *O.R.,* ser. 1, vol. 5, 1011; Joseph E. Brown to Jefferson Davis, February 18, 1863, *O.R.,* ser. 4, vol. 2, 404–5.

32. Stanley Lebergott, "Why the South Lost: Commercial Purpose in the Confederacy, 1861–1865," *Journal of American History* 70 (June 1983): 70–71.

33. R. E. Lee to J. L. Kemper, January 29, 1864, *O.R.,* ser. 1, vol. 33, 1127–28.

34. Richard D. Goff, *Confederate Supply* (Durham, NC: Duke University Press, 1969), 97–101.

35. Stanley Lebergott, "Why the South Lost: Commercial Purpose in the Confederacy, 1861–1865," *Journal of American History* 70 (June 1983): 74.

36. "An Act to Lay Taxes for the Common Defense and Carry on the Government of the Confederate States," passed April 24, 1863, *O.R.,* (1902), ser. 4, vol. 3, 140; Richard D. Goff, *Confederate Supply* (Durham, NC: Duke University Press, 1969), 89–90.

37. R. E. Lee to W. E. Jones, April 7, 1863, *O.R.,* ser. 1, vol. 25, pt. 2, 710–11; R. E. Lee to James A. Seddon, March 27, 1863, *O.R.,* ser. 1, vol. 25, pt. 2, 687.

38. R. E. Lee to James A. Seddon, March 27, 1863, *O.R.,* ser. 1, vol. 25, pt. 2, 687; Ella Lonn, *Desertion during the Civil War* (Lincoln: University of Nebraska Press, 1998), 13–14.

39. Z. B. Vance to J. A. Seddon, February 23, 1863, *O.R.,* ser. 4, vol. 2, 413; Richard D. Goff, *Confederate Supply* (Durham, NC: Duke University Press, 1969), 111–18.

40. R. E. Lee to James A. Seddon, March 27, 1863, *O.R.,* ser. 1, vol. 25, pt. 2, 687.

41. R. E. Lee to James A. Seddon, April 17, 1863, *O.R.,* ser. 1, vol. 25, pt. 2, 730.

42. J. F. H. Claiborne, as quoted in Robert F. Pace, " 'It Was Bedlam Let Loose': The Louisiana Sugar Country and the Civil War," *Louisiana History* 39 (Autumn 1998): 398; Paul W. Gates, *Agriculture and the Civil War* (New York: Al-

fred A. Knopf, 1965), 119; Richard D. Goff, *Confederate Supply* (Durham, NC: Duke University Press, 1969), 83–84; P. G. T. Beauregard to C. J. Villere, February 9, 1863, *O.R.*, ser. 4, vol. 2, 391; Z. B. Vance to J. A. Seddon, February 28, 1863, *O.R.*, ser. 4, vol. 2, 413; Jonathan Worth to J. J. Jackson, January 5, 1863, in J. G. de Roulhac Hamilton, ed., *The Correspondence of Jonathan Worth* 2 vols. (Raleigh: North Carolina Historical Commission, 1909), vol. 1, 222; J. A. Wroth to Jonathan Worth, January 23, 1863, J. G. de Roulhac Hamilton, ed., *The Correspondence of Jonathan Worth* 2 vols. (Raleigh: North Carolina Historical Commission, 1909), 1, 225.

3. BREAD RIOTS

1. Paul W. Gates, *Agriculture and the Civil War* (New York: Alfred A. Knopf, 1965), 38–39; Victoria Bynum, "'War within a War': Women's Participation in the Revolt of the North Carolina Piedmont," *Frontiers* 9 (1987), 44; Jerrold Northrop Moore, *Confederate Commissary General: Lucius Bellinger Northrop and the Subsistence Bureau of the Southern Army* (Shippensburg, PA: White Mane Publishing Co., 1996), 170–71.

2. *Charleston Mercury,* March 23, 1863, p. 1; *New York Herald*, April 13, 1863, 4.

3. *Charleston Mercury,* March 25, 1863, p. 2; *Louisville Daily Journal*, April 15, 1863, 3; Paul W. Gates, *Agriculture and the Civil War* (New York: Alfred A. Knopf, 1965), 39; W. Buck Yearns and John G. Barrett, ed., *North Carolina Civil War Documentary* (Chapel Hill: University of North Carolina Press, 1980), 94; Victoria Bynum, "'War within a War': Women's Participation in the Revolt of the North Carolina Piedmont," *Frontiers* 9 (1987), 44; "A Female Raid," *Carolina Watchman*, March 26, 1863; Christopher A. Graham, "Women's Revolt in Rowan County," *Columbiad* 3 (Spring 1999): 131–47; *Richmond Sentinel*, April 7, 1863; *Raleigh Standard*, March 25, 1863, as reprinted in "Bread Riot in Raleigh, N.C.," *New York Times*, April 19, 1863, 1, and *New York Herald*, April 13, 1863, p. 4.

4. "A Female Raid," *Carolina Watchman*, March 26, 1863; and Michael Brown to Governor Vance, March 16, 1863, as at North Carolina Digital History, http://www.learnnc.org/lp/editions/nchist-civilwar/4187, accessed December 13, 2009.

5. Greensborough *Patriot,* February 19, 1863, and March 12, 1863, as cited in Victoria Bynum, "'War within a War': Women's Participation in the Revolt of the North Carolina Piedmont," *Frontiers* 9 (1987), 47; Victoria E. Bynum, *Unruly Women: The Politics of Social and Sexual Control in the Old South* (Chapel Hill: University of North Carolina Press, 1992), 145; *Baltimore American*, April 7, 1863, as reprinted in The *New York Times*, April 10, 1863, 1; *New York Herald,* April 10, 1863, 4; *Boston Herald*, April 10, 1863, 4; *Louisville Daily Journal*,

April 10, 1863, 3; Augusta *Chronicle,* April 4, 1863; *Southern Confederacy,* April 16, 1863, 2; Geo. U. Morris to Theodorus Bailey, May 1, 1863, *O.R.*, ser. 1, vol. 17, 432; *Raleigh Standard,* March 25, 1863, as reprinted in "Bread Riot in Raleigh, N.C.," *New York Times,* April 19, 1863, p. 1.

6. Thomas C. DeLeon, *Four Years in the Rebel Capitals: An Inside View of Life in the Southern Confederacy* (Mobile, AL: Gossip Print Co., 1890), 86.

7. City Council Minutes, February 23, 1863, Emory M. Thomas, *The Confederate State of Richmond: A Biography of the Capital* (Baton Rouge: Louisiana State University Press, 1998), 113; *Richmond Whig,* February 16, 1863, as quoted in Ernest B. Furgurson, *Ashes of Glory: Richmond at War* (New York: Vintage Civil War Library, 1996), 192.

8. *New York Herald,* April 11, 1863, as reprinted in Frank Moore [Edward Everett, ed.], *The Rebellion Record,* 8 vols. (New York: G. P. Putnam, 1863), 6, 523; John B. Jones, *A Rebel War Clerk's Diary at the Confederate States Capital,* 2 vols. (Philadelphia: Lippincott, 1866), 1, 277.

9. John B. Jones, *A Rebel War Clerk's Diary at the Confederate States Capital,* 2 vols. (Philadelphia: Lippincott, 1866), 1, 277–80; John Landstreet to his wife, March 22, 1863, as quoted in William Blair, *Virginia's Private War: Feeding Body and Soul in the Confederacy, 1861–1865* (New York: Oxford University Press, 1998), 73.

10. Edward Younger, ed., *Inside the Confederate Government; The Diary of Robert Garlick Hill Kean* (New York: Oxford University Press, 1957), 41; *Southern Illustrated News,* March 14, 1863, as cited in David J. Eicher, *The Longest Night: A Military History of the Civil War* (New York: Simon & Schuster, 2001), 449.

11. Clement Clay, as quoted in Virginia Clay-Clopton [Ada Sterling, ed.], *A Belle of the Fifties: Memoirs of Mrs. Clay of Alabama* (New York: Doubleday, Page & Co., 1904), 194; "Diary of Edmund Ruffin," as quoted in Charles W. Ramsdell, "General Robert E. Lee's Horse Supply, 1862–1865," *American Historical Review* 35 (July 1930): 762; Richard D. Goff, *Confederate Supply* (Durham: Duke University Press, 1969), 87; John B. Jones, *A Rebel War Clerk's Diary at the Confederate States Capital,* 2 vols. (Philadelphia: Lippincott, 1866), 1, 282; Edward Younger, ed., *Inside the Confederate Government; The Diary of Robert Garlick Hill Kean* (New York: Oxford University Press, 1957), 47.

12. John B. Jones, *A Rebel War Clerk's Diary at the Confederate States Capital,* 2 vols. (Philadelphia: Lippincott, 1866), 2, 280.

13. Sara Agnes Rice Pryor, *Reminiscences of Peace and War* (New York: Macmillan Co., 1904), 238.

14. Hal Tutwiler to Nettie, April 3, 1863, Stephen E. Ambrose, ed., "The Bread Riots in Richmond," *Virginia Magazine of History and Biography* 71 (April 1963): 203.

15. Judith White Brockenbrough McGuire, *Diary of a Southern Refugee,* 3rd ed. (Richmond: J. W. Randolph, 1889), 202–3; Richmond City Council Minutes, April 12–13, 1863, as cited in Emory M. Thomas, *The Confederate State of Richmond: A Biography of the Capital* (Baton Rouge: Louisiana State University Press, 1998), 120.

16. *Richmond Sentinel,* April 7, 1863, and the *Richmond Whig,* April 8, 1863, as quoted in The *New York Times,* April 19, 1863, 1; *New York Herald,* April 11, 1863, as reprinted in Frank Moore [Edward Everett, ed.], *The Rebellion Record,* 8 vols. (New York: G. P. Putnam, 1863), 6, 523–24; John B. Jones, *A Rebel War Clerk's Diary at the Confederate States Capital,* 2 vols. (Philadelphia: Lippincott, 1866), 1, 284–86; Sarah Woolfolk Wiggins, ed., *The Journals of Josiah Gorgas, 1857–1878* (Tuscaloosa: University of Alabama Press, 1995), 59; E. D. Keys to H. W. Halleck, April 9, 1863, *O.R.,* ser. 1, vol. 51, pt. 1, 1002.

17. Varina Davis, *Jefferson Davis, Ex-President of the Confederate States of America,* 2 vols. (New York: Belford Co., 1890), 2, 375; *Richmond Whig,* May 10, 1878; The *New York Times,* April 30, 1889, 10; *Richmond Dispatch,* December 30, 1888; John B. Jones, *A Rebel War Clerk's Diary at the Confederate States Capital,* 2 vols. (Philadelphia: Lippincott, 1866), 1, 285; Sara Agnes Rice Pryor, *Reminiscences of Peace and War* (New York: Macmillan Co., 1904), 239; *New York Herald,* April 11, 1863, as reprinted in Frank Moore [Edward Everett, ed.], *The Rebellion Record,* 8 vols. (New York: G. P. Putnam, 1863), 6, 523; Michael B. Chesson, "Harlots or Heroines? A New Look at the Richmond Bread Riot," *Virginia Magazine of History and Biography* 92 (April 1984): 139.

18. Michael B. Chesson, "Harlots or Heroines? A New Look at the Richmond Bread Riot," *Virginia Magazine of History and Biography,* 92 (April 1984): 139.

19. Judith White Brockenbrough McGuire, *Diary of a Southern Refugee,* 3rd ed. (Richmond: J. W. Randolph, 1889), 203–4; Arnold Elzey to James L. Longstreet, April 6, 1863, *O.R.,* ser. 1, vol. 18, 965.

20. *Richmond Sentinel,* April 7, 1863, as republished in The *New York Times,* April 19, 1863, 1; John M. Daniel and Peter Bridges, *Pen of Fire: John Moncure Daniel* (Kent, OH: Kent State University Press, 2002), 201; Jno. Winters to the President of the Telegraph Company, April 2, 1863, and Jno. Winters to the Richmond Press, April 2, 1863, *O.R.,* ser. 1, vol. 18, 958.

21. *Richmond Sentinel,* April 7, 1863; *Clarke County Journal,* April 23, 1863, 2; *Montgomery Weekly Advertiser,* April 15, 1863, 1; "Letter from Richmond," *Memphis Daily Appeal,* April 11, 1863, 1.

22. *Richmond Examiner,* April 4, 1863, as quoted in Michael B. Chesson, "Harlots or Heroines? A New Look at the Richmond Bread Riot," *Virginia Magazine of History and Biography,* 92 (April 1984): 132; *Southern Confederacy* [Atlanta, Ga],

April 16, 1863, p. 2; *Montgomery Weekly Advertiser*, April 15, 1863, 1; John B. Jones, *A Rebel War Clerk's Diary at the Confederate States Capital* 2 vols. (Philadelphia: Lippincott, 1866), 1, 286.

23. "Letter from Richmond," *Memphis Daily Appeal,* April 11, 1863, 1.

24. "Federal War Policy," *Memphis Daily Appeal,* April 15, 1863, 2; *Charleston Mercury*, June 6, 1863.

25. *Richmond Sentinel*, April 7, 1863, as quoted in The *New York Times*, April 19, 1863, 1; Judith White Brockenbrough McGuire, *Diary of a Southern Refugee,* 3rd ed. (Richmond: J. W. Randolph, 1889), 203.

26. Sallie A. Brock, *Richmond during the War: Four Years of Personal Observation* (New York: G. W. Carlston & Co., 1867), 210.

27. *The New York Times*, April 26, 1863, 1; Geo. U. Morris to Theodorus Bailey, May 1, 1863, *O.R.*, ser. 1, vol. 17, 432.

28. William Howard Russell, *My Diary North and South* (New York: Harper & Brothers, 1863), 108; E. S. Dargan to James A. Seddon, March 29, 1863, *O.R.*, ser. 1, vol. 52, pt. 2, 448; E. S. Dargan, as cited in John B. Jones, *A Rebel War Clerk's Diary at the Confederate States Capital,* 2 vols. (Philadelphia: Lippincott, 1866), 1, 194; "Pemberton's Official Report," dated August 2, 1863, *O.R.*, ser. 1, vol. 24, pt. 1, 289–90; "Do You Mean to Starve Us?" *Mobile Register*, February 4, 1863.

29. *Louisville Daily Journal*, April 25, 1863, 3.

30. The *New-Orleans New Era,* as reprinted in The *New York Times*, April 26, 1863, 1.

31. The *New-Orleans Era*, Sept. 21, 1863, as reprinted in The *New York Times*, October 1, 1863, p. 4; "Rioting in Mobile," The *New York Times*, September 15, 1863, 5; *Harper's Weekly* 7 (October 10, 1863): 643.

32. Kate Cumming, *A Journal of Hospital Life in the Confederate Army of Tennessee* (Louisville, KY: John P. Morton and Co., 1866), 122.

33. *The Appeal*, October 15, 1863, as quoted in Thomas H. Baker, "Refugee Newspaper: The *Memphis Daily Appeal,* 1862–1865," *Journal of Southern History* 29 (August 1963): 341; Paul W. Gates, *Agriculture and the Civil War* (New York: Alfred A. Knopf, 1965), 40; "The 'Riot' in North Carolina," *Raleigh Progress,* as reprinted in *Memphis Daily Appeal*, March 10, 1863, 1.

34. "Female Bread Riot in Savannah," *The New York Times*, May 8, 1864, 8; *New York Herald*, May 8, 1864; *Columbus Gazette*, May 20, 1864, 3; Drew Gilpin Faust, "Altars of Sacrifice: Confederate Women and the Narratives of War," *Journal of American History* 76 (March 1990): 1227; *News,* as reprinted in Howard Zinn and Anthony Arnove, *Voices of a People's History of the United States* (New York: Seven Stories Press, 2004), 208.

35. Paul W. Gates, *Agriculture and the Civil War* (New York: Alfred A. Knopf, 1965), 40; "Interesting Information from a Federal Spy in Secessia," *Boston Herald*, January 14, 1864, 4.

36. *Southern Confederacy*, as reprinted in *Boston Herald*, February 11, 1865, 4, and quoted in U. S. Grant to E. M. Stanton, February 6, 1865, *O.R.*, ser. 1, vol. 46, pt. 2, 475.

37. "Joint Resolution to the Production of Provisions," passed April 4, 1863, *O.R.*, ser. 4, vol. 2, 468; Jefferson Davis, "Address to the People of the Confederate States," April 10, 1863, *O.R.*, ser. 4, vol. 2, pt. 1, 476.

38. *Atlanta Intelligencer*, as reprinted in *The New York Times*, April 26, 1863, 1.

39. General Bragg, as quoted in *Harper's New Monthly Magazine* 28 (December 1863): 128.

40. Ibid.

41. John B. Jones, *A Rebel War Clerk's Diary at the Confederate States Capital*, 2 vols. (Philadelphia: Lippincott, 1866), 1, 240.

42. *Richmond Dispatch*, April 8, 1863; *Richmond Dispatch*, April 13, 1863; William Blair, *Virginia's Private War: Feeding Body and Soul in the Confederacy, 1861–1865* (New York: Oxford University Press, 1998), 75; *Richmond Sentinel*, April 7, 1863; "Bread Destitution," *Richmond Whig*, April 8, 1863; Robert Tomes and Benjamin G. Smith, *The War with the South: A History of the Late Rebellion*, 3 vols. (New York: Virtue & Yorston, 1867), 3, 295; "Richmond City Council Minutes," as cited in Emory M., Thomas *The Confederate State of Richmond: A Biography of the Capital* (Baton Rouge: Louisiana State University Press, 1998), 146.

43. *New York Herald*, April 8, 1863, 1; *New York Herald*, April 11, 1863, as reprinted in Frank Moore [Edward Everett, ed.], *The Rebellion Record*, 8 vols. (New York: G. P. Putnam, 1863), 6, 523.

44. "Famine at the South," *The New York Times*, April 20, 1863, 4; *New York Herald*, September 15, 1863, 3.

45. Cincinnati *Commercial*, as quoted in the *Daily Times* [Leavenworth, Kansas], January 31, 1864, 2; "More Bread Riots," *Village Record*, April 24, 1863, 2; "Food Wanted Instead of Cotton: The Bread Riot in Richmond," *Boston Herald*, April 9, 1863, 2; "The Rebel Cry for Help," *Louisville Daily Journal*, April 15, 1863, 3.

46. "The Food Question Down South," *Harper's Weekly* 7 (May 9, 1863): 304; "Important Revelations from Rebellion," *New York Herald*, May 11, 1863, 4; "Sowing and Reaping," *Frank Leslie's Illustrated Newspaper*, May 23, 1863, 141.

47. J. P. Benjamin to John P. Slidell, March 21, 1863, *O.R.*, ser. 2, vol. 3, 724; J. P. Benjamin to John P. Slidell, March 21, 1863, *O.R.*, ser. 2, vol. 3, 724; John Milton to Jefferson Davis, April 15, 1863, *O.R.*, ser. 4, vol. 2, 487.

4. Abundance and Organization

1. H. C. Symonds, *Report of a Commissary of Subsistence 1861–65* (Sing Sing, NY: The Author, 1888), 85–86.

2. H. C. Symonds, *Report of a Commissary of Subsistence 1861–65* (Sing Sing, NY: The Author, 1888), 147–48.

3. Paul W. Gates, *Agriculture and the Civil War* (New York: Alfred A. Knopf, 1965), 138–39, 146–47, 149–50.

4. Emerson D. Fite, "The Agricultural Development of the West during the Civil War," *The Quarterly Journal of Economics* 20 (February 1906): 271–72; Leo Rogin, *The Introduction of Farm Machinery in Its Relation to the Productivity of Labor in the Agriculture of the United States during the Nineteenth Century* (Berkeley: University of California Press, 1931), 91; Wayne D. Rasmussen, "The Civil War: A Catalyst of Agricultural Revolution," *Agricultural History* 39 (October 1965): 189–90; Paul W. Gates, *Agriculture and the Civil War* (New York: Alfred A. Knopf, 1965), 228–29, 232, 241.

5. D. Eldon Hall, *A Condensed History of the Origination, Rise, Progress and Completion of the "Great Exhibition of the Industry of All Nations," Held in the Crystal Palace, London, during the Summer of the Year 1851* (New York: Redfield, 1852), 77; William T. Hutchinson, *Cyrus Hall McCormick Seed-Time, 1809–1856*, 2 vols. (New York: The Century Co., 1930), 1, 466, 2, 97–98; Paul W. Gates, *Agriculture and the Civil War* (New York: Alfred A. Knopf, 1965), 232–33; Leo Rogin, *The Introduction of Farm Machinery in Its Relation to the Productivity of Labor in the Agriculture of the United States during the Nineteenth Century* (Berkeley: University of California Press, 1931), 91.

6. Paul W. Gates, *Agriculture and the Civil War* (New York: Alfred A. Knopf, 1965), 237. Ralph W. Sanders, *Ultimate John Deere: The History of the Big Green Machines* (Stillwater, MN: Voyageur Press, 2001), 36; Robert Leslie Jones, "The Introduction of Farm Machinery into Ohio Prior to 1865," *Ohio Archaeological and Historical Publications* 58 (January 1949): 13–14; *Annual Report of the Ohio State Board of Agriculture for 1863* (Columbus: C. Scott's Steam Press, 1864), xix–xx, as quoted in Wayne D. Rasmussen, "The Civil War: A Catalyst of Agricultural Revolution," *Agricultural History* 39 (October 1965): 190.

7. Wayne D. Rasmussen, "The Civil War: A Catalyst of Agricultural Revolution," *Agricultural History* 39 (October 1965): 193.

8. Thomas Weber, *The Northern Railroads in the Civil War, 1861–1865* (Bloomington: Indiana University Press, 1999), 138; Rudolf A. Clemen, *The American Livestock and Meat Industry* (New York: Ronald Press Co., 1923), 90–91.

9. Henry Crittenden Morris, *The History of the First National Bank of Chicago* (Chicago: R. R. Donnelley & Sons Co., 1902), 181–82; "Nelson Morris Dead:

Financier and Pioneer Meat Packer Dies at His Home in Chicago," The *New York Times*, August 28, 1907, 7.

10. Emerson D. Fite,"The Agricultural Development of the West during the Civil War," *The Quarterly Journal of Economics* 20 (February 1906): 267; Emerson David Fite, *Social and Industrial Conditions in the North during the Civil War* (New York: Peter Smith, 1930), 78–79; Howard Copeland Hill, "The Development of Chicago as a Center of the Meat Packing Industry," *Mississippi Valley Historical Review* 10 (December 1923): 262.

11. Oscar Edward Anderson, *Refrigeration in America: A History of a New Technology and Its Impact* (Princeton NY: Princeton University Press, 1953), 25, 35; David O. Whitten and Bessie E. Whitten, *The Birth of Big Business in the United States, 1860–1914: Commercial, Extractive, and Industrial Enterprise* (Westport, CT: Praeger, 2006), 167; Paul W. Gates, *Agriculture and the Civil War* (New York: Alfred A. Knopf, 1965), 176.

12. Paul B. Frederic, *Canning Gold: Northern New England's Sweet Corn Industry* (Lanham, MD: University Press of America, 2002), 27; Hugh S. Orem, "Baltimore: Master of the Art of Canning," in Arthur I. Judge, ed., *A History of the Canning Industry: Souvenir of the Seventh Annual Convention of the National Canners' Association and Allied Associations* (Baltimore: The Canning Trade, 1914), 10; Earl Chapin May, *The Canning Clan: A Pageant of Pioneering Americans* (New York: Macmillan Co., 1937), 23.

13. "Startling Exposure of the Milk Trade of New York and Brooklyn," *Frank Leslie's Illustrated Newspaper* 5 (May 8, 1858): 353–54, 359.

14. Joe B. Frantz, "Gail Borden as a Businessman," *Bulletin of the Business Historical Society* 22 (December 1948): 123–33; Joe B. Frantz, *Gail Borden, Dairyman to a Nation* (Norman: University of Oklahoma Press, 1951), 254–55; James J. Nagle, "Borden's Passes Its First Century," *The New York Times*, January 4, 1957, Business & Finance, 35; John Leander Bishop, *A History of American Manufactures from 1608 to 1860,* 3rd ed., 3 vols. (Philadelphia: Edward Young & Co., 1868), 2, 546.

15. Earl Chapin May, *The Canning Clan: A Pageant of Pioneering Americans* (New York: Macmillan Co., 1937), 24, 212–23, 287; Thomas Wilson, *Notes on Canned Goods* (Washington, D.C.: Commissary of General Subsistence, 1870), 1–2.

16. Richard H. Collidge, "Report," September 11, 1862, *O.R.*, ser. 1, vol. 19, pt. 2, 260–62; "Reports of Surg. Thomas A. McParlin, U. S. Army, Medical Director, Including Operations January 14-July 31," June 6, 1864, *O.R.*, ser. 1, vol. 36, pt. 1, 262, 275; Thos. McParlin, November 28, 1864, *O.R.*, ser. 1, vol. 36, pt. 1, 212, 215, 229; James H. Carlton to Christopher Carlson, May 4, 1865, *O.R.*, ser. 1, vol. 48, pt. 2, 317; "Report of Capt. Milton Burns," February 6, 1865, *O.R.*, ser. 1, vol. 48, pt. 1, 94; Charles E. Davis, *Three Years in the Army: the*

Story of the Thirteenth Massachusetts (Boston: Estes and Lauriat, 1894), 117; C. S. Spear, "Report of Fleet Surgeon Wood, U. S. Navy, on the Sanitary Condition of the James River Flotilla. Off Norfolk, Va.," August 2, 1862, *O.R.N.*, ser. 1, vol. 7, 618; Charles E. Davis, *Three Years in the Army: The Story of the Thirteenth Massachusetts* (Boston: Estes and Lauriat, 1894), 117.

17. "An Act to Prohibit the Importation of Luxuries or of Articles Not Necessaries or of Common Use," June 14, 1864, *OR* ser. 4, vol. 3, 486; Wm. W. Orme to Edwin M. Stanton, December 7, 1863, *O.R.*, ser. 2, vol. 6, 6, 660; "List of Articles which Sutlers may be Permitted to Sell to Prisoners of War," *O.R.*, ser. 2, vol. 6, 1014–5; John Hussey, November 7, 1863, *O.R.*, ser. 2, vol. 6, 483.

18. Erna Risch, *Quartermaster Support of the Army 1775–1939* (Washington, Quartermaster Historian's Office, Office of the Quartermaster General, 1962), 383; George B. McClellan, *McClellan's Own Story* (New York: C. L. Webster & Co., 1886), 42–43; Fred Albert Shannon, *The Organization and Administration of the Union Army, 1861–1865,* 2 vols. (Gloucester, MA: Peter Smith, 1965), 1, 54, 70; Mark Snell, "Commissary," David S. Heidler, Jeanne T. Heidler, and David J. Coles, eds., *Encyclopedia of the American Civil War: A Political, Social, and Military History* (New York: W. W. Norton & Co., 2000), 473–74.

19. Fred Albert Shannon, *The Organization and Administration of the Union Army, 1861–1865,* 2 vols. (Gloucester, MA: Peter Smith, 1965), 1, 76, 79–80.

20. Fred Albert Shannon, *The Organization and Administration of the Union Army, 1861–1865,* 2 vols. (Gloucester, MA: Peter Smith, 1965), 1, 73; *Harper's Weekly* 5 (August 17, 1861): 528; Edwin M. Stanton to Andrew Johnson, November 14, 1866, " *O.R.*, ser. 3, vol. 5, 1039.

21. William H. Seward, May 28, 1867, as in Clayton Colman Hall, ed., *Baltimore: Its History and Its People* 3 vols. (New York: Lewis Historical Publishing Co., 1912), 3, 559.

22. *British Sessional Papers* 55 (1865): 40–45, as reprinted in Robert H. Jones, "Long Live the King?" *Agricultural History* 37 (July 1963): 167.

23. *Louisville Daily Journal*, November 2, 1861, 2; "The Immense Present Importation of Corn," *The Economist* 20 (October 25, 1862): 1179–80.

24. Louis B. Schmidt, "The Influence of Wheat and Cotton on Anglo-American Relations during the Civil War," *Iowa Journal of History and Politics* 16 (July 1918): 437.

25. Ephraim Douglass Adams, *Great Britain and the American Civil War,* 2 vols. (New York: Longmans, Green and Co., 1925), vol. 2, 13; Frank Lawrence Owsley [Harriet Chappell Owsley, ed.], *King Cotton Diplomacy: Foreign Relations of the Confederate States of America,* 2nd ed. (Chicago: The University of Chicago Press, 1959), 547–48.

26. Paul W. Gates, *Agriculture and the Civil War* (New York: Alfred A. Knopf, 1965), 225–27; Ethel D. Hoover, "Retail Prices after 1850," in *Trends in the American Economy in the Nineteenth Century* (Princeton: Princeton University Press, 1960), vol. 24, pp. 141–90.

27. There were exceptions to the "well-fed" Union army, such as in Missouri and western Virginia at the beginning of the war. See Ella Lonn, *Desertion during the Civil War* (Lincoln: University of Nebraska Press, 1998), 129–30; Lewis Henry Steiner, *A Sketch of the History, Plan of Organization, and Operations of the U. S. Sanitary Commission* (Philadelphia: J. B. Rodgers, 1866); Emerson David Fite, *Social and Industrial Conditions in the North during the Civil War* (New York: Peter Smith, 1930), 276–78; John William De Forest [James Henry Croushore, ed.], *A Volunteer's Adventures: A Union Captain's Record of the Civil War* (London: Oxford University Press, 1946), 162.

5. GIBRALTAR OF THE MISSISSIPPI

1. Samuel Carter III, *The Final Fortress: The Campaign for Vicksburg 1862–1863* (New York: St. Martin's Press, 1980), 16, 21.

2. "Pemberton's Official Report," dated August 2, 1863, *O.R.*, ser. 1, vol. 24, pt. 1, 280–81.

3. G. T. Beauregard to Jefferson Davis, in *O.R.*, ser. 1, vol. 10, pt. 1, 776; Alfred Roman, *The Military Operations of General Beauregard in the War Between the States, 1861 to 1865*, 2 vols. (New York: Harper & Brothers, 1884), vol. 1, 540; *The Medical Times and Gazette* 2 (July 13, 1867): 51; Charles Janeway Stillé, *History of the United States Sanitary Commission* (New York: Hurd and Houghton, 1868), 322.

4. U. S. Grant, *Personal Memoirs of U. S. Grant*, 2 vols. (New York: C. L. Webster & Co., 1885), 1, 435.

5. U. S. Grant, "Special Field Order No. 21," December 12, 1862, *O.R.*, ser. 1, vol. 17, pt. 2, 405.

6. U. S. Grant, *Personal Memoirs of U. S. Grant*, 2 vols. (New York: C. L. Webster & Co., 1885), 1, 435.

7. Samuel Carter III, *The Final Fortress: The Campaign for Vicksburg 1862–1863* (New York: St. Martin's Press, 1980), 140; W. T. Sherman to John Sherman, January 6, 1863, as in Rachel Sherman Thorndike, ed., *The Sherman Letters* (New York: Charles Scribners' Sons, 1894), 179–80; Bell Irvin Wiley, *The Life of Billy Yank* (Indianapolis, IN: Bobbs-Merrill 1951), 227.

8. Sylvanus Cadwallader, *Three Years with Grant: As Recalled by War Correspondent Sylvanus Cadwallader* (Lincoln: University of Nebraska Press, 1996), 40; U. S.

Grant, *Personal Memoirs of U. S. Grant,* 2 vols. (New York: The Century Co., 1903), 1, 362, 365; Grant to Halleck, December 25, 1862, *O.R.,* ser. 1, vol. 17, pt. 1, 478.

9. Mark A. Weitz, *More Damning than Slaughter: Desertion in the Confederate Army* (Lincoln: University of Nebraska Press, 2005), 66.

10. Robert F. Pace, " 'It was Bedlam Let Loose': The Louisiana Sugar Country and the Civil War," *Louisiana History* 39 (Autumn 1998): 391–92, 396; N. P. Banks to Halleck, May 4, 1863, *O.R.,* ser. 1, vol. 15, 309–10; "Report of Colonel Joseph S. Morgan, Ninetieth New York Infantry, commanding Provisional Brigade," May 28, 1863, *O.R.,* ser. 1, vol. 26, pt. 1, 40–41; Lawrence L. Hewitt and Arthur W. Bergeron, eds., *Louisianians in the Civil War* (Columbia: University of Missouri Press, 2002), 181.

11. James Kendall Hosmer, *The Color-Guard, Being a Corporal's Notes of Military Service in the Nineteenth Army Corps* (Boston, Walker, Wise, and Co., 1864), 103.

12. Walter Lynwood Fleming, *Civil War and Reconstruction in Alabama* (New York: The Columbia University Press, 1905), 75–76; Kate Cumming, *A Journal of Hospital Life in the Confederate Army of Tennessee* (Louisville, Ky: John P. Morton and Co., 1866), 156.

13. Mark Grimsley, *The Hard Hand of War: Union Military Policy toward Southern Civilians 1861–1865* (New York: Cambridge University Press, 1995), 151–52; B. H. Liddell Hart, *Sherman: Soldier, Realist, American* (New York: Da Capo Press, 1993), 183; U. S. Grant to Stephen A. Hurlbut, May 5, 1863, *O.R.,* ser. 1, vol. 24, pt. 3, 275.

14. Jean Edward Smith, *Grant* (New York: Simon & Schuster, 2001), 288.

15. Charles Anderson Dana, *Recollections of the Civil War* (New York: D. Appleton & Co., 1898), 47–48; Charles A. Dana to the War Department, May 4, 1863, *O.R.,* ser. 1, vol. 24, pt. 1, 84.

16. Sylvanus Cadwallader [Benjamin P. Thomas, ed.], *Three Years with Grant: As Recalled by War Correspondent Sylvanus Cadwallader* (Lincoln: University of Nebraska Press, 1996), 72; Isaac Jackson, *"Some of the Boys," The Civil War Letters of Isaac Jackson, 1862–1865* (Carbondale: Southern Illinois University Press, 1960), 90.

17. Byron Cloyd Bryner, *Bugle Echoes: The Story of Illinois 47th* (Springfield, IL: Phillips [*sic*] Bros., 1905), 80.

18. Samuel Carter III, *The Final Fortress: The Campaign for Vicksburg 1862–1863* (New York: St. Martin's Press, 1980), 76.

19. John C. Pemberton, *Pemberton: Defender of Vicksburg* (Chapel Hill: University of North Carolina Press, 1942), 175; "Pemberton's Official Report," dated Au-

gust 2, 1863, as *O.R.*, ser. 1, vol. 24, pt. 1, 271; Samuel Carter III, *The Final Fortress: The Campaign for Vicksburg 1862–1863* (New York: St. Martin's Press, 1980), 140; Ibid., 76.

20. General Edward Tracy, as quoted in Virginia Clay-Clopton [Ada Sterling, ed.], *A Belle of the Fifties: Memoirs of Mrs. Clay of Alabama* (New York: Doubleday, Page & Co., 1904), 193; W. H. Johnson to L. B. Northrop, August 10, 1863, *O.R.*, ser. 1, vol. 24, pt. 3, 1052.

21. John C. Pemberton, *Pemberton: Defender of Vicksburg* (Chapel Hill: University of North Carolina Press, 1942), 173; Emma Balfour, Diary, Mississippi Archives, p. 1, as quoted in Scott Walker, *Hell's Broke Loose in Georgia: Survival in a Civil War Regiment* (Athens: University of Georgia Press, 2005), 85–86.

22. Emma Balfour, Diary, Mississippi Archives, p. 1, as quoted in Scott Walker, *Hell's Broke Loose in Georgia: Survival in a Civil War Regiment* (Athens: University of Georgia Press, 2005), 85–86; Emma Balfour and John C. Pemberton, as quoted in Samuel Carter III, *The Final Fortress: The Campaign for Vicksburg 1862–1863* (New York: St. Martin's Press, 1980), 210.

23. "Special Orders, No. 141," May 26, 1863, *O.R.*, ser. 1, vol. 24, pt. 3, 352; U. S. Grant, *Personal Memoirs of U. S. Grant,* 2 vols. (New York: C. L. Webster & Co., 1885), 1, 454–45; Samuel Carter III, *The Final Fortress: The Campaign for Vicksburg 1862–1863* (New York: St. Martin's Press, 1980), 243.

24. Samuel Carter III, *The Final Fortress: The Campaign for Vicksburg 1862–1863* (New York: St. Martin's Press, 1980), 242.

25. Ibid. William H. Tunnard, *A Southern Record the History of the Third Regiment, Louisiana Infantry* (Baton Rouge: Printed for the Author, 1866), 245; "Pemberton's Official Report," dated August 2, 1863, *O.R.*, ser. 1, vol. 24, pt. 1, 279.

26. Ephraim Anderson, *Memoirs: Historical and Personal, including the Campaigns of the First Missouri Confederate Brigade* (Saint Louis, MD: Times Printing Co., 1868), 337–38.

27. Alexander St. Clair-Abrams, *A Full and Detailed History of the Siege of Vicksburg* (GA: Intelligencer Steam Power Presses, 1863), 67; Ephraim Anderson, *Memoirs: Historical and Personal, including the Campaigns of the First Missouri Confederate Brigade* (Saint Louis, MO: Times Printing Co., 1868), 358; *Vicksburg Citizen*, as quoted in Adolph A. Hoehling, *Vicksburg: 47 Days of Siege* (Englewood Cliffs, NJ: Prentice-Hall, 1969), 252–53.

28. *Chicago Tribune*, July 25, 1863, 3; *Southern Punch*, August 22, 1863.

29. S. H. Lockett, "The Defense of Vicksburg," *Battles and Leaders of the Civil War,* 4 vols. (New York: The Century Co., 1888), 3, 492; George W. Cable, ed., "A

Woman's Diary of the Siege of Vicksburg," *The Century* 30 (September 1885): 774; Mary Elizabeth Massey, "The Food and Drink Shortage on the Confederate Homefront," *North Carolina Historical Review* 26 (April 1949): 313–16; *Vicksburg Citizen*, as quoted in Adolph A. Hoehling, *Vicksburg: 47 Days of Siege* (Englewood Cliffs, NJ: Prentice-Hall, 1969), 252–53.

30. Alexander St. Clair-Abrams, *A Full and Detailed History of the Siege of Vicksburg* (GA: Intelligencer Steam Power Presses, 1863), 67.

31. Ashbel Smith, "Report of Colonel Ashbel Smith, Second Texas Infantry. City of Galveston, Tex. July, 1864," *O.R.*, ser. 1, vol. 24, pt. 2, 392; Captain Claiborne, as quoted in Adolph A. Hoehling, *Vicksburg: 47 Days of Siege* (Englewood Cliffs, NJ: Prentice-Hall, 1969), 264. Claiborne did not die of starvation, but was hit by a Union shell fragment on June 24, 1863, ten days before Vicksburg surrendered.

32. Communication dated June 28, 1863, and signed "Many soldiers," in Richard Wheeler, *Voices of the Civil War* (New York: Meridian, 1976), 346.

33. C. A. Dana letter to E. M. Stanton, Secretary of War, dated June 29, 1863, *O.R.*, ser. 1, vol. 24, pt. 3, page 112.

34. U. S. Grant, *Personal Memoirs of U. S. Grant,* 2 vols. (New York: C. L. Webster & Co., 1885), 1, 444; J. H. Jones, "Rank and File at Vicksburg," as in Franklin L. Reilly, ed., *Publications of the Mississippi Historical Society* (Oxford, MS: Mississippi Historical Society, 1903), 7, 30.

35. J. H. Jones, "Rank and File at Vicksburg," as in Franklin L. Reilly, ed., *Publications of the Mississippi Historical Society* (Oxford, MS: Mississippi Historical Society, 1903), 7, 30.

36. Samuel Carter III, *The Final Fortress: The Campaign for Vicksburg 1862–1863* (New York: St. Martin's Press, 1980), 243; W. H. Tunnard, "Reminiscences of the Third Louisiana (Confederate) Infantry in the Trenches in Front of Logan's Division," in Osborn Hamiline Oldroyd, *A Soldier's Story of the Siege of Vicksburg* (Springfield, IL: For the author, 1885), 142; Ephraim Anderson, *Memoirs: Historical and Personal, including the Campaigns of the First Missouri Confederate Brigade* (Saint Louis, MO: Times Printing Co., 1868), 359; W. H. Tunnard, "Reminiscences of the Third Louisiana (Confederate) Infantry in the Trenches in Front of Logan's Division," in Osborn Hamiline Oldroyd, *A Soldier's Story of the Siege of Vicksburg* (Springfield, IL: For the author, 1885), 142.

37. *The New York Times*, August 17, 1863, 2.

38. U. S. Grant to William T. Sherman, July 13, 1863, *O.R.*, ser. 1, vol. 24, pt. 3, 507.

39. W. T. Sherman to U. S. Grant, July 14, 1863, *O.R.*, ser. 1, vol. 24, pt. 2, 526; Sylvanus Cadwallader [Benjamin P. Thomas, ed.], *Three Years with Grant: As*

Recalled by War Correspondent Sylvanus Cadwallader (Lincoln: University of Nebraska Press, 1996), 124–25.

40. "Pemberton's Official Report," dated August 2, 1863, *O.R.*, ser. 1, vol. 24, pt. 1, 286.

41. Ibid., 292.

42. Sarah Woolfolk Wiggins, ed., *The Journals of Josiah Gorgas, 1857–1878* (Tuscaloosa: University of Alabama Press, 1995), 74–75; Sylvanus Cadwallader [Benjamin P. Thomas, ed.], *Three Years with Grant: As Recalled by War Correspondent Sylvanus Cadwallader* (Lincoln: University of Nebraska Press, 1996), 124–25.

43. Bell Irvin Wiley, *The Life of Johnny Reb: the Common Soldier of the Union* (Baton Rouge: Louisiana State University Press, 1978), 94; Abraham Lincoln to James C. Conklin, August 16, 1863, as in Paul Selby, *Stories and Speeches of Abraham Lincoln* (Chicago: Thompson and Thomas, 1900), 270.

44. L. B. Northrop to Robert E. Lee, July 23, 1863, *O.R.*, ser. 1, vol. 51, pt. 2, 738.

6. TRADERS OR TRAITORS

1. S. Bassett French to L. B. Northrop, August 3, 1863, *O.R.*, ser. 1, vol. 29, pt. 2, 656; L. B. Northrop to Robert E. Lee, July 23, 1863, *O.R.*, ser. 1, vol. 51, pt. 2, 738; Maxwell Woodhall, October 7, 1862, *O.R.N.*, ser. 1, vol. 13, 369; P. W. White to Office of Chief Commissary, November 2, 1863, *New York Herald*, February 20, 1864, *New York Herald*, February 23, 1864, *O.R.*, ser. 1, vol. 35, pt. 2, 392–96.

2. Sarah Woolfolk Wiggins, ed., *The Journals of Josiah Gorgas, 1857–1878* (Tuscaloosa: University of Alabama Press, 1995), 75, 76, 84; *Richmond Examiner*, October 30, 1863; *Richmond Whig*, October 30, 1863, as cited in Emory M. Thomas, *The Confederate State of Richmond: A Biography of the Capital* (Baton Rouge: Louisiana State University Press, 1998), 146.

3. Stanley Lebergott, "Why the South Lost: Commercial Purpose in the Confederacy, 1861–1865," *Journal of American History* 70 (June 1983): 72; Ludwell H. Johnson, "Contraband Trade during the Last Year of the Civil War," *Mississippi Valley Historical Review* 49 (March 1963): 642; Ludwell H. Johnson, "Trading with the Union: The Evolution of Confederate Policy," *Virginia Magazine of History and Biography* 78 (July 1970): 324.

4. Abraham Lincoln, "Proclamation," August 16, 1861, *OR* ser. 1, vol. 6, 90.

5. Ludwell H. Johnson, "Trading with the Union: The Evolution of Confederate Policy," *Virginia Magazine of History and Biography* 78 (July 1970): 308–9; F. G. Ruffin, "A Chapter in Confederate History," *North American Review* 134 (January 1882): 103.

6. Ludwell H. Johnson, "Contraband Trade during the Last Year of the Civil War," *Mississippi Valley Historical Review* 39 (March 1962): 635.

7. E. Merton Coulter, "Effects of Secession upon the Commerce of the Mississippi Valley," *Mississippi Valley Historical Review* 3 (December 1916): 283–98; D. J. G. to the Secretary of War, January 7, 1863, *O.R.*, ser. 4, vol. 2, 302; John Christopher Schwab, *The Confederate States of America, 1861–1865* (New York: C. Scribner's Sons, 1901), 259–60; Michael G. Mahon, *The Shenandoah Valley 1861–1865: The Destruction of the Granary of the Confederacy* (Mechanicsburg, PA: Stackpole Books, 1999), 46; Sallie A. Brock, *Richmond during the War: Four Years of Personal Observation* (New York: G. W. Carlston & Co., 1867), 203–7.

8. Edward Younger, ed., *Inside the Confederate Government: The Diary of Robert Garlick Hill Kean* (New York: Oxford University Press, 1957), 32.

9. Ludwell H. Johnson, "Contraband Trade during the Last Year of the Civil War," *Mississippi Valley Historical Review* 39 (March 1962): 636.

10. Benjamin F. Butler to Reverdy Johnson, July 21, 1862, *O.R.*, ser. 3, vol. 2, 239.

11. Ludwell H. Johnson, "Contraband Trade during the Last Year of the Civil War," *Mississippi Valley Historical Review* 49 (March 1963): 642; James Ford Rhodes, *History of the United States from the Compromise of 1850,* 9 vols. (New York: Macmillan Co., 1920), 5, 278–79, 307–8.

12. E. R. S. Canby to the Secretary of War, December 7, 1864, as *O.R.*, ser. 1, vol. 41, pt. 4, 786.

13. Joseph H. Parks, "A Confederate Trade Center under Federal Occupation: Memphis, 1862 to 1865," *Journal of Southern History* 7 (August 1941): 292; William T. Sherman, *Memoirs of General W. T. Sherman Written by Himself,* 2 vols. (New York: D. Appleton, 1891), 1, 267.

14. F. G. Ruffin, "A Chapter in Confederate History," *North American Review* 134 (January 1882): 99–100; George Randolph to Jefferson Davis, October 30, 1862, *O.R.*, ser. 4, vol. 2, 151; Jerrold Northrop Moore, *Confederate Commissary General: Lucius Bellinger Northrop and the Subsistence Bureau of the Southern Army* (Shippensburg, PA: White Mane Publishing Co., 1996), 169.

15. F. G. Ruffin, "A Chapter in Confederate History," *North American Review* 134 (January 1882): 102; James A. Seddon to S. G. French, February 20, 1863, *O.R.*, ser. 1, vol. 51, pt. 2, 682.

16. W. T. Sherman to Grant, August 17, 1862, *O.R.*, ser. 1, vol. 17, pt. 2, 178; James Ford Rhodes, *History of the United States from the Compromise of 1850,* 9 vols. (New York: Macmillan Co., 1920), 5, 286.

17. U. S. Grant, "General Orders No. 11," December 17, 1862, *O.R.*, ser. 1, vol. 17, pt. 2, 424.

18. U. S. Grant to Salmon P. Chase, July 21, 1863, *O.R.*, ser. 1, vol. 24, pt. 3, 538; U. S. Grant, "Trade with the Rebellious States," *The New York Times*, October 11, 1863, 6.

19. C. C. Washburn, "Trade with the Confederacy," May 10, 1864, *O.R.*, ser. 1, vol. 39, pt. 2, 22–23; Joseph H. Parks, "A Confederate Trade Center under Federal Occupation: Memphis, 1862 to 1865," *Journal of Southern History* 7 (August 1941): 304–5.

20. *The Record of Benjamin F. Butler* (Boston, 1883), 18–50.

21. Judith F. Gentry, "White Gold: The Confederate Government and Cotton in Louisiana," *Louisiana History* 33 (Summer 1992): 231–35; Ludwell H. Johnson, "Contraband Trade during the Last Year of the Civil War," *Mississippi Valley Historical Review* 39 (March 1962): 636; Ludwell H. Johnson, "Trading with the Union: The Evolution of Confederate Policy," *Virginia Magazine of History and Biography* 78 (July 1970): 312; Jerrold Northrop Moore, *Confederate Commissary General: Lucius Bellinger Northrop and the Subsistence Bureau of the Southern Army* (Shippensburg, PA: White Mane Publishing Co., 1996), 242–43.

22. Ludwell H. Johnson, "Trading with the Union: The Evolution of Confederate Policy," *Virginia Magazine of History and Biography* 78 (July 1970): 642; Abraham Lincoln, John George Nicolay, and John Hay, eds., *The Complete Works of Abraham Lincoln*, 2nd ed., 12 vols. (New York: Francis D. Tandy Co., 1905), 11, 49; Ludwell H. Johnson, "Contraband Trade during the Last Year of the Civil War," *Mississippi Valley Historical Review* 39 (March 1962): 640, 643.

23. Ludwell H. Johnson, "Commerce between Northeastern Ports and the Confederacy, 1861–1865," *Journal of American History* 54 (June 1967): 34, 36–37; John B. Jones, *A Rebel War Clerk's Diary at the Confederate States Capital*, 2 vols. (Philadelphia: Lippincott, 1866), 1, 343; Stephen R. Wise, *Lifeline of the Confederacy: Blockade Running During the Civil War* (Columbia: University of South Carolina Press, 1988), 195.

24. L. B. Northrop, "Report on Subsistence," November 20, 1863, *O.R.*, ser. 4, vol. 2, 970; John Johns, "Wilmington during the Blockade," *Harper's New Monthly Magazine* 33 (September 1866): 498; F. G. Ruffin, "A Chapter in Confederate History," *North American Review* 134 (January 1882): 106–7; Richard D. Goff, *Confederate Supply* (Durham, NC: Duke University Press, 1969), 153; James Sprunt, *Chronicles of the Cape Fear River* (Raleigh, NC: Edwards and Broughton Printing Co., 1914), 353–54.

25. Frank G. Ruffin, November 9, 1864, *O.R.*, ser. 4, vol. 3, 785–6; Stephen R. Wise, *Lifeline of the Confederacy: Blockade Running During the Civil War* (Columbia: University of South Carolina Press, 1988), 7; Thomas E. Taylor, *Running the Blockade* (London: John Murray, 1896), 139–40.

26. These estimates are from Stanley Lebergott, "Through the Blockade: The Profitability and Extent of Cotton Smuggling, 1861–1865," *Journal of Economic History* 41 (December 1981): 884.

27. Ibid., 882.

28. *Congressional Globe*, 38th Congress, 1st Session, vol. 2, 2823; Merton Coulter, "Commercial Intercourse with the Confederacy in the Mississippi Valley, 1861–1865," *Mississippi Valley Historical Review*, 5 (March 1919): 387–88; E. Merton Coulter, "Effects of Secession upon the Commerce of the Mississippi Valley," *Mississippi Valley Historical Review* 3 (December 1916): 389–90.

29. *House Reports of Committees,* 38th Congress, 2nd Session, no. 24, 1–4, as quoted in E. Merton Coulter, "Effects of Secession upon the Commerce of the Mississippi Valley," *Mississippi Valley Historical Review* 3 (December 1916): 390; James Ford Rhodes, *History of the United States from the Compromise of 1850,* 9 vols. (New York: Harper, 1904), 5, 420; Ludwell H. Johnson, "Trading with the Union: The Evolution of Confederate Policy," *Virginia Magazine of History and Biography* 78 (July 1970): 324–25.

7. The Confederacy's Breadbasket

1. U. S. Grant to Sheridan, August 26, 1864, *O.R.*, ser. 1, vol. 43, pt. 1, 917.

2. P. H. Sheridan to Grant, October 7, 1864, *O.R.*, ser. 1, vol. 43, pt. 2, 308. A slightly different version of this letter appears in *Appleton's Annual Cyclopaedia and Register of Important Events of the Year 1864* (New York: D. Appleton & Co., 1866), 4, 154.

3. Michael G. Mahon, "The Shenandoah Valley of Virginia as a Source of Subsistence for the Confederacy during the American Civil War: A New Perspective," MA thesis (University of North Carolina at Charlotte, 1989), 12; Michael G. Mahon, *The Shenandoah Valley, 1861–1865: The Destruction of the Granary of the Confederacy* (Mechanicsburg, PA: Stackpole Books, 1999), 42–43, 68.

4. M. R. Kaufman to James A. Seddon, January 10, 1863, *O.R.*, ser. 3, vol. 3, 13–14.

5. Mann Spitler *et al.* to Jefferson Davis, August 23, 1861, *O.R.*, ser. 1, vol. 4, 820–21.

6. David Hunter Strother [Cecil B. Eby, ed.], *A Virginia Yankee in the Civil War: The Diaries of David Hunter Strother* (Chapel Hill: University of North Carolina Press 1961), 254.

7. Michael G. Mahon, "The Shenandoah Valley of Virginia as a Source of Subsistence for the Confederacy during the American Civil War: A New Perspective," MA thesis (University of North Carolina at Charlotte, 1989), iii, 48; Michael G. Mahon, *The Shenandoah Valley, 1861–1865: The Destruction of the Granary of the Confederacy* (Mechanicsburg, PA: Stackpole Books, 1999), 31–32.

8. Elizabeth Preston Allan, *The Life and Letters of Margaret Junkin Preston* (Boston: Houghton, Mifflin & Co., 1903), 155; Diary of Jedediah Hotchkiss, as quoted in Michael G. Mahon, *The Shenandoah Valley 1861–1865: The Destruction of the Granary of the Confederacy* (Mechanicsburg, PA: Stackpole Books, 1999), 73; Michael G. Mahon, *The Shenandoah Valley, 1861–1865: The Destruction of the Granary of the Confederacy* (Mechanicsburg, PA: Stackpole Books, 1999), 95–96.

9. *Richmond Examiner,* as reprinted in *Staunton Spectator,* May 3, 1864, 1.

10. M. R. Kaufman to James A. Seddon, January 10, 1863, *O.R.*, ser. 3, vol. 3, 13–14; Josephine F. Roedel, Diary, manuscript diary in the Library of Congress, as quoted in Michael G. Mahon, "The Shenandoah Valley of Virginia as a Source of Subsistence for the Confederacy during the American Civil War: A New Perspective," M.A. thesis (University of North Carolina at Charlotte, 1989), 43.

11. Sarah Strickler Fife, Diary, March 16, 1862, as quoted in William Blair, *Virginia's Private War: Feeding Body and Soul in the Confederacy, 1861–1865* (New York: Oxford University Press, 1998), 77; James F. Huntington, "Operations in the Shenandoah Valley, from Winchester to Port Republic, 1862," *Papers of the Military Historical Society of Massachusetts* 6 (1907): 3–29.

12. Thad. J. Walker, "Scouting in the Shenandoah Valley," in George Morley Vickers, ed., *Under Both Flags: A Panorama of the Great Civil War* (Richmond: B. F. Johnson Publishing Co., 1896), 172.

13. Michael G. Mahon, "The Shenandoah Valley of Virginia as a Source of Subsistence for the Confederacy during the American Civil War: A New Perspective," M.A. Thesis (University of North Carolina at Charlotte, 1989), 59.

14. D. Hunter, May 24, 1864, as in Thomas L. Wilson, *Sufferings Endured for a Free Government: Or, a History of the Cruelties and Atrocities of the Rebellion* (Philadelphia: Smith & Peters, 1864), 236; *New York Herald,* May 14, 1864.

15. Benjamin Shroder Schneck, *The Burning of Chambersburg, Pennsylvania* (Philadelphia: Lindsay & Blakiston, 1864), 65.

16. Charles Carleton Coffin, *Abraham Lincoln* (New York: Harper & Brothers, 1893), 445; U. S. Grant to Halleck, July 11, 1864, *O.R.*, ser. 1, vol. 40, pt. 3, 223; U. S. Grant to D. Hunter, August 5, 1864, *O.R.*, ser. 1, vol. 38, pt. 1, 18–19.

17. U. S. Grant to Sheridan, August 26, 1864, *O.R.*, ser. 1, vol. 43, pt. 1, 917.

18. Whitelaw Reid, *Ohio in the War: Her Statesmen, Her Generals, and Her Soldiers,* 2 vols. (New York: Moore, Wilstach & Baldwin, 1868), 1, 801.

19. P. H. Sheridan to Halleck, October 1, 1864, *O.R.*, ser. 1, vol. 43, pt. 2, 250; Horace Greeley, *The American Conflict: A History of the Great Rebellion in the*

United States of America, 1860–'65, 2 vols. (Hartford: O. D. Case & Co, 1866), vol. 2, 610–11.

20. Matthella Harrison as quoted in Michael G. Mahon, *The Shenandoah Valley 1861–1865: The Destruction of the Granary of the Confederacy* (Mechanicsburg, PA: Stackpole Books, 1999), 115; Edward J. Stackpole, *Sheridan in the Shenandoah: Jubal Early's Nemesis,* 2nd ed. (Harrisburg, PA: Stackpole Books, 1992), 348–49.

21. Thomas Smith Gregory Dabney, October 22, 1864, as in Susan Dabney Smedes, *A Southern Planter: Social Life in the Old South* (New York: Pott, 1887), 225; G. W. Nichols, *A Soldier's Story of His Regiment* (Jesup, GA, 1898), 192; William G. Thomas, "Nothing Ought to Astonish Us: Confederate Civilians in the 1864 Shenandoah Valley Campaign," in Gary W. Gallagher, ed., *The Shenandoah Valley Campaign of 1864* (Chapel Hill: University of North Carolina Press, 2006), 238.

22. *Valley Spirit,* August 31, 1864, 1; Charles A. Page, *Letters of a War Correspondent* (Boston: L. C. Page and Co., 1899), 269.

23. *Rockingham Register,* as reprinted in the *Staunton Vindicator,* November 18, 1864, 2.

24. William G. Thomas, "Nothing Ought to Astonish Us: Confederate Civilians in the 1864 Shenandoah Valley Campaign," in Gary W. Gallagher, ed., *The Shenandoah Valley Campaign of 1864* (Chapel Hill: University of North Carolina Press, 2006), 246.

25. Jas. W. Forsyth to Wesley Merritt, November 27, 1864, *O.R.,* ser. 1, vol. 43, pt. 2, 679; Jeffry D. Wert, *Mosby's Rangers* (New York: Simon and Schuster, 1990), 261–63; Sheridan to Stevenson, November 28, 1864, *O.R.,* ser. 1, vol. 43, pt. 2, 687.

26. *The Vindicator,* December 2, 1864, 2; H. W. Halleck to Sheridan, December 27, 1864, *O.R.,* ser. 1, Vol. 43, 831; Stephen V. Ash, *When the Yankees Came: Conflict and Chaos in the Occupied South, 1861–1865* (Chapel Hill: University of North Carolina Press, 1995), 103.

27. A. L. Long, *Memoirs of Robert E. Lee: His Military and Personal History* (New York: J. N. Stoddard, 1886), 367–68; William G. Thomas, "Nothing Ought to Astonish Us: Confederate Civilians in the 1864 Shenandoah Valley Campaign," in Gary W. Gallagher, ed., *The Shenandoah Valley Campaign of 1864* (Chapel Hill: University of North Carolina Press, 2006), 237; Andre M. Fleche, "Uncivilized War: The Shenandoah Campaign, the Northern Democratic Press and the Election of 1864," in Gary W. Gallagher, ed., *The Shenandoah Valley Campaign of 1864* (Chapel Hill: University of North Carolina Press, 2006), 203.

28. "Report of Major General Sheridan to the Hon. Committee on the Conduct of the War," *Supplemental Report of the Joint Committee on the Conduct of the War,*

Supplemental to Senate Report no. 142, 38th Congress, 2nd session. 2 vols. (Washington: Government Printing Office, 1866), 2, 31.

8. Giving Thanks and No Thanks

1. Abraham Lincoln, "No. 21. Appointing the last Thursday of November a Day of Thanksgiving and Praise," October 20, 1864, George P. Sanger, ed., *The Statutes at Large, Treaties, and Proclamations of the United States of America* (Boston: Little, Brown, & Co., 1866), 13, 749; G. W. B. [George W. Blunt], "Our Soldiers and Sailors and Thanksgiving," The *New York Times*, October 27, 1864, 4; George W. Blunt, letter to Abraham Lincoln, dated November 11, 1864.

2. *New York Observer,* November 17, 1864, as quoted in Emerson David Fite, *Social and Industrial Conditions in the North During the Civil War* (New York: Peter Smith, 1930), 283.

3. W. T. Crane, "Thanksgiving Festivities at Fort Pulaski, Georgia, Thursday, November 27th, 1862," *Frank Leslie's Illustrated Weekly* 15 (January 3, 1863): 38; Malcolm Dana, *Norwich Memorial: The Annals of Norwich, New London County, Connecticut, in the Great Rebellion of 1861–65* (Norwich, CT: J. H. Jewett and Co., 1873), 187; Winslow Homer, "Thanksgiving in Camp," *Harper's Weekly* 6 (November 29, 1862): 764; W. T. Crane, "Thanksgiving Festivities at Fort Pulaski, Georgia, Thursday, November 27th, 1862," *Frank Leslie's Illustrated Newspaper,* January 3, 1863, 38; *Godey's Lady's Book* 71 (November 1865): 445; Sarah Josepha Hale to Lincoln, September 28, 1863, as at the Library of Congress; Gideon Wells, *Diary,* 3 vols. (New York: W. W. Norton, 1960), 1, 450; John G. Nicolay to John Hay, Friday, April 1, 1864, at the Library of Congress: http://memory.loc.gov/cgi-bin/ampage?collId=mal&fileName=mal2/428/4283000/malpage.db&recNum=0, accessed December 25, 2009.

4. *Trenton Daily State Gazette,* November 24, 1864, as quoted in Paul A. Cimbala, "Soldiering on the Home Front: The Veteran Reserve Corps and the Northern People," in Paul A. Cimbala and Randall M. Miller, eds., *Union Soldiers and the Northern Home Front: Wartime Experiences, Postwar Adjustments* (New York: Fordham University Press, 2002), 214; James S. Robbins, "Giving Thanks in Wartime," The Soldiers' and Sailors' Thanksgiving 1864," National Review Online, November 24, 2004 at: http://www.nationalreview.com/robbins/robbins200411240851.asp, accessed December 31, 2009.

5. Malcolm McG. Dana, *Norwich Memorial: The Annals of Norwich, New London County, Connecticut, in the Great Rebellion of 1861–65* (Norwich, CT: J. H. Jewett and Co., 1873), 187–88.

6. *Trenton Daily State Gazette,* November 24, 1864, as quoted in Paul A. Cimbala, "Soldiering on the Home Front: The Veteran Reserve Corps and the Northern

People," in Paul A. Cimbala and Randall M. Miller, eds., *Union Soldiers and the Northern Home Front: Wartime Experiences, Postwar Adjustments* (New York: Fordham University Press, 2002), 214.

7. Frank Boott Goodrich, *The Tribute Book: A Record of the Munificence, Self-Sacrifice and Patriotism of the American People* (New York: Derby & Miller, 1865), 436, 439.

8. "The Thanksgiving Dinner," *The New York Times*, November 18, 1864, 8; "Scene at Delmonico's Restaurant: Preparing Poultry to be Cooked for Soldiers' Thanksgiving Dinner," *Frank Leslie's Illustrated Weekly* 19 (December 3, 1864): 161.

9. Theodore Roosevelt, "Soldiers' and Sailors' Thanksgiving Dinner," *The New York Times*, November 23, 1864, 8; *Report of the Committee on Providing a Thanksgiving Dinner for the Soldiers and Sailors. Presented December 14th, 1864* (New York: Union League Club, 1865), 3–4, 25; "Thanksgiving Dinner for the Soldiers and Sailors," *The New York Times*, November 8, 1864, 2; Frank Boott Goodrich, *The Tribute Book: A Record of the Munificence, Self-Sacrifice and Patriotism of the American People* (New York: Derby & Miller, 1865), 435.

10. George F. Williams, "Preparation for Thanksgiving," *The New York Times*, November 28, 1864, 4.

11. Rutherford B. Hayes [Charles Richard Williams, ed.], *The Diary and Letters of Rutherford B. Hayes* (Columbus, OH: Ohio State Archeological and Historical Society, 1922), 2, 533, 540.

12. Robert Laird Stewart, *History of the One Hundred and Fortieth Regiment Pennsylvania Volunteers* (Philadelphia: Printed by the Franklin Bindery, 1912), 245; "From Sheridan's Army; Thanksgiving Day Military Matters," *The New York Times*, December 1, 1864, 1; Robert Laird Stewart, *History of the One Hundred and Fortieth Regiment Pennsylvania Volunteers* (Philadelphia: Printed by the Franklin Bindery, 1912), 245; "From Sheridan's Army; Thanksgiving Day Military Matters," *The New York Times*, December 1, 1864, 1.

13. Aldace Freeman Walker, *The Vermont Brigade in the Shenandoah Valley, 1864* (Burlington, VT: Free Press Association, 1869), 165; *Report of the Committee on Providing a Thanksgiving Dinner for the Soldiers and Sailors* (New York: Union League Club, 1865), 19; Sergeant Walker, "Diary," as quoted in Thomas Francis Wildes, *Record of the One Hundred and Sixteenth Regiment, Ohio Infantry Volunteers in the War of the Rebellion* (Sandusky, OH: I. F. Mack & Bros., 1884), 99.

14. Joseph Gould, *The Story of the Forty-Eighth* (Philadelphia: Regimental Association, 1908), 279; Howard Aston, *History and Roster of the Fourth and Fifth Independent Battalions and Thirteenth Regiment Ohio Cavalry Volunteers* (Columbus, OH: Press of F. J. Heer, 1902), 25.

15. Robert Tilney, *My Life in the Army* (Philadelphia: Ferris & Leach, 1912), 156–57.

16. Alfred Seelye Roe, *The Ninth New York Heavy Artillery* (Worcester, MA: The author, 1899), 202.

17. "Affairs at Nashville," *The New York Times*, December 11, 1864, p. 2.

18. Faunt Le Roy Senour, *Major General William T. Sherman, and His Campaigns* (Chicago: H. M. Sherwood, 1865), 328–29; "The Thanksgiving Feast," *The New York Times*, November 24, 1864, 4; James S. Robbins, "Giving Thanks in Wartime," The Soldiers' and Sailors' Thanksgiving 1864," National Review Online, November 24, 2004 at: http://www.nationalreview.com/robbins/robbins200411240851.asp, accessed December 25, 2009.

19. Frank Boott Goodrich, *The Tribute Book: A Record of the Munificence, Self-Sacrifice and Patriotism of the American People* (New York: Derby & Miller, 1865), 437.

20. Oliver Willcox Norton, *Army Letters, 1861–1865: Being Extracts from Private Letters to Relatives* (Chicago: O. L. Deming, 1903), 243; Robert Laird Stewart, *History of the One Hundred and Fortieth Regiment Pennsylvania Volunteers* (Philadelphia: Printed by the Franklin Bindery, 1912), 245.

21. Malcolm McG. Dana, *Norwich Memorial: The Annals of Norwich, New London County, Connecticut, in the Great Rebellion of 1861–65* (Norwich, CT: J. H. Jewett and Co., 1873), 188–89; Frank Boott Goodrich, *The Tribute Book: A Record of the Munificence, Self-Sacrifice and Patriotism of the American People* (New York: Derby & Miller, 1865), 431, 436.

22. Frank Boott Goodrich, *The Tribute Book: A Record of the Munificence, Self-sacrifice and Patriotism of the American People* (New York: Derby & Miller, 1865), 433.

23. Charles J. House, "First Maine Heavy Artillery in Fall of 1864," *The Maine Bugle* 4 (April 1897): 136.

24. "The Soldiers' Thanksgiving," *The New York Times*, December 6, 1864, 1.

25. "Turkeys for the Sailors," *The New York Times,* November 24, 1864, 1; Robert Laird Stewart, *History of the One Hundred and Fortieth Regiment Pennsylvania Volunteers* (Philadelphia: Printed by the Franklin Bindery, 1912), 245; "From Sheridan's Army; Thanksgiving Day Military Matters," *The New York Times*, December 1, 1864, 1.

26. Abram P. Smith, *History of the Seventy-sixth Regiment New York Volunteers: What it Endured* (Cortland, NY: Truair, Smith & Miles, 1867), 320.

27. *New York Herald*, November 27, 1864.

28. *Richmond Dispatch*, November 25, 1864.

29. *Richmond Whig*, November 25, 1864; *Richmond Examiner*, December 22, 1864; *Charleston Mercury,* January 4, 1865, 1.

30. G. F. J. O'Brien, "James A. Seddon, Statesman of the Old South," Ph.D. thesis (University of Maryland, 1963), 480; Mike Wright, *City under Siege: Richmond in the Civil War* (New York: Cooper Square Press, 2002), 218.

31. *Richmond Examiner*, December 22, 1864; Henry Edward Young to his mother, December 1864, as quoted in J. Tracy Power, *Lee's Miserables* (Chapel Hill: University of North Carolina Press, 1998), 230.

32. *Richmond Examiner,* December 31, 1864.

33. *Richmond Examiner*, December 31, 1864; Mrs. Robert E. Lee to Mrs. Williams, January 2, 1865, as quoted in Mike Wright, *City under Siege; Richmond in the Civil War* (New York: Cooper Square Press, 2002), 218.

34. Mary Bandy Daughtry, *Gray Cavalier: The Life and Wars of General W. H. F. "Rooney" Lee* (Cambridge, MA: Da Capo Press, 2002), 258; G. F. J. O'Brien, "James A. Seddon, Statesman of the Old South," Ph.D. thesis (University of Maryland, 1963), 480.

35. J. Tracy Power, *Lee's Miserables: Life in the Army of Northern Virginia from the Wilderness to Appomattox* (Chapel Hill: University of North Carolina Press, 1998), 232–33; Mike Wright, *City under Siege: Richmond in the Civil War* (New York: Cooper Square Press, 2002), 219.

36. Harry G. Townsend, "Townsend's Diary, January-May 1865," in R. A. Brock, ed., *Southern Historical Papers* 34 (January-December 1906): 99.

37. A. B. C., "The Soldiers' New-Year's Dinner," *Richmond Dispatch*, January 6, 1865.

38. *Richmond Enquirer*, January 3, 1865, as quoted in Mike Wright, *City under Siege: Richmond in the Civil War* (New York: Cooper Square Press, 2002), 218; *Richmond Examiner*, January 5, 1865.

39. Frank Boott Goodrich, *The Tribute Book: A Record of the Munificence, Self-Sacrifice and Patriotism of the American People* (New York: Derby & Miller, 1865), 3.

40. *New York Herald*, November 21, 1864.

41. J. Tracy Power, *Lee's Miserables: Life in the Army of Northern Virginia from the Wilderness to Appomattox* (Chapel Hill: University of North Carolina Press, 1998), 233.

9. Hard War

1. "Reports of Captain Orlando Poe," December 26, 1864, *O.R.*, ser. 1, vol. 44, pt. 1, 56; W. T. Sherman to Grant, October 9, 1864, *O.R.*, ser. 1, vol. 39, pt. 3, 162.

2. Stephen E. Bower, "The Theology of the Battlefield: William Tecumseh Sherman and the U.S. Civil War," *The Journal of Military History* 64 (October

2000): 1020; W. T. Sherman to John Sherman, January 25, 1863, in "Letters of Two Brothers," *Century Magazine* 45 (January 1893): 434.

3. W. T. Sherman to Ellen Sherman, May 6, 1863, in M. A. De Wolfe Howe, ed., *Home Letters of General Sherman* (New York: C. Scribner's Sons, 1909), 260; W. T. Sherman to H. W. Hill, September 7, 1863, The *New York Times*, January 17, 1864, 6.

4. W. T. Sherman to R. M. Sawyer, January 18, 1864, as reprinted in William Jewett Tenney, *The Military and Naval History of the Rebellion in the United States* (New York: D. Appleton & Co., 1865), 499–500; John Townsend Trowbridge, *The South: A Tour of its Battlefields and Ruined Cities, a Journey Through the Desolated States, and Talks with the People* (Hartford, CT: L. Stebbins, 1866), 440.

5. Bobby Leon Roberts and Carl H. Moneyhon, *Portraits of Conflict: A Photographic History of Mississippi in the Civil War* (Fayetteville: University of Arkansas Press, 1993), 275; William I. Nugent, March 13, 1864, to his wife, as in J. K. Bettersworth, ed., *Mississippi in the Confederacy as They Saw It*, 2 vols. (Baton Rouge: Published for the Mississippi Dept. of Archives and History, Jackson, by Louisiana State University Press, 1961), 1, 213.

6. Sherman to Grant, as quoted in Charles Edmund Vetter, *Sherman, Merchant of Terror, Advocate of Peace* (Gretna, LA: Pelican Pub. Co., 1992), 182; Sherman to Halleck, February 29, 1864, *O.R.*, ser. 1, vol. 32, pt. 2, 498; Paul W. Gates, *Agriculture and the Civil War* (New York: Alfred A. Knopf, 1965), 121.

7. E. D. Townsend to Nathaniel P. Banks, April 30, 1864, *O.R.*, ser. 1, vol. 34, pt. 3, 358.

8. Francis F. McKinney, *Education in Violence: The Life of George H. Thomas and the History of the Army of the Cumberland* (Detroit, MI: Wayne State University Press, 1961), 316.

9. R. M. Collins, *Chapters from the Unwritten History of the War between the States* (St. Louis: Nixon-Jones Printing Co., 1893), 223; The *New York Times*, June 22, 1864, 2.

10. Sherman to Edwin M. Stanton, October 20, 1864, *O.R.*, ser. 1, vol. 39, pt. 3, 369.

11. Lee B. Kennett, *Marching through Georgia: The Story of Soldiers and Civilians during Sherman's Campaign* (New York: HarperPerennial, 1995), 217–18.

12. W. T. Sherman to Grant, October 9, 1864, *O.R.*, ser. 1, vol. 39, pt. 3, 162; The *Cincinnati Commercial*, November 12, 1864, as reprinted in the *Richmond Dispatch*, November 18, 1864, 1.

13. William T. Sherman, *Memoirs of General W. T. Sherman Written by Himself*, 2 vols. (New York: D. Appleton, 1891), 2, 175–76.

14. A. Beckwith to Sherman, November 11, 1864, *O.R.*, ser. 1, vol. 39, pt. 3, 741; H. C. Symonds, *Report of a Commissary of Subsistence, 1861–65* (Sing Sing, NY: The Author, [1888]), 148–150, 158; B. H. Liddell Hart, *Sherman: Soldier, Realist, American* (New York: Dodd, Mead & Co., 1929), 236; Lee B. Kennett, *Marching through Georgia: The Story of Soldiers and Civilians during Sherman's Campaign* (New York: HarperPerennial, 1995), 239; Noah Andre Trudeau, *Southern Storm: Sherman's March to the Sea* (New York: HarperCollins, 2008), 538.

15. William T. Sherman, *Memoirs of General W. T. Sherman Written by Himself,* 2 vols. (New York: D. Appleton, 1891), 2, 183.

16. *New York Herald*, December 22, 1864, as quoted in J. Cutler Andrews, *The North Reports the Civil War* (Pittsburgh: Pittsburgh University Press, 1985), 577–78.

17. Paper read before the Loyal Legion in Boston, September 17, 1900, as quoted in James Ford Rhodes, *History of the United States from the Compromise of 1850,* 9 vols. (New York: Macmillan Co., 1920), 5, 23.

18. Jefferson Davis, speech at Macon, as in Frank Moore, ed., *The Rebellion Records: A Diary of American Events* (New York: Van Nostrand, 1867), 148; P. G. T. Beauregard, Proclamation dated November 18, 1864, as in Thomas Prentice Kettell, *History of the Great Rebellion, from Its Commencement to Its Close* (Hartford, CT: L. Stebbins; Cincinnati, F. A. Howe, 1865), 681.

19. Robert Hill to his sister, January 8, 1865, as quoted in Victor Davis Hanson, *The Soul of Battle: From Ancient Times to the Present Day, How Three Great Liberators Vanquished Tyranny* (New York: Free Press, 1999), 173; Lee B. Kennett, *Marching through Georgia: The Story of Soldiers and Civilians during Sherman's Campaign* (New York: HarperPerennial, 1995), 297; B. H. Liddell Hart, *Sherman: Soldier, Realist, American* (New York: Dodd, Mead & Co., 1929), 340.

20. A. P. Mason to Joseph Wheeler, October 22, 1864, Joseph Wheeler, *Campaigns of Wheeler and His Cavalry. 1862–1865* (Atlanta: Hudgins Publishing Co., 1899), 276; *Augusta Constitutionalist*, November 22, 1864, as quoted in Faunt Le Roy Senour, *Major General William T. Sherman, and His Campaign* (Chicago: H. M. Sherwood, 1865), 306.

21. P. G. T. Beauregard, Proclamation dated November 18, 1864, as in Thomas Prentice Kettell, *History of the Great Rebellion, from Its Commencement to Its Close* (Hartford, CT: L. Stebbins; Cincinnati, F. A. Howe, 1865), 681, 682.

22. William T. Sherman, *Memoirs of General W. T. Sherman Written by Himself,* 2 vols. (New York: D. Appleton, 1891), 2, 181–82; Ibid. 2, 183; B. H. Liddell Hart, *Sherman: Soldier, Realist, American* (New York: Dodd, Mead & Co., 1929), 332; Ibid., 339.

23. Paul W. Gates, *Agriculture and the Civil War* (New York: Alfred A. Knopf, 1965), 93; Robert F. Hawes Jr., *One Nation, Indivisible? A Study of Secession and the Constitution* (Palo Alto, CA: Fultus, 2006), 155.

24. William T. Sherman, *Memoirs of General W. T. Sherman Written by Himself,* 2 vols. (New York: D. Appleton, 1891), 2, 184.

25. Samuel Merrill, *The Seventieth Indiana Volunteer Infantry in the War of the Rebellion* (Indianapolis: Bowen-Merrill Co., 1900), 223.

26. Faunt Le Roy Senour, *Major General William T. Sherman, and His Campaign* (Chicago: H. M. Sherwood, 1865), 322–23, 328–29.

27. Erna Risch, *Quartermaster Support of the Army 1775–1939* (Washington, Quartermaster Historian's Office, Office of the Quartermaster General, 1962), 419; Sherman to William J. Hardee, December 17, 1864, *O.R.,* ser. 1, vol. 44, 737; Diary of Capt. E. J. Sherlock, as quoted in Bell Irvin Wiley, *The Life of Billy Yank* (Indianapolis: Bobbs-Merrill 1952), 232.

28. W. T. Sherman, "Reports of Major General William T. Sherman," December 22, 1864, *O.R.,* ser. 1, vol. 44, 13; B. H. Liddell Hart, *Sherman: Soldier, Realist, American* (New York: Dodd, Mead & Co., 1929), 338, 346; Lee B. Kennett, *Marching through Georgia: The Story of Soldiers and Civilians during Sherman's Campaign* (New York: HarperPerennial, 1995), 309.

29. George S. Bradley, *The Star Corps or, Notes of an Army Chaplain, During Sherman's Famous "March to the Sea"* (Milwaukee: Jermain & Brightman, 1865), 207; Noah Andre Trudeau, *Southern Storm: Sherman's March to the Sea* (New York: HarperCollins, 2008), 271; Edward M. Alfriend, "Social Life in Richmond During the War," *Cosmopolitan* 12 (December 1891): 230.

30. William T. Sherman, *Memoirs of General W. T. Sherman Written by Himself,* 2 vols. (New York: D. Appleton, 1891), 2, 227.

31. Ibid. Sherman to Halleck, October 19, 1964, *O.R.,* ser. 1, vol. 39, pt. 3, 358. vol. 2, 223, 227; George Ward. Nichols, *The Story of the Great March* (New York: Harper & Brothers, 1865), 35.

32. Charles F. Morse, *Letters Written during the Civil War, 1861–1865* (Boston, MA: T. R. Martin, 1898), 210; W. W. Lord, Jr., "In the Path of Sherman," *Harper's Monthly Magazine* 120 (February 1910): 445.

33. *Emma LeConte's Diary, 1864–1865* (Academic Affairs Library, University of North Carolina at Chapel Hill, 1998), 56, as at: http://docsouth.unc.edu/fpn/leconteemma/leconte.html, accessed December 31, 2009.

34. W. W. Lord, Jr., "In the Path of Sherman," *Harper's Monthly Magazine* 120 (February 1910): 444–45.

35. Jefferson Davis [Lynda Laswell Crist, *et al,* ed], *The Papers of Jefferson Davis: September 1864-May 1865,* 5 vols. (Baton Rouge: Louisiana State University Press, 1985), 2, 441.

36. Charles F Morse, *Letters Written during the Civil War, 1861–1865* (Boston, MA: T. R. Martin, 1898), 213; *New York Daily Tribune,* April 1, 1865, as

quoted in J. Cutler Andrews, *The North Reports the Civil War* (Pittsburgh: Pittsburgh University Press, 1985), 626.

37. Lee to Z. B. Vance, February 24, 1865, as in Armistead Lindsay Long, Marcus Joseph Wright, eds., *Memoirs of Robert E. Lee* (New York: J. M. Stoddart & Co., 1887), 686.

38. Sherman's obituary in the *Americus* (Georgia) *Daily Times*, as quoted in Victor Davis Hanson, *The Soul of Battle: From Ancient Times to the Present Day, How Three Great Liberators Vanquished Tyranny* (New York: Free Press, 1999), 149.

10. Capital Hunger

1. "Diary of Edmund Ruffin," as quoted in Charles W. Ramsdell, "General Robert E. Lee's Horse Supply, 1862–1865," *American Historical Review* 35 (July 1930): 768.

2. Paul W. Gates, *Agriculture and the Civil War* (New York: Alfred A. Knopf, 1965), 116.

3. *Rockingham Register,* as quoted in Michael G. Mahon, *The Shenandoah Valley, 1861–1865: The Destruction of the Granary of the Confederacy* (Mechanicsburg, PA: Stackpole Books, 1999), 100; Mary Elizabeth Massey, "The Food and Drink Shortage on the Confederate Homefront," *North Carolina Historical Review* 26 (April 1949): 313–16; *Raleigh Daily Progress*, January 23, 1864, as reprinted in *Franklin Repository*, January 27, 1864, 1; *Franklin Repository*, January 27, 1864, 1.

4. *New York Herald*, May 31, 1864; John B. Jones, *A Rebel War Clerk's Diary at the Confederate States Capital*, 2 vols. (Philadelphia: Lippincott, 1866), 2, 190, 318; Judith White Brockenbrough McGuire, *Diary of a Southern Refugee*, 3rd ed. (Richmond: J. W. Randolph, 1889), 247.

5. R. E. Lee to J. Longstreet, January 16, 1864, *O.R.*, ser. 1, vol. 32, pt. 2, 566; R. E. Lee to J. Longstreet, March 28, 1864, *O.R.*, ser. 1, vol. 52, pt. 2, 649; R. E. Lee to Jefferson Davis, January 2, 1864, *O.R.*, ser. 1, vol. 33, 1061; R. E. Lee to L. B. Northrop, January 5, 1864, *O.R.*, ser. 1, vol. 33, 1064; Sam Jones to R. E. Lee, January 17, 1864, *O.R.*, ser. 1, vol. 33, 1093.

6. R. E. Lee to the Secretary of War, August 22, 1864, *O.R.*, ser. 1, vol. 42, pt. 2, 1194–95; Hugh Henderson Scott, "The Story of a Scout Told in His Own Way," in U. R. Brooks, *Butler and His Cavalry in the War of Secession, 1861–1865* (Columbia, SC: The State Co., 1909), 315.

7. R. E. Lee to James A. Seddon, January 22, 1864, *O.R.*, ser. 1, vol. 33, pt. 1, 1114; Charles W. Ramsdell, "The Confederate Government and the Railroads," *American Historical Review* 22 (July 1917): 806; Frank G. Ruffin to James A.

Seddon, February 8, 1864, *O.R.*, ser. 4, vol. 3, 88; S. B. French to L. B. Northrop, February 8, 1864, *O.R.*, ser. 4, vol. 3, 89; A. R. Lawton to J. Longstreet, March 9, 1864, *O.R.*, ser. 1, vol. 32, pt. 3, 598; A. R. Lawton to R. E. Lee, March 21, 1864, *O.R.*, ser. 1, vol. 33, pt. 1, 1236–37; Richard D. Goff, *Confederate Supply* (Durham, NC: Duke University Press, 1969), 214.

8. John William Jones, *Life and Letters of Robert Edward Lee* (New York and Washington: Neale Publishing Co., 1906), 314; *Richmond Dispatch*, May 19, 1864; *New York Herald*, November 27, 1863; *New York Herald*, November 6, 1863; John Tyler to Sterling Price, July 9, 1864, *O.R.*, ser. 1, vol. 40, pt. 3, 759; Jefferson Davis, "The Senate and House of Representatives of the Confederate States of America," November 7, 1864, *O.R.* Ser. 4, vol. 3, 792.

9. Sara Agnes Rice Pryor, *Reminiscences of Peace and War* (New York: Macmillan Co., 1904), 283; Wm. Smith, December 7, 1864, *O.R.*, ser. 4, vol. 3, pt. 3, 918; *Utica Daily Observer*, November 13, 1863.

10. R. E. Lee to Hampton, September 3, 1864, *O.R.*, ser. 1, vol. 42, pt. 2, 1233–34.

11. Considerable debate has swirled about how many actually participated in the raids. Figures range from 2,500 to 3,500 to 4,000 men. See Richard Lykes, "Hampton's Cattle Raid, September 14–17, 1864," *Military Affairs* 21 (Spring 1957): 7, 11; Hugh Henderson Scott, "The Story of a Scout Told in His Own Way," in U. R. Brooks, ed., *Butler and His Cavalry in the War of Secession, 1861–1865* (Columbia, SC: The State Co., 1909), 111.

12. Chiswell Dabney, "The Beefsteak Feast," in Maud Carter Clement, ed., *War Recollections of Confederate Veterans of Pittsylvania County* (Chatham, VA: Pittsylvania Historical Society, 1982), 63; David Cardwell, "A Brilliant Coup. How Wade Hampton Captured Grant's Entire Beef Supply," *News and Courier* (Charleston, S.C.), October 10, 1894, as in *Southern Historical Society Papers* 22 (January-December 1894): 163; Shadburne to Hampton, September 5, 1864, *O.R.*, ser. 1, vol. 42, pt. 2, 1236; David Cardwell, "A Brilliant Coup. How Wade Hampton Captured Grant's Entire Beef Supply," *News and Courier* (Charleston, S.C.), October 10, 1894, as in *Southern Historical Society Papers* 22 (January-December 1894): 147–56; Edward Laight Wells, *Hampton and His Cavalry in '64* (Richmond: B. F. Johnson Pub. Co., 1899), 287–311); Paul W. Gates, *Agriculture and the Civil War* (New York: Alfred A. Knopf, 1965), 94.

13. U. S. Grant, *Personal Memoirs of U. S. Grant*, 2 vols. (New York: Charles L. Webster & Co., 1894), 1, 592; Horace Porter, "Campaigning with Grant," *Century Magazine* 54 (June 1897): 209.

14. Virginia Clay-Clopton [Ada Sterling, ed.], *A Belle of the Fifties: Memoirs of Mrs. Clay of Alabama* (New York: Doubleday, Page & Co., 1904), 168; Edward M. Alfriend, "Social Life in Richmond During the War," *Cosmopolitan* (December 1891): 134; Timothy J. Regan, David C. Newton, and Kenneth J. Pluskat, *The Lost*

Civil War Diaries: the Diaries of Corporal Timothy J. Regan. (Victoria, BC: Trafford, 2003), 137; Dallas Tucker, "The Fall of Richmond," *Richmond Dispatch*, February 3, 1902, as in *Southern Historical Society Papers* 29 (January-December 1901): 154.

15. Edward M. Alfriend, "Social Life in Richmond during the War," *Cosmopolitan* (December 1891): 134–37; Mary Boykin Chesnut [Isabella D. Martin and Myrta Lockett Avary, eds.], *A Diary from Dixie* (New York: D. Appleton and Co., 1905), 260; Basil L. Gildersleeve, "A Southerner in the Peloponnesian War," *Atlantic Monthly* 80 (September 1897): 339–40.

16. Mrs. M. P. Handy, "Confederate Make-Shifts," *Harper's New Monthly Magazine* 52 (March 1876): 579–80.

17. Virginia Clay-Clopton [Ada Sterling, ed.], *A Belle of the Fifties: Memoirs of Mrs. Clay of Alabama* (New York: Doubleday, Page & Co., 1904), 185.

18. Mary Boykin Chesnut [Isabella D. Martin and Myrta Lockett Avary, eds.], *A Diary from Dixie* (New York: D. Appleton and Co., 1905), 201, 281–83.

19. Fitzgerald Ross, "A Visit to the Cities and Camps of the Confederate States, 1863–64," *Blackwood's Edinburgh Magazine* 97 (February 1865): 158.

20. Thomas E. Taylor, *Running the Blockade* (London: John Murray, 1896), 138–40.

21. John S. Wise, *The End of an Era* (Boston: Houghton, Mifflin & Co., 1899), 410; Mike Wright, *City under Siege: Richmond in the Civil War* (New York: Cooper Square Press, 2002), 283.

22. *New York Herald*, March 13, 1891.

23. Grant, as quoted in "Testimony of Charles A. Dana," *Southern Historical Society Papers* 1 (March, 1876): 151–52.

24. Northrop, as quoted in James Grant Wilson and John Fiske, eds., *Appleton's Cyclopædia of American Biography*, 5 vols. (New York: D. Appleton and Co., 1888), 4, 535; Augustus Choate Hamlin, *Martyria: Or, Andersonville Prison* (Boston: Lee & Shepard, 1866), 80; Norton Parker Chipman, *The Horrors of Andersonville Rebel Prison* (San Francisco: Bancroft Co., 1891), 69.

25. Northrop, as quoted in James Grant Wilson and John Fiske, eds., *Appleton's Cyclopædia of American Biography*, 5 vols. (New York: D. Appleton and Co., 1888), 4, 535; Augustus Choate Hamlin, *Martyria: Or, Andersonville Prison* (Boston: Lee & Shepard, 1866), 80; Norton Parker Chipman, *The Horrors of Andersonville Rebel Prison* (San Francisco: Bancroft Co., 1891), 69; William Franklin Lyon, *In and Out of Andersonville Prison* (Detroit, MI: G. Harland Co., 1905), 97. What was just as disgraceful was the large number of Confederate soldiers who died in Union prisoner-of-war camps. The North, with its abundance of food and its good transportation system, could easily have provided liberally for its prisoners, and no Southerner should have died due to illnesses exacerbated by malnutrition and hunger.

26. L. B. Northrop to John C. Breckenridge, February 9, 1865, *O.R.*, ser. 1, vol. 46, pt. 2, 1211; Edward Younger, ed., *Inside the Confederate Government: The Diary of Robert Garlick Hill Kean* (New York: Oxford University Press, 1957), 230; W. W. Myers, November 24, 1863, *O.R.*, ser. 2, vol. 6, 570–71, passim.

27. R. E. Lee to James A. Seddon, January 11, 1865, as in *O.R.*, ser. 1, vol. 46, pt. 2, 1035; Sarah Woolfolk Wiggins, ed., *The Journals of Josiah Gorgas, 1857–1878* (Tuscaloosa: University of Alabama Press, 1995), 147–48.

28. George Edgar Turner, *Victory Rode the Rails: The Strategic Place of the Railroads in the Civil War* (Lincoln: University of Nebraska Press, 1992), 365–66.

29. John B. Jones, *A Rebel War Clerk's Diary at the Confederate States Capital*, 2 vols. (Philadelphia: Lippincott, 1866), 2, 384; Frank Everson Vandiver, "The Food Supply of the Confederate Armies, 1865," *Tyler's Quarterly Historical and Genealogical Magazine* 26 (October 1944): 78; William Lamb, "The Defense of Fort Fisher," *Battles and Leaders of the Civil War*, 4 vols. (New York: The Century Co., 1888), 4, 642; R. E. Lee, "To the Farmers East of the Blue Ridge and South of James River," *O.R.*, ser. 1, vol. 46, pt. 2, 1075; R. E. Lee to the Secretary of War, January 16, 1865, *O.R.*, ser. 1, vol. 46, pt. 2, 1075; Frank Everson Vandiver, "The Food Supply of the Confederate Armies, 1865," *Tyler's Quarterly Historical and Genealogical Magazine* 26 (October 1944): 79–80.

30. R. E. Lee to James A. Seddon, February 8, 1865, *O.R.*, ser. 1, vol. 56, pt. 2, 1210.

31. J. Longstreet to R. E. Lee, February 14, 1865, *O.R.*, ser. 1, vol. 46, pt. 2, 1233–34; R. E. Lee to J. Longstreet, February 22, 1865, *O.R.*, ser. 1, vol. 46, pt. 2, 1250.

32. Grant to Elihu A. Washburne, February 23, 1865, as in John Y. Simon, *et al*, eds., *The Papers of Ulysses S. Grant* (Carbondale: Southern Illinois University Press, 1985), 14, 31; Grant to E. R. S. Canby, February 27, 1865, as in John Y. Simon *et al*, eds., *The Papers of Ulysses S. Grant* (Carbondale: Southern Illinois University Press, 1985), 14, 61–63; *New York Herald*, March 13, 1865.

33. R. E. Lee to Jefferson Davis, April 12, 1865, *O.R.*, ser. 1, vol. 46, pt. 1, 1265; Frank Everson Vandiver, "The Food Supply of the Confederate Armies, 1865," *Tyler's Quarterly Historical and Genealogical Magazine* 26 (October 1944): 86.

34. Douglas Southall Freeman, *R. E. Lee: A Biography*, 4 vols. (New York: Charles Scribner's Sons, 1934), 4, 509; Frank Everson Vandiver, "The Food Supply of the Confederate Armies, 1865," *Tyler's Quarterly Historical and Genealogical Magazine* 26 (October 1944): 86; George Edgar Turner, *Victory Rode the Rails: The Strategic Place of the Railroads in the Civil War* (Lincoln: University of Nebraska Press, 1992), 372–75; U. S. Grant, *Personal Memoirs of U. S. Grant*, 2 vols. (New York: C. L. Webster & Co., 1886), 2, 625.

35. John B. Jones, *A Rebel War Clerk's Diary at the Confederate States Capital*, 2 vols. (Philadelphia: Lippincott, 1866), 2, 464, 474; "Strength of the Army of

Northern Virginia, General Robert F. Lee commanding, December 31, 1864," as in *O.R.*, ser. 1, vol. 42, pt. 3, 1362.

36. Ella Lonn, *Desertion during the Civil War* (Lincoln: University of Nebraska Press, 1998), 13; J. Tracy Power, *Lee's Miserables: Life in the Army of Northern Virginia from the Wilderness to Appomattox* (Chapel Hill: University of North Carolina Press, 1998), 236, 308; "Statement of John Johnson," February 8, 1865, *O.R.*, ser. 1, vol. 46, pt. 2, 387; J. H. Duncan to Joseph Finegan, January 21, 1865, *O.R.*, ser. 1, vol. 46, pt. 2, 1144.

37. Joseph E. Johnston, *Narrative of Military Operations Directed During the Late War between the States* (New York: D. Appleton and Co., 1874), 424–45; Stanley Lebergott, "Why the South Lost: Commercial Purpose in the Confederacy, 1861–1865," *Journal of American History* 70 (June 1983): 70–71.

38. R. E. Lee to the Secretary of War, January 27, 1865, as quoted in J. S. McNeilley, "A Mississippi Brigade in the Last Days of the Confederacy," in Franklin L. Reilly, ed., *Publications of the Mississippi Historical Society* (Oxford, MS: Mississippi Historical Society, 1903), vol. 7, 39–40; J. Tracy Power, *Lee's Miserables: Life in the Army of Northern Virginia from the Wilderness to Appomattox* (Chapel Hill: University of North Carolina Press, 1998), 237.

EPILOGUE

1. Abby Fisher, *What Mrs. Fisher Knows about Old Southern Cooking* (San Francisco: Women's Co-operative Printing Office, 1881).

2. Gaillard Hunt, *Life in America One Hundred Years Ago* (New York: Harper & Brothers Publishers, 1914), 218–19.

3. Tom Dicke, "Red Gold of the Ozarks: The Rise and Decline of Tomato Canning, 1885–1955," *Agricultural History* 79 (Winter 2005): 1–2.

4. Emerson David Fite, *Social and Industrial Conditions in the North during the Civil War* (New York: Peter Smith, 1930), 267; Jimmy M. Skaggs, *Prime Cut: Livestock Raising and Meatpacking in the United States, 1607–1983* (College Station: Texas A&M University Press, 1986), 78.

5. "Tomatoes from California," *American Agriculturist* 28 (August 1869): 283; *Chicago Tribune*, October 20, 1870; *Chicago Tribune* March 4, 1871, as cited in Richard Osborn Cummings, *The American and His Food: A History of Food Habits in the United States* (Chicago: University of Chicago Press, 1940), 62; Edward F. Keuchel Jr., "The Development of the Canning Industry in New York State to 1960," Ph.D. dissertation (Cornell University, 1970), 40; Neptune Fogelberg and Andrew W. McKay, *The Citrus Industry and the California Fruit Growers Exchange System* (Washington, D.C.: Farm Credit Administration, 1940), 13; Ralph J. Roske, *Everyman's Eden: A History of California* (New

York: Macmillan, 1968), 398–99; Kevin Starr, *Inventing the Dream: California through the Progressive Era* (New York: Oxford University Press, 1985), 133; Steven Stoll, *The Fruits of Natural Advantage; Making the Industrial Countryside in California* (Berkeley: University of California Press, 1998), 50–51.

6. Edward Danforth Eddy, Jr., *Colleges for Our Land and Time: The Land-Grant Idea in American Education* (New York: Harper, 1957), 33.

AFTERWORD

1. Eli N. Evans, *Judah P. Benjamin, the Jewish Confederate* (New York: Free Press, 1988), 334.

2. *Public School Methods*, new ed. (Chicago: Methods Co., 1918), 396; George Earlie Shankle, *American Nicknames: Their Origin and Significance* (New York: Wilson, 1955), 186.

3. E. Lee Trinkle, "Cyrus Hall McCormick: A Distinguished Virginian Who Has Contributed to World Progress," July 29, 1931.

4. Kevin H. Siepel, *Rebel: The Life and Times of John Singleton Mosby* (Lincoln: University of Nebraska Press, 2008), x.

Bibliography

Abrams, Alex. St. Clair. *A Full and Detailed History of the Siege of Vicksburg.* Atlanta, GA: Intelligencer Steam Power Presses, 1863.

Adams, Ephraim Douglass. *Great Britain and the American Civil War.* New York: Russell & Russell, 1958.

Ambrose, Stephen E. "The Bread Riots in Richmond," *Virginia Magazine of History and Biography* 71 (April 1963): 203.

Anderson, Ephraim. *Memoirs of the First Missouri Confederate Brigade.* 1868.

Anderson, Stuart. "1861: Blockade vs. Closing the Confederate Ports," *Military Affairs* 41 (December 1977): 190–94.

Andreano, Ralph. *The Economic Impact of the Civil War.* Cambridge, MA: Schenkman Publishing Co., 1967.

Andrews, J. Cutler. *The North Reports the Civil War.* Pittsburgh: Pittsburgh University Press, 1985.

Ash, Stephen V. *When the Yankees Came: Conflict and Chaos in the Occupied South, 1861–1965.* Chapel Hill: University of North Carolina Press, 1995.

Ayers, Edward L. *In the Presence of Mine Enemies: War in the Heart of America, 1859–1863.* New York: W. W. Norton, 2003.

Bacon, Benjamin W. *Sinews of War: How Technology, Industry, and Transportation Won the Civil War.* Novato, CA : Presidio, 1997.

Baker, Thomas H. "Refugee Newspaper: The Memphis Daily Appeal, 1862–1865," *Journal of Southern History* 29 (August 1963): 326–344.

Ballard, Michael B. *Pemberton: The General Who Lost Vicksburg*. Jackson: University Press of Mississippi, 1991.

Barrett, John Gilchrist. *The Civil War in North Carolina*. Chapel Hill: University of North Carolina Press, 1963.

————. *Sherman's March through the Carolinas*. Chapel Hill: University of North Carolina Press, 1956.

Beringer, Richard E., Herman Hattaway, Archer Jones, and William H. Still, Jr. *Why the South Lost the Civil War*. Athens: University of Georgia Press, 1986.

Billings, John D. *Hardtack and Coffee: The Unwritten Story of Army Life*. Lincoln: University of Nebraska Press, 1993.

Black, Robert C. III. *The Railroads of the Confederacy*. Chapel Hill: University of North Carolina, 1998.

Black, Robert W. *Cavalry Raids of the Civil War*. Mechanicsburg, PA: Stackpole Books, 2004.

Blair, William. *Virginia's Private War: Feeding Body and Soul in the Confederacy, 1861–1865*. New York: Oxford University Press, 1998.

Bower, Stephen E. "The Theology of the Battlefield: William Tecumseh Sherman and the U.S. Civil War," *The Journal of Military* 64 (October 2000): 1005–34.

Bridges, Peter. *Pen of Fire: John Moncure Daniel*. Kent, OH: Kent State University Press, 2002.

Brooks, U. R. *Butler and His Cavalry in the War of Secession, 1861–1865*. Columbia, SC: The State Co., 1909.

Browne, Ray B., and Lawrence A. Kreiser. *The Civil War and Reconstruction*. Westport, CT: Greenwood Press, 2003.

Burroughs, Frances M. "The Confederate Receipt Book: A Study of Food Substitution in the American Civil War," *South Carolina Historical Magazine* 93 (January 1992): 31–50.

Bynum, Victoria E. *Unruly Women: The Politics of Social and Sexual Control in the Old South*. Chapel Hill: University of North Carolina Press, 1992.

Cadwallader, Sylvanus [Benjamin P. Thomas, ed.]. *Three Years with Grant*. Lincoln: University of Nebraska Press, 1955.

Canfield, Cass. *The Iron Will of Jefferson Davis*. New York: Harcourt Brace Jovanovich, 1978.

Cardwell, David. "A Brilliant Coup. How Wade Hampton Captured Grant's Entire Beef Supply," *News and Courier* (Charleston, S.C.), October 10, 1894, as in *Southern Historical Society Papers* 22 (January-December 1894): 147–56.

Carse, Robert. *Blockade: The Civil War at Sea*. New York: Rinehart & Co., 1958.

Carter, Samuel III. *The Final Fortress: The Campaign for Vicksburg 1862–1863*. New York: St. Martin's Press, 1980.

Chesnut, Mary Boykin Miller [Isabella D. Martin, Myrta Lockett Avary, eds.], *A Diary from Dixie*. New York: D. Appleton and Co., 1905.

Chesson, Michael B. "Harlots or Heroines? A New Look at the Richmond Bread Riot," *Virginia Magazine of History and Biography* 92 (April 1984): 131–75.

Cimbala, Paul A., and Randall M. Miller, eds. *Union Soldiers and the Northern Home Front: Wartime Experiences, Postwar Adjustments*. New York: Fordham University Press, 2002.

Clark, John E. Jr. *Railroads in the Civil War: The Impact of Management on Victory and Defeat*. Baton Rouge: Louisiana State University Press, 2001.

Claussen, Martin P. "Peace Factors in Anglo-American Relations, 1861–1865," *Mississippi Valley Historical Review* 75 (March 1940): 511–22.

Clay-Clopton, Virginia [Ada Sterling, ed.]. *A Belle of the Fifties: Memoirs of Mrs. Clay of Alabama.* New York: Doubleday, Page & Co., 1904.

Collins, R. M. *Chapters from the Unwritten History of the War between the States.* St. Louis, MD: Nixon-Jones Printing Co., 1893.

Coombe, Jack D. *Thunder along the Mississippi: The River Battles that Split the Confederacy.* New York: Sarpedon, 1996.

Coulter, E. Merton. *The Confederate States of America, 1861–1865.* Baton Rouge: Louisiana State University Press, 1950.

———. "Effects of Secession upon the Commerce of the Mississippi Valley," *Mississippi Valley Historical Review* 3 (December 1916): 275–300.

———. "The Movement for Agricultural Reorganization in the Cotton South during the Civil War," *Agricultural History* 1 (January 1927): 3–17.

Craig, Lee A., and Thomas Weiss, "Agricultural Productivity Growth during the Decade of the Civil War," *Journal of Economic History* 53 (September 1993): 527–48.

Daughtry, Mary Randy. *Gray Cavalier: The Life and Wars of General W. H. F. "Rooney" Lee.* Cambridge, MA: Da Capo Press, 2002.

Davis, Burke. *Sherman's March.* New York: Vintage Books, 1988.

Davis, William C. *A Taste for War: The Culinary History of the Blue and Gray.* Mechanicsburg, PA: Stackpole Books, 2003.

Day, Samuel Phillips. *Down South: Or, an Englishman's Experience at the Seat of the American War.* 2 vols. Vol. 1, 267. London: Hurat and Blackett, 1862.

DeLeon, Thomas C. *Four Years in the Rebel Capitals: An Inside View of Life in the Southern Confederacy.* Mobile, AL: Gossip Print Co., 1890.

Downing, Alexander G. [Olynthus Burroughs, ed]. *Clark Downing's Civil War Diary.* Des Moines: The Historical Dept. of Iowa, 1916.

Dufour, Charles L. *Nine Men in Grey*. Lincoln: University of Nebraska Press, 1993.

Eaton, Clement. *A History of the Southern Confederacy*. New York: Free Press, 1965.

Eicher, David J. *The Longest Night: A Military History of the Civil War*. New York: Simon & Schuster, 2001.

Eisenhower, John S. D. *Agent of Destiny: The Life and Times of General Winfield Scott*. Norman: University of Oklahoma Press, 1997.

Ekelund, Robert B. Jr. *Tariffs, Blockades, and Inflation: The Economics of the Civil War*. Wilmington, DE: Scholarly Resources, Inc., 2004.

Emory, Thomas M. *The Confederate State of Richmond: A Biography of the Capital*. Baton Rouge: Louisiana State University Press, 1998.

Estaville, Lawrence E. Jr., "A Strategic Railroad: The New Orleans, Jackson and Great Northern in the Civil War," *Louisiana History* 14 (Spring 1973): 117–36.

Evans, Eli N. *Judah P. Benjamin, the Jewish Confederate*. New York: Free Press, 1988.

Fellman, Michael. *Citizen Sherman: A Life of William Tecumseh Sherman*. New York: Random House, 1995.

Fite, Emerson David. "The Agricultural Development of the West During the Civil War," *Quarterly Journal of Economics* 20 (February 1906): 259–78.

———. *Social and Industrial Conditions in the North during the Civil War*. New York: Peter Smith, 1930.

Fleche, Andre M. "Uncivilized War: The Shenandoah Campaign, the Northern Democratic Press and the Election of 1864," in Gary W. Gallagher, ed., *The Shenandoah Valley Campaign of 1864*. Chapel Hill: University of North Carolina Press, 2006.

Fleming, Walter Lynwood. *Civil War and Reconstruction in Alabama*. New York: Columbia University Press, 1905.

Flood, Charles Bracelen. *Grant and Sherman: The Friendship that Won the Civil War*. New York: HarperPerennial, 2005.

Foster, Buck T. *Sherman's Mississippi Campaign*. Tuscaloosa: University of Alabama Press, 2006.

Furgurson, Ernest B. *Ashes of Glory: Richmond at War*. New York: Vintage, 1996.

Gallagher, Gary W., ed. *The Shenandoah Valley Campaign of 1864*. Chapel Hill: University of North Carolina Press, 2006.

Gates, Paul W. *Agriculture and the Civil War*. New York: Alfred A. Knopf, 1965.

Gentry, Judith F. "White Gold: The Confederate Government and Cotton in Louisiana," *Louisiana History* 33 (Summer 1992): 229–40.

Ginzberg, Eli. "The Economics of British Neutrality during the American Civil War," *Agricultural History* 10 (October 1936): 147–56.

Glatthaar, Joseph. *General Lee's Army: From Victory to Collapse*. New York: Free Press, 2008.

———. *The March to the Sea and Beyond: Sherman's Troops in the Savannah and Carolinas Campaigns*. New York: New York University Press, 1985.

Goff, Richard D. *Confederate Supply*. Durham, NC: Duke University Press, 1969.

———. "Logistics and Supply Problems of the Confederacy." Ph.D. dissertation, Duke University, 1963.

Grant, U. S. *Personal Memoirs of U. S. Grant*. 2 vols. New York: C. L. Webster & Co., 1885–86.

Grimsley, Mark, and Brooks D. Simpson, eds. *The Collapse of the Confederacy*. Lincoln: University of Nebraska Press, 2001.

Grimsley, Mark. *The Hard Hand of War: Union Military Policy toward Southern Civilians 1861–1865.* New York: Cambridge University Press, 1995.

Hague, Parthenia Antoinette. *A Blockaded Family: Life in Southern Alabama during the War.* Boston and New York: Houghton Mifflin, 1888.

Hanson, Victor Davis. *The Soul of Battle: From Ancient Times to the Present Day, How Three Great Liberators Vanquished Tyranny.* New York: Free Press, 1999.

Hart, B. H. Liddell. *Sherman: Soldier, Realist, American.* New York: Da Capo Press, 1993.

Hattaway, Herman, and Archer Jones. *How the North Won: A Military History of the Civil War.* Urbana: University of Illinois Press, 1991.

Heidler, David Stephen, Jeanne T. Heidler, and David J. Coles. *Encyclopedia of the American Civil War: A Political, Social, and Military History.* New York: W. W. Norton, 2002.

Herbert, Donald David, ed. *Why the North Won the Civil War: Six Authoritative Views on the Economic, Military, Diplomatic, Social, and Political Reasons behind the Confederacy's Defeat.* New York: Touchstone, 1996.

Hertzler, Ann. "Civil War Heroines: Wilmington Soldiers' Aid Society; Mrs. Alfred Martin," *Lower Cape Fear Historical Society Bulletin* 50 (October 2006): 1–5.

Hoehling, Adolph A. *Vicksburg: 47 Days of Siege.* Englewood Cliffs, NJ: Prentice-Hall, 1969.

Huse, Caleb. *The Supplies for the Confederate Army.* Boston: T. R. Marvin, 1906.

Hutton, Paul Andrew. *Phil Sheridan and His Army.* Norman: University of Oklahoma Press, 1999.

Johnson, Ludwell H. "Commerce between Northeastern Ports and the Confederacy, 1861–1865," *Journal of American History* 54 (June 1967): 30–42.

———. "Contraband Trade during the Last Year of the Civil War," *Mississippi Valley Historical Review* 39 (March 1962): 635–52.

———. "Trading with the Union: The Evolution of Confederate Policy," *Virginia Magazine of History and Biography* 78 (July 1970): 308–25.

Johnson, Timothy D. *Winfield Scott: The Quest for Military Glory*. Lawrence: University Press of Kansas, 1998.

Johnston, Joseph E. *Narrative of Military Operations During the Late War Between the States*. New York: D. Appleton and Co., 1874.

Jones, Archer. *Civil War Command and Strategy: The Process of Victory and Defeat*. New York: Free Press, 1992.

Jones, John B. *A Rebel War Clerk's Diary at the Confederate States Capital*. 2 vols. Philadelphia: J. B. Lippincott & Co., 1866.

Jones, Robert H. "Long Live the King?," *Agricultural History* 37 (July 1963): 166–69.

Kelter, Christian B. "Pennsylvania and Virginia Germans during the Civil War: A Brief History and Comparative Analysis," *Virginia Magazine of History and Biography* 109 (2001): 37–86.

Kennett, Lee B. *Marching Through Georgia: The Story of Soldiers and Civilians During Sherman's Campaign*. New York: HarperPerennial, 1995.

Khasigian, Amos. "Economic Factors and British Neutrality, 1861–1865," *Historian* 25 (August 1963): 451–65.

Kimball, William J. "The Bread Riot in Richmond, 1863," *Civil War History* 7 (1961): 149–54.

Lebergott, Stanley. "Through the Blockade: The Profitability and Extent of Cotton Smuggling, 1861–1865," *Journal of Economic History* 41 (December 1981): 867–88.

———. "Why the South Lost: Commercial Purpose in the Confederacy, 1861–1865," *Journal of American History* 70 (June 1983): 58–74.

Lester, Richard I. *Confederate Finance and Purchasing in Great Britain*. Charlottesville: University Press of Virginia, 1975.

Lonn, Ella. *Desertion during the Civil War*. Lincoln: University of Nebraska Press, 1998.

———. *Salt as a Factor in the Confederacy*. Southern Historical Publications #4. University, AL: University of Alabama, 1965.

Loughborough, Mary Ann. *My Cave Life in Vicksburg*. New York: D. Appleton and Co., 1864.

Luaghi, Raimondo [Paolo E. Coletta, trans.]. *A History of the Confederate Navy*. Annapolis, MD: Naval Institute Press, 1996.

Lykes, Richard. "Hampton's Cattle Raid, September 14–17, 1864," *Military Affairs* 21 (Spring 1957): 1–20.

Mahin, Dean B. *One War at a Time; The International Dimensions of the American Civil War*. Washington, D.C.: Brassey's, 2000.

Mahon, Michael G. *The Shenandoah Valley, 1861–1865: The Destruction of the Granary of the Confederacy*. Mechanicsburg, PA: Stackpole Books, 1999.

———. "The Shenandoah Valley of Virginia as a Source of Subsistence for the Confederacy during the American Civil War: a New Perspective." MA thesis, University of North Carolina at Charlotte, 1989.

Martin, Bessie. *A Rich Man's War, a Poor Man's Fight*. Tuscaloosa: The University of Alabama Press, 2003.

Massey, Mary Elizabeth. "The Effect of Shortages on the Confederate Homefront," *Arkansas Historical Quarterly* 9 (Autumn 1950): 172–93.

———. *Ersatz in the Confederacy: Shortages and Substitutes on the Southern Homefront*. Columbia: University of South Carolina Press, 1993.

———. "The Food and Drink Shortage on the Confederate Homefront," *North Carolina Historical Review* 26 (April 1949): 306–34.

McClellan, George B. *McClellan's Own Story*. New York: C. L. Webster & Co., 1886.

McGuire, Judith White Brockenbrough. *Diary of a Southern Refugee*. 3rd ed. Richmond: J. W. Randolph, 1889.

McKinney, Francis F. *Education in Violence: The Life of George H. Thomas and the History of the Army of the Cumberland*. Detroit, MI: Wayne State University Press, 1961.

McPherson, James M., ed. *The Atlas of the Civil War*. Philadelphia: Courage Books, 2005.

McPherson, James M. *Battle Cry of Freedom: The Civil War Era*. New York: Oxford University Press, 1988.

McPherson, James M., and William J. Cooper, eds. *Writing the Civil War: the Quest to Understand*. Columbia: University of South Carolina Press, 1998.

Merritt, Wesley. "Sheridan in the Shenandoah," *Battles and Leaders of the Civil War*. 4 vols. New York: The Century Co., 1884. Vol. 4, 500–21.

Miller, David W. *Second Only to Grant: Quartermaster General Montgomery C. Meigs*. Shippensburg, PA: White Mane Books, 2000.

Minter, Winfred Pleasants. "Supplying the Confederate Armies: A Study in War Administration." Ph.D. dissertation, University of Chicago, 1954.

Mitchell, Patricia B. *Yanks, Rebels, Rats & Rations: Scratching for Food in Civil War Prison Camps*. Chatham, Virginia: self-published, 1993.

Moore, Jerrold Northrop. *Confederate Commissary General: Lucius Bellinger Northrop and the Subsistence Bureau of the Southern Army*. Shippensburg, PA: White Mane Publishing Co., 1996.

Moore, John G. "Mobility and Strategy in the Civil War," *Military Affairs* 24 (Summer 1960): 68–77.

Morris, Roy. *Sheridan: The Life and Wars of General Phil Sheridan.* New York: Vintage, 1993.

Netzley, Patricia D. *The Greenhaven Encyclopedia of the Civil War.* San Diego, CA: Greenhaven Press, 2004.

Newton, Steven H. *Joseph E. Johnston and the Defense of Richmond.* Lawrence: University Press of Kansas, 1998.

Nichols, G. W. *A Soldier's Story of his Regiment.* Jesup, GA: 1898.

Nichols, George Ward. *The Story of the Great March.* New York: Harper & Brothers, 1865.

O'Brien, G. F. J. "James A. Seddon, Statesman of the Old South." Ph.D. thesis, University of Maryland, 1963.

Otto, John. *Southern Agriculture during the Civil War Era, 1860–1880.* Westport, CT: Greenwood Press, 1994.

Owsley, Frank Lawrence [Harriet Chappell Owsley, ed.]. *King Cotton Diplomacy: Foreign Relations of the Confederate States of America.* 2nd ed. Chicago: University of Chicago Press, 1959.

Pace, Robert F. " 'It was Bedlam Let Loose': The Louisiana Sugar Country and the Civil War," *Louisiana History* 39 (Autumn 1998): 389–409.

Parks, Joseph H. "A Confederate Trade Center under Federal Occupation: Memphis, 1862 to 1865," *Journal of Southern History* 7 (August 1941): 289–314.

Patchan, Scott C. *Shenandoah Summer: The 1864 Valley Campaign.* Lincoln: University of Nebraska Press, 2007.

Pember, Phoebe Yates. *A Southern Woman's Story: Life in Confederate Richmond.* Wilmington, NC: Broadfoot Publishing Co., 1991.

Pemberton, John C. *Pemberton: Defender of Vicksburg.* Chapel Hill: University of North Carolina Press, 1942.

Power, J. Tracy. *Lee's Miserables: Life in the Army of Northern Virginia from the Wilderness to Appomattox*. Chapel Hill: University of North Carolina Press, 1998.

Pryor, Sara Agnes Rice. *Reminiscences of Peace and War*. New York: Macmillan Co., 1904.

Ramsdell, Charles W. "Materials for Research in the Agricultural History of the Confederacy," *Agricultural History* 4 (January 1930): 18–22.

Rasmussen, Wayne D. "The Civil War: A Catalyst of Agricultural Revolution," *Agricultural History* 39 (October 1965): 187–95.

Rhodes, James Ford. *History of the United States from the Compromise of 1850*. New York: Harper, 1904.

Risch, Erna. *Quartermaster Support of the Army 1775–1939*. Washington, DC: Quartermaster Historian's Office, Office of the Quartermaster General, 1962.

Rogin, Leo. *The Introduction of Farm Machinery in Its Relation to the Productivity of Labor in the Agriculture of the United States during the Nineteenth Century*. Berkeley: University of California Press, 1931.

Roland, Charles Pierce. *Louisiana Sugar Plantations during the Civil War*. Baton Rouge: Louisiana State University Press, 1997.

Roman, Alfred. *The Military Operations of General Beauregard in the War Between the States 1861 to 1865*. 2 vols. New York: Harper & Brothers, 1884.

Royster, Charles. *The Destructive War: William Tecumseh Sherman, Stonewall Jackson, and the Americans*. New York: Vintage Books, 1993.

Ruffin, F. G. "A Chapter in Confederate History," *North American Review* 134 (January 1882): 97–110.

Sargent, Fitzwilliam. *England, the United States, and the Southern Confederacy*. 2nd ed. London: Hamilton, Adams, and Co., 1864.

Scharf, J. Thomas. *History of the Confederate States Navy: From its Organization to the Surrender of its Last Vessel*. New York: The Fairfax Press, 1977.

Schlesinger, Arthur Meier. "A Dietary Interpretation of American History," *Proceedings of the Massachusetts Historical Society*, 3rd Series, 68 (October 1944 -May 1947): 199–227.

Schmidt, Louis B. "The Influence of Wheat and Cotton on Anglo-American Relations during the Civil War," *Iowa Journal of History and Politics* 16 (July 1918): 400–39.

———. "Internal Commerce and the Development of National Economy before 1860," *Journal of Political Economy* 47 (December 1939): 798–822.

———. "The Internal Grain Trade of the United States, 1850–1860," *Iowa Journal of History and Politics* 18 (January 1920): 94–124.

———. "The Internal Grain Trade of the United States, 1860–1880," *Iowa Journal of History and Politics* 19 (1921): 414–55.

Schwab, John Christopher. *The Confederate States of America, 1861–1865*. New York: C. Scribner's Sons, 1901.

Sears, Stephen W. *The Civil War Papers of George B. McClellan. Selected Correspondence 1860–1865*. New York: Da Capo Press, 1992.

———. *George B. McClellan: The Young Napoleon*. New York: Da Capo Press, 1999.

Sellers, James A. "The Economic Incidents of the Civil War in the South," *Mississippi Valley Historical Review* 14 (September 1927): 179–91.

Shannon, Fred Albert. *The Organization and Administration of the Union Army, 1861–1865*. 2 vols. Gloucester, MA: Peter Smith, 1965.

Shea, William L., and Terrence J. Winschel. *Vicksburg Is the Key: The Struggle for the Mississippi River*. Lincoln: University of Nebraska Press, 2003.

Sheehan-Dean, Aaron, ed. *Struggle for a Vast Future*. Oxford, UK: Osprey Publishing, 2006.

Sherman, William Tecumseh. *General Sherman's Official Account of His Great March through Georgia and the Carolinas*. New York: Bunce & Huntington, 1865.

Shorto, Russell. *David Farragut and the Great Naval Blockade*. Englewood Cliffs, NJ: Silver Burdett Press, 1991.

Simon, John Y. "The Politics of the Morrill Act," *Agricultural History* 37 (1963): 103–11.

Simpson, Brooks D. *Ulysses S. Grant: Triumph over Adversity, 1822–1865*. Boston: Houghton Mifflin, 2000.

Simson, Jay W. *Naval Strategies of the Civil War: Confederate Innovations and Federal Opportunism*. Nashville, TN: Cumberland House, 2001.

Smith, Jean Edward. *Grant*. New York: Simon & Schuster, 2001.

Spaulding, Lily May, and John Spaulding, eds. *Civil War Recipes: Receipts from the Pages of Godey's Lady's Book*. Lexington: University of Kentucky Press, 1999.

Stackpole, Edward J. *Sheridan in the Shenandoah; Jubal Early's Nemesis*. 2nd ed. Harrisburg, PA: Stackpole Books, 1992.

Stephens, George Ware. "Some Aspects of Early Intersectional Rivalry for the Commerce of the Upper Mississippi Valley," *Washington University Studies* 10 (April 1923): 277–300.

Stephenson, Nathaniel W. *The Day of the Confederacy*. New Haven, CT: Yale University Press; 1919.

Surdam, David G. "King Cotton: Monarch or Pretender? The State of the Market for Raw Cotton on the Eve of the American Civil War," *Economic History Review* 51 (1998): 113–32.

———. *Northern Naval Superiority and the Economics of the American Civil War*. Columbia: University of South Carolina Press, 2001.

Symonds, H. C. *Report of a Commissary of Subsistence, 1861–65*. Sing Sing, NY: self-published, 1888.

Tanner, Adelph. *Encouragement of Food Crops in the Confederacy*. n.l.: n.p., 1928.

Tatum, Georgia Lee. *Disloyalty in the Confederacy*. Lincoln: University of Nebraska Press, 2000.

Taylor, Robert A. *Rebel Storehouse: Florida's Contribution to the Confederacy*. Tuscaloosa: University of Alabama, 2003.

Taylor, Thomas E. *Running the Blockade*. London: John Murray, 1896.

Thomas, Emory M. *The Confederate Nation: 1861–1865*. New York: Harper & Row, 1979.

Thomas, William G. "Nothing Ought to Astonish Us: Confederate Civilians in the 1864 Shenandoah Valley Campaign," in Gary W. Gallagher, ed., *The Shenandoah Valley Campaign of 1864* (Chapel Hill: University of North Carolina Press, 2006), 237.

Thompson, Samuel Bernard. *Confederate Purchasing Operations Abroad*. Gloucester, MA: Peter Smith, 1973.

Tice, Douglas O. "Bread or Blood!: The Richmond Bread Riots," *Civil War Times Illustrated* 12 (February 1974): 12–9.

Tilden, Arnold. *The Legislation of the Civil-War Period*. Los Angeles: University of Southern California Press, 1937.

Torisky, Danielle. "Feeding the Family Homefront: Challenges during the American Civil War." Shenandoah Valley Regional Studies Seminar, February 19, 1999.

———. Reginald R. Foucar-Szocki, and Jacqueline B. Walker. "Quantity Feeding during the American Civil War." *Marriage & Family Review* 28 (October 1998): 69–91.

Trudeau, Noah Andre. *Southern Storm: Sherman's March to the Sea*. New York: HarperCollins, 2008.

Turner, George Edgar. *Victory Rode the Rails: The Strategic Place of the Railroads in the Civil War.* Lincoln: University of Nebraska Press, 1992.

Van der Zee, Jacob. "The Roads and Highways of Territorial," *Iowa Journal of History and Politics* 3 (1903): 175–225.

Vandiver, Frank E. "The Food Supply of the Confederate Armies, 1865," *Tyler's Quarterly Historical and Genealogical Magazine* 26 (October 1944): 77–89.

———. *Their Tattered Flags; The Epic of the Confederacy.* New York: Harper's Magazine Press Book, 1970.

Vetter, Charles Edmund. *Sherman, Merchant of Terror, Advocate of Peace.* Gretna, LA: Pelican, 1992.

Volo, Dorothy Denneen, and James M. Volo. *Daily Life in Civil War America.* 2nd ed. Santa Barbara, CA: Greenwood Press, 2009.

Washburn, Benjamin M. "An Analysis of Confederate Subsistence Logistics," MS thesis, Air Force Institute of Technology, Air University, Wright-Patterson Air Force Base, Ohio, 1989.

Weber, Thomas. *The Northern Railroads in the Civil War, 1861–1865.* Bloomington: Indiana University Press, 1999.

Weitz, Mark A. *A Higher Duty; Desertion among Georgia Troops during the Civil War.* Lincoln: University of Nebraska, 2000.

———. *More Damning than Slaughter: Desertion in the Confederate Army.* Lincoln: University of Nebraska Press, 2005.

Wesley, Charles H. *The Collapse of the Confederacy.* Columbia: University of South Carolina Press, 2001.

Wheeler, Richard. *Voices of the Civil War.* New York: Meridian, 1990.

Wiggins, Sarah Woolfolk, ed. *The Journals of Josiah Gorgas, 1857–1878.* Tuscaloosa: University of Alabama Press, 1995.

Wilde, Mark W. "Industrialization of Food Processing in the United States, 1860–1960." Ph.D. dissertation, University of Delaware, 1988.

Wiley, Bell Irvin. *The Life of Billy Yank: The Common Soldier of the Union.* Baton Rouge: Louisiana State University Press, 1978.

———. *The Life of Johnny Reb: The Common Soldier of the Union.* Baton Rouge: Louisiana State University Press, 1978.

Williams, David. *Bitterly Divided: The South's Inner Civil War.* New York: New Press, 2008.

Williams, Roger L. *The Origins of Federal Support for Higher Education: George W. Atherton and the Land-Grant College Movement.* University Park: Pennsylvania State University Press, 1991.

Wise, Stephen R. *Lifeline of the Confederacy: Blockade Running During the Civil War.* Columbia: University of South Carolina Press, 1988.

Wright, Mike. *City under Siege: Richmond in the Civil War.* New York: Cooper Square Press, 2002.

Younger, Edward, ed. *Inside the Confederate Government: The Diary of Robert Garlick Hill Kean.* New York: Oxford University Press, 1957.

Index